Slavery and the Numbers Game

BLACKS IN THE NEW WORLD
August Meier, Series Editor

HERBERT G. GUTMAN

Slavery and the Numbers Game

A Critique of
Time on the Cross

UNIVERSITY OF ILLINOIS PRESS
Urbana   Chicago   London

© 1975 by Herbert G. Gutman
Manufactured in the United States of America

Library of Congress Cataloging in Publication Data

Gutman, Herbert George, 1928-
Slavery and the numbers game.

(Blacks in the New World)
Includes bibliographical references and index.
1. Fogel, Robert William. Time on the cross.
2. Slavery in the United States — Economic aspects.
3. Slavery in the United States — Condition of slaves.
I. Title. II. Series.
E449.F653G87 1975   331.1'1734'0973   75-15899
ISBN 0-252-00564-3
ISBN 0-252-00565-1 (pbk.)

This work originally appeared in slightly different form in *The Journal of Negro History* (January 1975) under a different title. The journal is edited by Lorraine A. Williams and is published by the Association for the Study of Afro-American Life and History, Washington, D.C.; the executive director is J. Rupert Picott.

For Marta and Nell
who are making their own worlds
and know what counts

Contents

List of Tables

Preface

Time on the Cross: The Economics of American Negro Slavery should be read as theater because it deals with two performances: the performance of the slave economy and the performance of enslaved Afro-Americans. It is the relationship between these two performances that makes this work so controversial: slavery lasted so long and worked so well because the ordinary enslaved Afro-American internalized the standards of social and economic behavior pressed upon him (or her) by slaveowners. The acceptance of such standards is the true but neglected record of "black achievement under adversity." *Time on the Cross* promises to set that record straight. Its authors attack "the traditional interpretation of slavery" to "correct the perversion of the history of blacks" and to destroy "myths that turned diligent and efficient workers into lazy loafers and bunglers, that turned love of family into a disregard for it, that turned those who struggled for self-improvement in the only way they could into 'Uncle Toms.' " The enslaved and their owners perform as actors and actresses in a drama written, directed, and produced by the "free market." That is the main theme of *Time on the Cross*, its essential message. But a critical and analytical examination of the relevant evidence in *Time on the Cross* shows that its novel patterns of slave belief and behavior bear little if any relationship to the common, real-life experiences that made up the daily drama of Afro-American social history prior to the general emancipation.

"What is set forth," co-authors Robert W. Fogel and Stanley L. Engerman explain, "represents the honest efforts of scholars whose central aim has been the discovery of what really happened." I believe that is true. Fogel and Engerman are former colleagues, and few persons have been more helpful to me in my own work and more generous with their time than Stanley Engerman. I remain greatly in his debt. Nevertheless, as the pages which follow make clear time and time again, I am convinced that *Time on the Cross* is a profoundly flawed work. It is not merely that the book contains errors of fact and interpretation. All books that promise to revise our understanding of important aspects of the past exaggerate their findings and entice readers with bold and often extreme statements. It is rather that the *essential* evidence does not sustain the authors' arguments reevaluating *slave performance*. The evidence does not make the case that enslaved Afro-Americans worked hard because they wanted to work hard.

My debts are several, and my apologies, one. The editors of the *Journal of Negro History*, and especially Mary F. Berry, encouraged a lengthy review of *Time on the Cross*. They got more than they bargained for, I fear, but nevertheless published the entire review at some expense in the January, 1975, issue. I greatly appreciate that decision. The haste involved in publishing so long a review-essay to meet a journal deadline made for some typographical errors in the *Journal* version. None of these errors affect any of the larger arguments, but they did affect readability and sometimes strained the eye. I apologize to the *Journal's* editors and readers and also to the book's authors for these errors. David Brion Davis ended up in footnote twenty-six. He belongs in many places, but not there, and readers of his magnificent *The Problem of Slavery in the Age of Revolution* will know why. I have corrected a number of errors in the present version and hope that none remain. Leslie Rowland deserves thanks for letting me use some of the data she gathered in her splendid research on Kentucky Afro-Americans during and just after the Civil War. Stanley Engerman made available to me birth registers for the Good Hope and Stirling plantations and household lists for the Watson plantation; he deserves thanks, too. Mary F. Berry, Paul David, Charles Dew, Eric Foner, Judith Mara Gutman, and William Eric Perkins made unusually helpful comments on an early version of this critique. It is better for that reason. Whatever shortcomings it has are entirely of my own making. Much in the Afro-American experience before the general emancipation is now being studied afresh. I like to think that this critique of *Time on the Cross* contributes in some way to that long-needed reexamination. Some may wonder what a "labor historian" is doing writing about enslaved Afro-Americans. I hope the answer to that question is clear by the time they finish reading this critique.

HERBERT G. GUTMAN
Nyack, New York
March 10, 1975

He who reads the inscrutable book of Nature as if it were a Merchant's Ledger is justly suspected of having never seen that Book, but only some School Synopsis thereof; from which if taken for the real book, more error than insight is to be derived.

Thomas Carlyle

... I have that all in figures — averages of deaths in the first cargoes, 25 per cent. — large average, certainly; they didn't manage the business exactly right; but then the rate of increase in a Christian country averages 25 per cent over what it would have been in Africa. Now, ... if these had been left in Africa, they would have been all heathen; by getting them over here, you have just as many, and all Christians to boot. Because, you see, the excess of increase balances the percentage of loss, and we make no deduction for interest in those cases.

Harriet Beecher Stowe[?]

$$F + E = T/C$$

Introduction

Few books in United States history, and certainly none about the history of enslaved Afro-Americans published in the past two decades, have attracted more popular notice and given more promise of provoking fierce controversy among historians and even lay persons than Robert William Fogel's and Stanley L. Engerman's *Time on the Cross: The Economics of American Negro Slavery*.[1] Controversial because it challenges many "conventional" views about enslaved Afro-Americans, it does so by a nearly promiscuous exposure of masses of quantitative data. Such data and the methods accompanying them are celebrated for supplying vast ranges of new information which in turn — at least according to Fogel and Engerman — finally allow us decisively to put aside racist myths and to see the enslaved as well as their owners in a new light. Sambo, it turns out, was really a black Horatio Alger, made so by his owner, who was nothing more than a rational profit-maximizer whose everyday decisions were determined by the powerful imperatives of the "free market."

Although *Time on the Cross* (hereafter referred to as T/C) contains many arguments and much data about the economics of slavery that are new, the work's importance as well as the popular notice it has attracted have much less to do with that subject than with Fogel's and Engerman's striking statements about slave belief and behavior. T/C may have unusual value as economic history. It may turn out that the expected return on an investment in slaves "compared favorably with the most outstanding investment opportunities in manufacturing," that slaveholders were "optimistic" on the eve of the Civil War, that southern plantations were more "efficient" and more "productive" than northern free farms, and that the southern economy and southern per capita income grew rapidly between 1840 and 1860. (Before the publication of T/C, cliometricians, Fogel and Engerman prominently among them, published revisionist findings on these and related matters — findings, not surprisingly, that help fill the pages of T/C.)[2] That

---

[1] Two vols., Boston: Little, Brown and Company, 1974, cited hereafter as T/C.

[2] See especially Robert Fogel and Stanley Engerman, "The Economics of Slavery,"

is for economic historians to dispute, and some have already done so.[3] But whatever the book's importance as economic history, detailed examination of T/C — its major arguments and the evidence supporting them — shows convincingly that it is poor social history, that its analysis of the beliefs and behavior of "ordinary" enslaved Afro-Americans is entirely misleading, that it uses a thoroughly inadequate model of slave socialization, and that it contains frequent and important errors of all kinds in its use of quantitative (not to mention literary) evidence essential to its major arguments.

T/C, however, is a serious work, and its authors are well-established and highly able economic historians. It is a work that draws heavily upon numerical evidence, and volume two, subtitled *Evidence and Methods — A Supplement,* is filled with algebraic equations, the results of computer runs, and arguments that only "specialists" seemingly can confront. Fogel and Engerman (hereafter referred to as F + E) insist that they manage "a more complete body of information on the operation of the slave system than has been available to anyone interested in the subject either during the antebellum era or since then." Readers learn that an "enormous body of evidence" is "the source of . . . new discoveries." The scope of the research project is awesome. It includes data from five other cliometricians with specialized skills, eleven resident University of Chicago graduate students, still other graduate students (perhaps as many as fifteen, and some heading smaller data collection teams), twenty or twenty-one persons (including this writer) who read an entire earlier draft, and another ninety-three persons — many among them distinguished economic historians and well-known and productive historians of slavery — who read earlier portions of the unpublished work.[4] Many of the data reported in T/C, moreover, have benefited from the modern computer. "We were able to do in five minutes, for $40," said Fogel to an admiring *Wall Street Journal* writer, "what would have taken 2,000 man days of work."[5]

Early reviewers, distinguished historians among them, got the message.

in *The Reinterpretation of American Economic History* (New York, 1971), pp. 311-341. Much that fills the pages in volume one of *Time on the Cross* and deals with the slave economy is found in that essay. The reader should compare that essay with chapters three and six in the first volume of *Time on the Cross.*

[3] See especially Paul A. David and Peter Temin, "Slavery: The Progressive Institution?" *Journal of Economic History,* 34 (September 1974), pp. 739-783; Thomas L. Haskell, "Were Slaves More Efficient? Some Doubts About 'Time on the Cross,' " *New York Review of Books,* 19 September 1974, 38-42; Martin Duberman, review of T/C, *Village Voice,* 18 July 1974, pp. 25-33; Allan Lichtman, review of T/C, *New Republic,* 6-13 July 1974, pp. 22-24; John Blassingame, review of T/C, *Atlantic Monthly,* August 1974, pp. 78-82.

[4] T/C, I, pp. 3-12, 265-270.

[5] *Wall Street Journal,* 28 March 1974.

In cautious reviews, David Brion Davis and C. Vann Woodward used similar metaphors. Davis noted that F + E "speak casually of their legions of research assistants, of their mobile SAM computers, of their electronic weaponry, of their occupation of every hidden site. . . . We are told that we are encircled, cut off, and cannot fight unless we have weapon-systems equal to those of the Cliometricians." Woodward found that "even in the 'nontechnical' volume of findings the rattle of electronic equipment is heard off stage, and the reader is coerced by references to . . . inconceivable mountains of statistical data." F + E themselves demonstrate a fierce capacity for combat in a tortuous, if tasteless, analysis of Kenneth Stampp's *The Peculiar Institution*. "They nail Kenneth Stampp to the cross," said Davis, "taunting him for his statistical errors [and] his nonscientific methodology." Woodward felt T/C an "all-out assault on American slavery historians, . . . a ruthless scourging of traditional historians of slavery, whether of the left or the right, for their slipshod and unscientific ways," including "the merciless clobbering of a few unfortunate victims." Reviewers less qualified than Davis and Woodward drove home a different point, one meant as a warning to "traditional" historians. T/C, said the *New York Times Book Review*, "is a different kind of history; its conclusions are based on reams of fresh data and sophisticated mathematical techniques borrowed from economics. . . . It just won't wash to feign moral outrage about quantitative whippings or about the number of slave women in brothels." The same point was made in *Time*. "Generally moderate," F + E were "quite merciless when dealing with what they regard as the fumbling ignorance of Stampp, Elkins, and Phillips on the subject of economics and statistics. . . . The message is perfectly clear. Historians who do not have these tools could grope for another hundred years in subjective confusion and never be able to evaluate or rebut the work of the cliometricians." The intelligent layman interested in Afro-American enslavement was even less fortunate. How could it be otherwise if the *Times Literary Supplement* warned potential T/C readers that "many of its graphs, equations, and symbols will be beyond the comprehension of most historians"?[6]

Computers are helpful, and so, no doubt, are complex mathematical techniques, but they are not prerequisites for understanding T/C, dealing with its central arguments, and examining its many uses and abuses of quantitative and literary evidence. The intelligent reader does not need to know the difference between a chi-square test and a multiple-regression analysis to learn that ordinary enslaved Afro-Americans did not conform to the patterns of beliefs and behavior emphasized in T/C.

[6] David Brion Davis, "Slavery and the Post–World War II Historians," *Daedalus* (Spring 1974), pp. 1-16; C. Vann Woodward, "The Jolly Institution," *New York Review of Books*, 2 May 1974, pp. 2-6; Peter Passell, review of T/C, *New York Times Book Review*, 28 April 1974, p. 4; Timothy Foote, review of T/C, *Time*, 17 June 1974, pp. 98-100; *Times Literary Supplement*, 31 May 1974.

An Overview of T/C

The Central Theme in T/C: "Black Achievement under Adversity"

Just as southern history has its "central theme," so, too, does T/C in dealing with the beliefs and behavior of enslaved Afro-Americans, that is, in dealing with their social history. Its major purpose is to chronicle anew "the record of black achievement under adversity." *Time*'s reviewer smartly noted that T/C describes "plantations as businesses administered in ways that suggest both a Victorian family and a paternalistic corporation eager to encourage worker morale in the interest of higher profits."[7] That reviewer failed only to mention that the eagerness of "most" slaves to work hard and diligently, according to F + E, matched the eagerness of "most" slaveowners to get them to do so.

In a review appropriately entitled "Capitalist Masters, Bourgeois Slaves," the economic historians Paul David and Peter Temin splendidly summarized the central theme of T/C: "The major part of 'the record of black achievement under adversity' which the book claims to have revealed consists simply in the alleged ability of black slaves to fully internalize the Protestant work ethic and the *mores* of Victorian family life, to assimilate and function within a market-oriented society, and — even though largely confined to the lowest levels of the socio-economic hierarchy — successfully to strive to make a profit for the enterprises which depended upon their labor. . . ." It is not merely that slavery was profitable. F + E are not the first to argue that point, and few historians would dispute it. It is rather that "the way the slaves . . . responded to the *positive* incentives their masters devised for maintaining nuclear families, caring for their young, and working diligently was responsible for the smooth and profitable operation of the system of slavery in the antebellum South." David and Temin go on: "This is seen by Fogel and Engerman as the main 'achievement' of the American Negro people in slavery. This is the view that distinguishes their book from every other major study of slavery published during the past three decades: Fogel and Enger-

[7] Foote, review of T/C, *Time*, 17 June 1974, pp. 98-100.

man reject not only the Sambo image, but also the conception that it was appropriate for the slaves to have resisted their bondage."[8] So goes the main thrust of T/C. A mass of evidence — some of it old and some of it new, some of it quantitative and some of it literary — seeks to show how well the slaves learned from their owners about how to labor efficiently and productively (the " 'Protestant' work ethic") and about how to live in normal nineteenth-century families (the mores of Victorian family life). An implicit model of slave socialization permeates the pages of T/C.

T/C and the Model of Slave Socialization: How Slaves Learned and What They Learned

The model of slave socialization in T/C is the traditional model, and it is an erroneous model that has greatly limited understanding of enslaved Afro-Americans and their beliefs and behavior. Put simply, F + E argue that enslavement successfully transformed the Afro-American into a hard-working, productive, and compliant specialized laborer. Planter-sponsored stimuli worked this transformation. That process had its origins in the policies and practices of slaveowners anxious to maximize profits. The model mixes two processes together: *how slaves learned* and *what slaves learned*. It is erroneous for two reasons.

First of all, it defines slave socialization by asking simply *what* enslavement *did* to Africans and to several generations of enslaved Afro-Americans. The methods used to answer this essential and important question are sometimes new, and so are many of the data. But the question asked is not new. It is the same question that has been asked by most historians and social scientists for three-quarters of a century. It does not differ from the question asked by such diverse students of slavery as U. B. Phillips, Stanley Elkins, and E. Franklin Frazier. Slaves learned only because of what was done to them. But just so much and no more can be learned about the enslaved by the

[8] David and Temin, *Journal of Interdisciplinary History*, 5 (Winter 1975), pp. 445-457, point out that "economic man" — either as slave or owner — makes no choices in T/C. The "market" determines his behavior: "[S]laveholders appear as indistinguishable from pure economic men. If they act benevolently, even compassionately towards their human chattel, it is not out of patriarchal commitment but because the workings of capitalism in a highly competitive industry happened to make such behavior most profitable, and because "the market" would have punished those owners who indulged in or failed to prevent the abusive treatment of their slaves."

The enslaved had just as little choice: "Fogel and Engerman . . . do not stop with the bourgeoisification of the southern slavocracy. For they hold that the slaves, too, learned to respond to a range of economic incentives that was created for them, seeking extra income, leisure, and occupational advance through cooperation and identification with the economic interests of their masters. In the underlying motivation of its members, then, the black slave community portrayed by Fogel and Engerman is thoroughly bourgeois, as much a part of capitalist society as was the white slave-owning class."

historian asking only this question. The quantity and the quality of the evidence examined hardly matter. The social history of the enslaved Afro-American still remains heavily shrouded by the the shadow of U. B. Phillips, the influential early-twentieth-century historian — a shadow cast by more than that historian's narrow racial assumptions. It has just as much to do with the larger analytic model Phillips worked with to explain how enslavement affected Africans and their many Afro-American descendants. Freed from its racist assumptions, that model still retains a powerful and wholly negative influence on the conceptualization of the Afro-American historical experience before the general emancipation. T/C is not free of that early-twentieth-century model. T/C is in no way a racist work. That should be clear at the start. But in seeking to explain "typical" slave beliefs and behavior, its authors cling tenaciously to the early-twentieth-century belief that enslaved Afro-Americans only learned from their owners. Phillips, of course, believed that slave culture (the source of slave belief and behavior) was "imitative." F + E reject that crude formulation. But slave socialization in T/C involves no more than slave conformity to master-sponsored external stimuli.

Second, the model of slave socialization in T/C is *static* and, therefore, *ahistorical*. That, too, is a common flaw in writing the history of enslaved Afro-Americans shared, for example, by F + E with such adversaries as Elkins, Kenneth Stampp, and Eugene Genovese. In T/C, the prices of cotton and slaves change over time, but the beliefs and behavior of enslaved Afro-Americans remain constant. The enslaved do not experience history. Time appears only in the book's title. Numbers and especially averages, which serve as critical indices of slave belief and behavior, are timeless in T/C. When the reader learns, for example, that the average age of a slave mother at the birth of a first surviving child was 22.5 years, there is no indication that F + E are dealing with enslaved women in 1720, 1770, 1810, or "over time."

The central flaw in most historical works on the enslaved Afro-American is a shared static model of how slaves learned. T/C does not differ from those works. It does no more than reinforce that flawed model of slave socialization. What gives T/C its novelty are its truly amazing "findings" about what slaves learned. In the pages which follow, we examine these findings as they affect F + E's explanation of slave beliefs and behavior. But a flawed model of slave socialization can greatly obscure and even distort accurate findings that hint at patterns of slave belief and behavior. A single example suffices to illustrate this point: "The average age at which slave women married was twenty." Three questions, among others, need to be answered about this statement. First, is this an *accurate finding?* Second, if it is accurate, *why* did most slave women marry at age twenty? And third, if it is accurate, what does this regularity in behavior tell us about slave beliefs and slave culture? A static model which assumes that slaves learned only from their owners promises to offer inaccurate answers to the second and third questions. It cannot be otherwise. But, as we shall see, the flaws in T/C have less to do with the second and third questions than with the first question. It is the findings in T/C that are so frequently in error, and especially the quantitative data essential to the following central themes in this study: owner-sponsored negative labor incentives, owner-sponsored positive labor incentives, slave urban and rural occupational distributions, slave mobility, owner attitudes and behavior toward slave marriage and the slave family, the effects of migration and sale on the slave family and slave marriage, and slave sexual behavior. On all of these important matters, the findings in T/C are either disappointingly slight and unconvincing, based upon flawed assumptions about slave culture and slave society, based upon the misuse of important quantitative data, or derived from inferences and estimates that are the result of a misreading of conventional scholarship.

The Essential Errors in T/C About What Enslaved Afro-Americans Learned

Listed below are some of the major errors in T/C:

I. Negative Labor Incentives

(1) F + E do not deny that slaveowners punished slaves, but they misuse a single piece of evidence — a list of whippings on the Bennet H. Barrow Louisiana cotton plantation in 1840 and 1841 — to argue that historians have greatly exaggerated the use of negative labor incentives such as whipping to spur slaves to work harder. That argument is made by computing the least significant measure of whipping.

(2) The whipping list, together with other documents left by Barrow, tells exactly the opposite of what F + E find. These documents tell that on an average a slave was whipped every 4.6 days, that most slaves were whipped for inefficient labor, that the most productive cotton pickers were also the most disorderly and the most frequently whipped slaves, that those who were whipped had not internalized the Protestant work ethic, and that F + E have misrepresented Barrow's disgust with the labor of his slaves.

II. Positive Labor Incentives

(1) The evidence offered by F + E to indicate patterns of short-run and intermediate rewards meant to get slaves to work harder shows no patterns.

(2) The reconstruction of urban and rural slave occupational structures "about 1850" convinces F + E that between 25 and 30 percent of rural slave males were neither field hands nor common laborers and that urban slaves had even greater opportunities. Slaves worked hard and internalized the Protestant work ethic because of the opportunity in the "long run" to climb the slave occupational ladder and become artisans, drivers, and overseers.

8

(3) Serious errors in overestimating the percentage of slaves with urban and rural skills, together with an entirely inappropriate comparison between the occupations of all slave males in 1850 and all males in 1870, invalidate this argument.

(4) The percentage of skilled and "managerial" slaves in southern cities is greatly exaggerated by the use of incomplete data on the antebellum southern white and free black urban occupational structure, by a misreading of Robert Starobin's study of industrial slavery, and especially by excessive reliance on a wholly inaccurate 1848 Charleston, South Carolina, census. It is impossible that 44 percent of southern urban artisans were blacks in 1860.

(5) The percentage of rural slaves who were neither common laborers nor field hands is also exaggerated because the so-called conventional ratio of slave drivers to slaves is based upon a misreading of other historians. The estimated percentage of slave overseers is based upon erroneous assumptions, and the estimated percentage of rural slave artisans is based upon a misreading of probate records. F + E estimate that 11.9 percent of rural slaves were artisans, but the occupations of twenty thousand Union Army Kentucky black soldiers fix that percentage at 1.6 percent. When corrections are made, it turns out that at least about 85 percent of rural male slaves were either common laborers or field hands, a percentage of change that greatly lessens the opportunities for slave advancement or achievement.

(6) The inflation of slave skills causes F + E to argue that a sharp drop in black skills followed emancipation. Racism, not slavery, is blamed for the low skill level among emancipated blacks and their children. That is an inaccurate explanation, because slave skills were far less important than suggested in T/C.

(7) The discussion of slave mobility in T/C is erroneous because mobility cannot be studied at a fixed moment in time. It can only be studied over time, and that is not done in T/C. It is possible that such a study will show that slaves in 1860 had a lower occupational status than their slave grandfathers in 1790.

III. Slave Marriage, the Slave Family, and Slave Sales

(1) T/C contains mostly data dealing with slave marriage (not the slave family) but regularly and erroneously uses data about "stable" slave marriages to describe "stable" slave families. The authors fail to distinguish between a slave marriage and a slave family in their analysis.

(2) The finding that "most slave sales were either of whole families or of individuals who were at an age when it would have been normal for them to have left the family" is not a finding at all. When an older child was separated involuntarily from its slave parents or siblings by sale, hire, gift transfer, or estate division, that separation involved the breakup of a slave family. And there was nothing "normal" about such an involuntary separation. Fail-

ure to examine how often children of any age were separated from immediate slave families flaws by default all arguments about the typicality of the "stable slave nuclear family."

(3) There is no positive evidence in T/C that slaves lived in stable nuclear families. There is only negative evidence — an apparent low incidence of sales that broke up slave marriages.

(4) Two arguments minimize the effects of interregional migration and sale on the stability of the slave family. Both are flawed. The belief that migration from the Upper to the Lower South with their owner did not break up immediate slave families is based upon the assumption that migrating owners owned all members of an immediate family. But it was common in the Upper South for a slave husband and wife to have separate owners. Migration without sale therefore broke up many slave families.

(5) A second argument shows infrequent marital breakups among women sold in the New Orleans slave market only because of the way in which F + E define a slave marriage. A comparison of the percentage of child-bearing women in the New Orleans slave market with child-bearing women in the slave-selling states is invalid because F + E construct familial slave relationships from the manuscript slave census. That cannot be done accurately.

(6) F + E make much use of William Calderhead's excellent study of slave sales in eight Maryland counties between 1830 and 1840, the only available study of slave sales in a particular population. F + E fail to point out that if Calderhead's data are typical for the entire South between 1820 and 1860, a slave was sold every 3.6 minutes and about two million slaves were sold between 1820 and 1860. Since most slaves lived in families, these data alone show how wrong it is to say that slaves lived in stable families. (Unless, of course, most slaves sold did not live in families.)

(7) Many essential "propositions" in T/C about the slave family are based upon scattered examples, not systematic evidence. They include arguments that slaveowners "promoted" stable slave families, that planters encouraged fertility by "promoting family formation," that slaves "apparently abandoned African family forms," and that "wives tended to play a much stronger role in black than in white families."

(8) The discussion of the slave family is marred by the failure to make such essential distinctions as the difference between a slave family and a slave household, by the absence of any discussion of slave kinship groupings, and by the failure to define words such as "nuclear."

IV. Slave Marital and Sexual Behavior

(1) The "average" age of slave women and men at marriage is fixed at twenty years for women and twenty-four years for men. F + E suggest that such information comes from probate records. It cannot.

(2) The striking argument that slave sexual mores were "prudish" is based upon a single source: scattered and unidentified probate records which fix the "average" age of slave women at the birth of a first surviving child in the household at 22.5 years and show that about 40.0 percent of slave mothers had a first surviving child when not yet 20 years old.

(3) A vast amount of other quantitative evidence drawn from the 1880 manuscript federal census fixes the average age of former slave women at the birth of a first surviving child at between 18.0 and 18.9 years and shows that between 8 and 13 percent of former slave women had a first child prior to a fifteenth birthday. About 60.0 percent had a first child prior to a twentieth birthday.

(4) If the 1880 data are correct and if what F + E report is accurate, it follows that one of the great consequences of the general emancipation was a significant drop in the age at which southern black women began having intercourse.

(5) But F + E err in their use of probate records. The historian cannot learn from a probate record whether the oldest child in a household is the first-born child. There is an upward bias in all probate records dealing with slave mothers. Plantation birth registers, not surprisingly, show an age of the mother at the birth of a first child that is consistent with the 1880 data.

(6) The age found in the probate records convinces F + E that prenuptial intercourse was rare among enslaved Afro-Americans. But the age of mothers at the birth of a first child was much lower than F + E realize, and a vast quantity of evidence shows that prenuptial intercourse was common among the enslaved. Such behavior, of course, is not evidence of promiscuity.

(7) Evidence in T/C that a narrow age spread separated most slave husbands and wives also is contradicted by a vast quantity of contemporary data, posing additional questions about the validity of the sources used by F + E.

(8) The argument that slave prostitution did not exist is based upon a misrepresentation of what the manuscript census schedules reveal and upon the creation of a non-fact.

The Quantity and Quality of Evidence in T/C

In the pages that follow, a variety of questions shall be asked about the evidence and the arguments in T/C dealing with what slaves learned. These questions are appropriate to all historical works and to all sorts of historical evidence. Have the authors asked the right question? Has the question asked been answered properly? Have the right sources been used? Have the sources used been properly studied? Are there conceptual errors in the use of the sources? Are there errors in what quantitative historians call "executional computations"? Has the work of other historians on similar subjects been properly used? Have the arguments of other historians on similar subjects been properly summarized? How do the new findings measure against the published findings of other historians and against other sources not examined by the author? What is the relationship between "hard" empirical findings and speculative inferences and estimates?

It is useful, furthermore, to indicate at the start some of the overall limitations in the evidence presented in T/C. The evidence, first of all, is quite uneven in quantity. Thirty-eight pages in volume two (pp. 87 to 125), for example, present supplementary evidence on the arguments in chapter four, "The Anatomy of Exploitation." That single chapter discusses at least fifteen different subjects, including the slave diet, slave shelter, slave clothing, slave medical care, slave mortality, slave morbidity, interracial and inter-status sexual contacts, slave sexual behavior, slave marital patterns, the slave family, slave punishments, short-run slave rewards, intermediate slave rewards, long-term slave rewards, and an estimated rate of slave "expropriation." The evidence offered on these diverse matters is greatly skewed. Three-fifths of the evidence in these thirty-eight pages discusses either the slave diet or a complicated measure of the rate of miscegenation. Second, much of volume two is filled with references to sources that are never carefully described. Manuscript plantation records and probate records, for example, are frequently cited, but the name of a single plantation record or probate record examined by F + E is never recorded in the text of this work. Third, and perhaps most important, there are assumptions that slip regularly into arguments otherwise surrounded by "averages" and "percentages." F + E explain at the beginning of volume two: "In the main text we attempted to weave these new findings into a fairly comprehensive reinterpretation of the nature of the slave economy. To do so we were obliged to invoke assumptions which, though plausible, cannot be verified at present, and to rely on additional evidence which is too fragmentary to be subjected to systematic statistical tests."[9] That is an honest admission of the weakness of much of the argument and evidence in T/C. It shall be seen in the pages that follow that some essential assumptions are not at all plausible and are, in fact, contradicted by vast quantities of evidence. It shall also be seen that fragmentary evidence appears again and again in explanations of the beliefs and behavior of both the owners of slaves and the enslaved themselves.

T/C is a very disappointing book. Although many monographs and specialized studies have been written about the enslaved Afro-American, an entire range of critical subjects — some inadequately studied and others still unstudied — needs fresh empirical examination. New work is needed on

[9] T/C, II, p. 4.

such subjects as the slave family and kinship system, slave demography, slave religion, slave work habits, the sale of slaves, the intimate texture of everyday slave life, and, most important, the processes by which an adaptive Afro-American slave culture emerged in the eighteenth and nineteenth centuries. New methodologies (some of them quantitative) have greatly advanced the writing of American social history in the past two decades but have not been used widely to study enslaved Afro-Americans. T/C is the first major study using such methods and relying primarily on quantitative data. Its authors celebrate the value of such methods and such data but do not use those data carefully. There is a danger, therefore, that their many errors will turn students of the Afro-American experience away from such techniques. That would be unfortunate, because such techniques are rather useful tools in describing regularities in social behavior and thereby allowing the social historian to begin reconstructing neglected or misinterpreted aspects of slave culture and slave beliefs.

Enslaved Afro-Americans and the
"'Protestant' Work Ethic"

We consider first the most important new "finding" in T/C: the conclusion that southern slave farms and plantations were much more efficient than southern free farms and northern farms because of the "quality of black labor." Summing up what they consider "some of the principal corrections of the traditional characterization of the slave economy," F + E assert: "The typical slave field hand was not lazy, inept, and unproductive. On an average he was harder-working and more efficient than his white counterpart."[10] All earlier historians of slavery — writers as different as U. B. Phillips, Stanley Elkins, and Kenneth Stampp — are severely criticized for failing to understand the "fact" that most *ordinary* slave workers had internalized what F + E call the "'Protestant' work ethic." This proposition about the "quality of black labor" is much, much more important to the general theme of T/C than F + E's discussion of slave material conditions such as food, clothing, shelter, and medical care and their discussion of "the slave family." F + E explain: "[M]aterial treatment is [not] the issue on which the economic analysis of slavery turns. Indeed, the resolution of none of the other issues depends on the resolution of the question of material treatment. Slavery could have been profitable, economically viable, highly efficient, and the southern economy could have been rapidly growing under either a cruel or a mild regime."[11] It was instead the productive labor of slaves that "explains" the relative efficiency of the plantation system.

Efficient Slave Labor Is Not the Same as an Efficient Plantation

The authors of T/C do much more than describe the relative efficiency of the antebellum plantation system. They attribute that efficiency to the

[10] T/C, I, pp. 4-5.
[11] T/C, II, pp. 219-220.

"quality of black labor" and, therefore, are describing the social character of the enslaved themselves. David and Temin put it well:

> Superior "efficiency" is . . . said to have characterized the work performance of the individual slaves, as well as the class of production organizations that utilized them.
> While they are analytically distinct, it is important to notice that the two types of statements involving comparisons of efficiency are *not empirically unconnected*. Fogel and Engerman have not developed *any independent quantitative support for their propositions regarding the comparative personal efficiencies of the typical slave and free worker* in agriculture. Instead, they have arrived at these conclusions essentially by the process of *eliminating some other conceivable explanations* for the measured factor productivity advantage of slave-using agriculture — such as differential economies of scale, technical knowledge[,] or managerial ability. . . . [Italics added.][12]

Econometricians are examining with care the measures by which F + E figure that "slave farms" were X percent more efficient than free southern or northern farms. David and Temin have begun that discussion and have suggested a number of biased estimates and erroneous assumptions that greatly exaggerate the productivity of slave farms as opposed to free farms.[13] The following pages examine in detail the evidence used by F + E to reveal the "comparative personal efficiencies of the typical slave . . . worker in agriculture" but do not discuss the relative efficiency of productive organizations worked with slave labor. David's and Temin's point that the "two types of statements involving comparisons of efficiency are not empirically unconnected" is important, but they neglect the critical quantitative data that F + E have assembled on the rural and urban slave occupational structures, the only new quantitative data meant to explain why slaves worked so hard and so well.

The Transformation of Slave Work Habits and the Protestant Work Ethic

F + E's most crucial arguments about the quality of slave labor and much of their least convincing evidence are found in a brief portion of chapter four entitled "Punishments, Rewards, and Expropriations." A short but controversial section, it has attracted the attention of nearly all reviewers and contains data essential to some of F + E's most startling conclusions.[14] It also uses evidence in ways that strikingly reveal the utter inadequacy of the old-fashioned model of slave society that tarnishes T/C. David and Temin vigorously dispute the low rate of expropriation estimated by F + E, insist-

[12] David and Temin, "Slavery: The Progressive Institution?" as cited.
[13] *Ibid.*
[14] T/C, I, pp. 144-153, 236-246.

ing that inaccurate estimates indicate a bias.[15] The focus here is different. It is on F + E's arguments and their use of evidence to show that enslaved Afro-Americans worked hard and diligently because they wanted to and because profit-maximizing owners skillfully mixed a few punishments with many rewards to encourage productive slave labor. We examine "punishments" and "rewards" — the positive and negative incentives used by slaveowners, especially planters, to improve slave labor and to increase productivity.[16] F + E do not deny that slaveowners used physical punishment, but they greatly minimize its significance in relation to the prevalence of positive labor incentives. The carrot counted more than the stick: "While whipping was an integral part of the system of punishment and rewards, it was not the totality of the system. What planters wanted was not sullen and discontented slaves who did just enough to keep from getting whipped. They wanted devoted, hard-working, responsible slaves who identified their fortunes with the fortunes of their masters. Planters sought to imbue slaves with a 'Protestant' work ethic and to transform that ethic from a state of mind into a high level of production. . . . Such an attitude could not be beaten into slaves. It had to be elicited."[17]

Convinced that a system of positive planter-sponsored labor incentives existed, F + E also insist that most slaves responded positively to the rewards offered them. The very last paragraph in T/C emphasizes this point. A high level of slave productivity resulted in the production of cotton, tobacco, sugar, and rice. But the "spikes of racism" — that is, "myths" — hid this "fact" from contemporaries and later historians. Racist beliefs turned slave high achievers into Uncle Toms.[18] The biased beliefs of antislavery advocates and so-called neo-abolitionist historians kept hidden from the American people, and especially from black Americans, truths about how the ancestors of twentieth-century Afro-Americans had been transformed as slaves into nineteenth-century "economic" men and women. Sambo really was Horatio Alger with a black skin.

Evidence supporting such a transformation is not found in T/C. If such a transformation actually occurred, *that* would be a social fact of great importance in understanding the behavior and beliefs of enslaved Afro-Americans and of their emancipated descendants. But most of the evidence in T/C about this important conclusion is not impressive. Much of it is circumstantial; none of it is substantial; most of it is quite traditional; hardly any of it comes from new sources; and, when used, such sources are often imprecisely and sometimes wildly exaggerated. To transform means "to change something to a different form," a change "in appearance, condition,

[15] David and Temin, "Slavery: The Progressive Institution?" as cited.
[16] T/C, I, pp. 144-153; II, pp. 116-119.
[17] T/C, I, p. 147.
[18] *Ibid.*, pp. 263-264.

nature, or character." Transformation, therefore, is a social process and has to occur over time. Something happens to someone. Slaves are made into "efficient" workers. The F + E model, however, is static and ahistorical. F + E never consider who was being transformed. Because there is no discussion of who the slaves were and how well they worked at the beginning of this social process, it is hardly possible to describe a transformation. Instead of that kind of needed and useful analysis, important evidence — especially that dealing with punishments, rewards, and mobility — is so badly used that it casts considerable and disturbing doubt upon the entire argument.

Scant Evidence on Negative Labor Incentives (or Slave Punishments)

Negative labor incentives, or punishments, are treated with a single and greatly misinterpreted quantitative example: Appendix C ("Misconduct and Punishments: 1840-1841") in Edwin Adams Davis, ed., *Plantation Life in the Florida Parishes of Louisiana, 1836-1846, as Reflected in the Diary of Bennet H. Barrow*.[19] The historian Davis apparently gathered cases of slave misconduct and punishment from the cotton planter Barrow's diary.[20] The Davis study contains one of the few easily accessible quantitative sources used by F + E. Cliometric theory is not needed to examine it. Analysis does not depend upon computer technology. Ordinary readers of T/C should examine these data, and draw their own conclusions about how accurately they have been used. My own analysis follows.

The Barrow punishment record serves to create a pseudostatistic that diminishes the importance of slave whippings. This record is the only evidence dealing with slave punishment, so it serves to trivialize planter-sponsored negative labor incentives. After a brief paragraph which tells that "whipping could be either a mild or a severe punishment" (an indisputable but hardly original generalization), a critical four-sentence paragraph based entirely on the Davis appendix follows: "Reliable data on the frequency of whipping is extremely sparse. The only systematic record of whipping now available for an extended period comes from the diary of Bennet Barrow, a Louisiana planter who believed that to spare the rod was to spoil the slave. His plantation numbered about 200 slaves, of whom about 120 were in the labor force. The record shows that over the course of two years a total of 160 whippings were administered, an average of 0.7 whippings per hand per year. About half the hands were not whipped at all during the period."[21]

19 New York, 1943, pp. 431-440.
20 The entire volume includes several other useful appendices, such as a brief but illuminating sketch of Barrow and his planter peers and Barrow's diary entries from 1836 to 1846, pp. 72-385.
21 T/C, I, p. 145.

Figure 40 — entitled "The Distribution of Whippings on the Bennet H. Barrow Plantation during a Two-Year Period Beginning in December, 1840" — which accompanies these few sentences, and which is reproduced here as Table 1, merely illustrates what the written word reports.

TABLE 1. DISTRIBUTION OF WHIPPINGS ON THE BENNET H. BARROW PLANTATION DURING A TWO-YEAR PERIOD BEGINNING IN DECEMBER, 1840

Whippings Per Hand	Estimated Percentage Whipped
0	45%
1	18%
2	14%
3	7%
4	11%
5	3%
6	1%
7	1%

The two brief paragraphs which follow the one quoted above do not enlarge upon these "findings" but examine whipping generally and offer some "comparative" observations.[22] The data drawn from the Barrow diary, then, are the only items of hard data dealing with negative labor incentives.

How the Historian Measures the Frequency of Slave Whippings, Figure 40

The sentence — "The record shows that over the course of two years a total of 160 whippings were administered, an average of 0.7 whippings per hand per year" — is examined first. Several questions come to mind. Is "0.7 whippings per hand per year" a useful average? Have the Barrow diary data and the appendices which accompany them been properly used? Have the right historical questions been asked of those data? It is assumed for the moment that Barrow owned 200 slaves, of whom about 120 were in the labor force. (It shall be seen below that each number — 200 and 120 — is wrong.) To report "an average of 0.7 whippings per hand per year" using these numbers is accurate. That is not, however, the significant average. The wrong question has been asked. The logic producing this average is

[22] A few sentences in volume two, p. 116, tell readers that "an adequate social history of whipping remains to be written" and that scattered historical writings indicate the persistence (despite a declining frequency) of whippings as a means of disciplining "members of the laboring classes" into the mid-nineteenth century in England, Russia, and even the American North. But what the British historian E. H. Carr calls the "economic whip" steadily replaced physical punishment in developing capitalist countries.

18

socially flawed along with the inferences suggested by it. The same logic could just as easily calculate the average number of whippings per hand per week (0.013). It is known, for example, that "on average" 127 blacks were lynched every year between 1889 and 1899.[23] How does one assess that average? Assume that 6 million blacks lived in the United States in 1889 and that 127 of them were lynched. Is it useful to learn that "the record shows an average of 0.0003 lynchings per black per year so that about 99.9997 percent of blacks were not lynched in 1889?" An accurate average, that is a banal statistic. Lynching as a form of social control cannot be evaluated by dividing the number of blacks (or whites) lynched into the number of living blacks (or whites). The absolute number of lynchings in a given time period and whether that number rose or fell later in time are important numbers. They measure the changing frequency with which this particular instrument of social violence was used. It is then possible to study that instrument's relative significance.

The same is true with slave whippings. Southern law permitted slaveowners to punish their chattel, and most historians agree that whipping served as the most common form of physical punishment, figuring as a central device in imposing order over troublesome slaves and in revealing the source of authority in a slave society. The essential statistic, therefore, is not the average number of whippings per hand per year.[24] Whether by the week or the year, such an average does not measure the utility of the whip as an instrument of social and economic discipline. It is much more relevant to know how often the whip was used: on Plantation X with Y slaves in Z years, how frequently was the whip used? That information is available in the Davis volume. In 1840-1841, Barrow's slaves were whipped 160 times. A slave — "on average" — was whipped every 4.56 days. Three slaves were whipped every two weeks. Among them, sixty (37.5 percent) were females. A male was whipped once a week, and a female once every twelve days. Are these averages "small" or "large"? That depends. And it depends upon much more than whether one is a "neo-abolitionist" or a "quantitative" historian. These are quite high averages, and for good reason. If whipping is viewed primarily as an instrument of labor discipline and not as the mere exercise of arbitrary power (or cruelty), whipping three slaves every two weeks means that this instrument of physical discipline had an adequate social visibility among the enslaved. Slave men and women were whipped frequently enough — whatever the size of the unit of ownership — to reveal

[23] C. Vann Woodward, *Origins of the New South, 1877-1913* (1951), pp. 351-352.

[24] Using the same data, interestingly, Eugene D. Genovese makes the same mistake. "Masters," he writes, "who were not slaves to their passions tried to hold corporal punishment to a minimum. The harsh Bennet H. Barrow of Louisiana used his whip more than most: his slaves averaged one whipping a month and many only once a year" (*Roll Jordan Roll* [1974], p. 64).

to them (and to us) that whipping regularly served Barrow as a negative instrument of labor discipline. Imagine reading the following argument:

> While whipping was an integral part of the system of punishment and rewards, it was not the totality of the system. What planters wanted was not sullen and discontented slaves who did just enough to keep from getting whipped. They wanted devoted, hard-working, responsible slaves who identified their fortunes with the fortunes of their masters. Planters sought to imbue slaves with a "Protestant" work ethic and to transform that ethic from a state of mind into a high level of production. . . . *Reliable data on the frequency of whipping is extremely sparse. The only systematic record of whipping now available comes from the diary of Bennet Barrow, a Louisiana planter who believed that to spare the rod was to spoil the slave. Over the course of two years, Barrow whipped a slave every 4.56 days. Women were whipped less frequently than men. On average, a male slave was whipped every 7.3 days and a female slave every 12.2 days.* [The "Protestant" work ethic] . . . could not be beaten into slaves. It had to be elicited.

A schoolboy would not take such an argument based on this evidence seriously. There is a *real* social difference between a slave being whipped every 4.56 days and "an average of 0.7 whippings per hand per year." And it rests on more than a mastery of long division.

Constructing a Whipping Table: Numerical Errors in Figure 40

So far, it has been pointed out that F + E asked the wrong question. That error is common among historians. But F + E also have inaccurately used the Barrow diary and the accompanying appendices. "His [Barrow's] plantation," they write, "numbered about 200 slaves, of whom about 120 were in the labor force." Both numbers are wrong. Whipping data are available for 1840-1841, but the Davis volume, including the diary itself, does not tell how many slaves Barrow owned in 1840-1841. An "Inventory of the Estate of Bennet H. Barrow," printed as an appendix, gives by name and age the slaves he owned when he died. About 200 men, women, and children are listed. But Barrow died in 1854, fourteen years after the recorded whippings, and it appears that F + E assume that Barrow owned "about 200 slaves" in 1840-1841. No data in the Davis volume warrant that assumption. Additional appendices — birth (1835-1846) and death (1831-1845) lists (pp. 427-431) — show that slightly more than twice as many slaves were born as died in these years. Since Barrow apparently sold few slaves, these records suggest that he owned far fewer than 200 slaves in 1840-1841. F + E, therefore, measured the actual number of recorded whippings against a total slave population far in excess of its real size. As a result, the frequency with which *individual* slaves were whipped is greatly underestimated. (After the publication of the journal version of this review-essay, Professor William Scarborough of the University of Southern Mississippi kindly supplied me with the number of slaves Barrow owned in 1840, a statistic drawn from his own research into the 1840 federal manuscript census. That document reveals that Barrow owned 129 [not 200] slaves in 1840. F + E estimate that 90 Barrow slaves were not whipped; the actual number is closer to 19, a drop of about 80 percent. Their inaccurate reckoning shows that 1 out of 2.2 Barrow slaves escaped the whip. Actually, only 1 out of 6.7 was not whipped. The ages of the Barrow slaves in 1840 are not known, but if they fit the typical age distribution given by F + E, then 89 were at least ten years old. F + E tell that Barrow whipped 110 individual slaves. If all slaves at least ten years old were whipped one or more times, we still would have to account for 21 slaves [110 − 89 = 21]. These 21 slaves had to be children under the age of ten. That means that half of slave children under ten were whipped at least once. If Barrow did not whip children under the age of five, and if children under the age of ten were fairly evenly distributed, that means that every child aged five to nine probably was whipped one or more times in 1840-1841. F + E's argument about relative absence of negative labor incentives would have been greatly strengthened if they had assumed that Bennet Barrow never lived rather than that he owned "200" slaves in 1840.)

Barrow's Diary Entries Compared to the Whipping List

The Barrow diary entries are just as valuable as the Davis whipping list.[25] There is some question whether the diary is complete.[26] The same volume also includes several valuable appendices and a sixty-seven-page essay on Barrow, his family, and his business, plantation, and social doings. Written in the Phillips tradition, the essay has some of the severe shortcomings characteristic of that genre but still contains much useful information. F + E rely heavily on the essay and Davis' list, "Misconduct and Punishments: 1840-1841," but for an unexplained reason none of the rich details describing plantation management and especially slave disciplining that stud the ten-year diary found their way into the pages of T/C. F + E possibly felt that this material was irrelevant to T/C's central themes. Extracts from the diary follow:[27]

[25] "The only systematic record of whipping now available for an extended period," write F + E, "comes from the diary of Bennett Barrow. . . ." The sentence more properly should read: . . .: "The only systematic record of whipping available to us for an extended period. . . ." F + E have not systematically searched plantation records for similar evidence. That much is clear from their list of sources. No one, to my knowledge, including F + E, has yet made a systematic search for such data. It is badly needed.

[26] Some of the whippings listed in the Davis appendix, for example, are not found in the published diary.

[27] Davis, *Plantation Life*, pp. 85-192 and 202-376, *passim*.

1836

Dec. 26   House Jerry & Isreal chained during Christmas Jerry for general bad conduct — for a year and better — Isreal bad conduct during cotten picking season

1837

Sept. 4   . . . had a general Whiping frollick

Oct. 2   More Whiping to do this Fall than alltogether in three years owing to my D mean Overseer

Dec. 31   ran two of Uncle Bats negros off last night — for making a disturbance — no pass — broke my sword Cane over one of their skulls

1838

Jan. 23   my House Servants Jane Lavenia & E. Jim broke into my store room — and helped themselves verry liberally to every thing — . . . I Whiped [them] . . . worse than I ever Whiped any one before

Sept. 28   Dennis and Tom *"Beauf"* ran off on Wednesday — . . . if I can see either of them and have a gun at the time will let them have the contents of it . . .

Oct. 12   [Tom ran off again] will Whip him more than I ever Whip one, I think he deserves more — the second time he has done so this year . . .

Oct. 20   Whiped about half to day

Oct. 26   Whiped 8 or 10 for weight to day — those that pick least weights generally most trash . . .

Oct. 27   Dennis ran off yesterday — & after I had Whiped him

Nov. 2   Dennis came in sick on Tuesday — ran off again yesterday — without my ever seeing him — will carry my Gun & small shot for him — I think I shall cure him of his rascallity

Nov. 7   Dennis came in last night — had him fasted — attempted to Escape. ran as far as the creek but was caught — the Ds rascal on the place

Dec. 30   Demps gave his wife Hetty a light cut or two & then locked her up to prevent her going to the Frollick — I reversed it turning her loose & fastning him

1839

Jan. 4   Whiped evry hand in the field this evening commencing with the driver

April 27   My hands worked verry badly — so far general Whipping yesterday

July 19   Gave L. Dave a good Whipping for some of his rascallity intend chaining him & Jack nights & Sunday till I think they are broke in — to behave

Sept. 9   Whiped G. Jerry & Dennis for their shirking

Sept. 30   Had G. Jerry T. Fill & Bts Nat up here washing all yesterday as punishment — generally dirty & ragged

Oct. 2   Lewis still out. no doubt but he is down at Uncle Bats Where his Father lives — which proves the impropiety of having slaves off the plantation

Oct.	3	told Dennis I intended to Whip him. [Dennis fled] . . . started Jack after him — to give him $50 if he catches him — I had rather a negro would do anything Else than runaway. Dennis & his Brother Lewis & G. Jerry the only ones that gives me any trouble to make do their part
Oct.	4	Boy Lewis came in last night — gave him the worst Whipping I ever gave any young negro. I predict he will not runaway *soon*. Building a Jail for him Dennis & Ginny Jerry — intend jailing them for Saturday nights 'till Monday mornings
Oct.	13	Put Darcas in Jail last night for pretending to be sick, repeatedly — the first one ever put in the Jail & G Jerry
Oct.	20	Gave my negros about my lot the worst Whipping they ever had
Oct.	23	Gave every cotten picker a Whipping last night for trash & of late my driver has lost considerable authority with them
[Dec.	23	Dennis caught]
Dec.	24	intend exhibiting Dennis during Christmas on a scaffold in the middle of the Quarter & with a red Flannel Cap on
Dec.	25	Let Darcas out of Jail — Dennis confined in Jail

1840

Jan.	9	Darcas began to sherk again — let her out of Jail Christmas she promised to do well &c.
April	18	gave my driver a few licks this evening, not knowing Who had done bad work
April	19	had a general Whipping among the House ones & two Carters for stealing, &c.
July	5	had Jack rigged out this evening with red flanel on his years [*sic*] & a Feather in them & sheet on, "in the Quarter." every negro up. Made Alfred and Betsey ride him round the Quarter dismount and take a kiss, for quarreling, Jack & Lize, Frank & Fanney the same.
July	30	[The cook Lavenia had run away and was found] Lavenia thought she had been whipped unjustly owing to Jane (the Cook), let Lavenia give her a good *drubing, &c.*
Oct.	13	I think my hands have Picked cotton worse this year than in several years picked it verry trashy & not better weights nor as good as *common*, intend Whipping them *straght*
Oct.	15	am sattisfied the best plan is to give them every thing they require for their comfort and never that they will do without Whipping or some punishment

1841

Jan.	3	[Barrow gave the Negroes a dinner] and afterwards inspected their manners in the Ballroom several acted very rude as usual. put them in Jail
Aug.	16	Ginney Jerry has been sherking about ever since Began to pick cotten. after Whipping him yesterday told him if ever he dodged about from me again would certainly shoot him. this morning at

Breakfast time Charles came & told me that Jerry was about to run off. took my Gun found him in the Bayou behind the Quarter, shot him in the thigh

Sept. 16   Ginney Jerry ran off Last Thursday to day a week, after being shot, Will shoot to kill him should I be fortunate enoughf [*sic*] to meet him, Will sell him &c.

Oct. 2   More hands attempting to sherk for two weeks past than I ever knew, Gave a number of them a good *floging*

1842

June 15   [Ginney Jerry ran away again] will shoot to kill him if an opportunity offers.... has not been touched this year, nor have I said a word to him, pray for a shot at him

Nov. 6   Friday night Jack Let Jerry slip for purpose of getting a pig thinking as Jerry was Jailed at night there would be no suspicion of him — for some reason told Alfred Jerry had a pig in his house A. went and found it as Jack thought. put him in Jail & in the stocks in the morning there was nothing of Jerry stocks Broke & door — no doubt some one turned him out — one concerned in the Pig — gave about a dozen severe Whipping in the Yard & all — Jack old Jenny & Darcas the most severe hand sawing

1844

Nov. 28   Whiped all my grown cotten pickers to day

Nov. 29   [Dennis ran off and was then caught] gave him the worst Whipping he ever had — & ducking

1845

May 27   [Darcas cut her husband with a hatchet in the hip] Very dangerous cut — will make her sick of the sight of a Hatchet as Long as she Lives

June 4   missed several of my young Hogs, found 8 or 10 Guilty, ducked & gave them a good thrashing, Mr. *Ginney* Jerry next morning Felt insulted at his treatment & put out, would give "freely" $100 to get a shot at him

Sept. 6   The negro hunters came this morning, Were not out long before we struck the trail of Ginny Jerry, ran and trailed for about a mile *treed* him, made the dogs pull him out of the tree, Bit him very badly, think he will stay home a while

Oct. 18   Fell quite unwell for two days past, effect of negro hunting

Oct. 27   Went with the negro Dogs to Hunt Ruffins runaways, & his small house boy Ed. ran off still out, 12 years of age — no Luck — negro dogs here — tired of them

Nov. 11   the negro dogs to Mrs Wades Quarter.... dogs soon tore him naked, took him Home Before the other negro & made the dogs give him another over hauling, has been drawing a knife & Pistol on persons about Town

It is surprising that as rich a source as these diary entries was entirely neglected. It reveals much about the labor incentives Barrow used with his slaves. More than once, for example, Barrow penned suggestive diary notations such as "had a general Whiping frolick," "whiped about half to day," "general Whipping yesterday," "intend Whipping them *straght*," "whiped all my grown cotton pickers to day." None of these general whippings counted in the list of whippings. The diary, in fact, reveals that general whippings of productive Barrow male and female slaves occurred quite regularly: there were at least six collective whippings — 1837, 1838, twice in 1839, 1840, and 1841 — between 1837 and 1841. The diary also listed other punishments. In his fine dissertation on the slave family, Bobby Jones concluded that Barrow resorted to "practically every known form of chastisement slaveholders used." Jones pointed out: "During his career, Barrow resorted to chains; extra work; whipping; humiliation, such as making a man wear women's clothing and parade around the quarters; imprisonment; stocks; 'raked several negro heads to day'; 'staking out'; 'hand-sawing'; and dousing or ducking in water which occurred in October and November." Jones figured that "hand-sawing" probably meant "a beating administered with the toothed-edge of a saw."[28] The diary extracts reprinted in these review-essay pages include yet other punishments, including the occasional shooting of a runaway. It is not inappropriate to ask — especially in a study which assesses the relative importance of slave physical punishments — why F + E failed to weigh the full punishment record reported in the diary. That source, after all, serves as the single piece of evidence on slave punishments.[29]

Barrow's Cotton Pickers (Field Hands) Were Frequently Whipped

The Davis appendix, it turns out, can measure the frequency with which an owner used a whip and, more importantly, suggest the relationship between whipping and slave labor "efficiency," even hinting that Barrow's field hands — the women as well as the men — had not internalized either Barrow's or F + E's conception of the " 'Protestant' work ethic." Only the Davis appendix "Misconduct and Punishments: 1840-1841" is used in their

[28] Bobby Jones, "A Cultural Middle Passage: Slave Marriage and Family in the Antebellum South," Ph.D. diss., University of North Carolina, 1965, pp. 57-58. This source is cited in the F + E bibliography so that if the authors missed such entries in examining the diary itself, they might have noticed them in reading this unusually important study.

[29] The fact that this is the single piece of evidence used by F + E to deal with physical punishment does not deter the economist Peter Passell from concluding that "Fogel and Engerman find no . . . pattern of abuse." The "economic" findings in T/C do not surprise that reviewer, but "what is surprising is the general level of dignity accorded the slaves in other aspects of life" (Passell, review of T/C, *New York Times Book Review*, 28 April 1974, p. 4).

arguments that follow. Other methods of negative labor discipline (such as ducking, jailing, and even "hand-sawing") are put aside, and it is assumed that the list is the full record of all slaves whipped. Slave misconduct and whippings are examined, but just for those slaves listed as cotton pickers by Barrow in other appendices published by Davis (two cotton picking lists dated November 3, 1838, and September 10, 1842). This analysis does not account for the misconduct and whipping of slaves who were not cotton pickers, particularly house servants. But it tells a good deal about those slaves who picked cotton, an activity of some importance on the Barrow plantation. Their misconduct and subsequent whipping indicate a pattern of slave and planter behavior entirely contradictory to the F + E thesis about slave punishments and slave work habits.

Table 2 indicates the frequency with which Barrow whipped his cotton

TABLE 2. FREQUENCY OF WHIPPINGS OF BARROW MALE AND FEMALE COTTON PICKERS, 1840-1841

Number of Times Whipped	Male Cotton Pickers		Female Cotton Pickers		All Cotton Pickers	
	Number	Percentage Whipped	Number	Percentage Whipped	Number	Percentage Whipped
0	7	19.4%	9	30.0%	16	24.2%
1	8	22.2%	5	16.7%	13	19.7%
2	10	27.8%	6	20.0%	16	24.2%
3–4	8	22.2%	8	26.6%	16	24.2%
5+	3	8.3%	2	6.7%	5	7.6%
Total	36	100.0%	30	100.0%	66	100.0%

pickers. Three out of four were whipped at least once during 1840-1841. Seven out of ten women felt the whip at least once. In all, fifty of sixty-six male and female cotton pickers were whipped at least once in this brief period. These fifty slaves together were whipped no fewer than 130 times during 1840-1841. The cotton pickers, incidentally, accounted for four out of five of the 160 whippings listed by the historian Davis. If we add to these data the names of women who gave birth to children during 1840-1841 (they were listed in a separate appendix), it is learned that twelve female cotton pickers gave birth to fourteen children in these years, and that seven were whipped in this period (two of them twice and a third no fewer than four times). Some cotton pickers, men and women alike, were not whipped at all. Let us consider them — about one in four of the Barrow cotton pickers — "efficient" field laborers. One in ten of the rest was whipped at least five times. Slightly more than two in five felt the whip at least three times.

The Reason Barrow Whipped Most Slave Men and Women: Inefficient Labor

The same appendix in which Davis listed whippings also includes evidence indicating the varieties of slave "misconduct" detected by Barrow, misconduct that led to physical punishment. Most of Barrow's slaves were whipped for not conforming to the Protestant work ethic. It is hardly a complete list of incidents of slave misconduct in 1840-1841, but it serves, nevertheless, as a most useful document bearing directly on the F + E thesis that slaveowners had successfully transformed the work ethic of their slaves. Barrow sometimes listed a disorderly slave but failed to describe the particular "disorder." Nevertheless, 267 individual disorderly acts were described, 80.9 percent of all those listed. Women committed slightly more than two in five (43 percent). A variety of disorderly acts were recorded, including familial quarrels, child neglect, theft, "impudence," visiting town, and running away. Failure to keep the evening curfew fixed by Barrow was a frequent disorder. But— most significantly—nearly three in four (73 percent) of the acts listed related directly to inefficient labor: "for not picking as well as he can," "not picking cotton," "very trashy cotton," "covering upon cotton limbs with ploughs," "for not bringing her cotton up," and so forth. A slight but not significant difference existed between the slave males and females: two in three acts of misconduct by females related to labor behavior, as contrasted to nearly four in five (78 percent) acts by males. The frequency of whippings among the cotton pickers has been examined, and now the frequency of recorded acts of misconduct among these same persons is studied (Table 3).

TABLE 3. FREQUENCY OF INDIVIDUAL ACTS OF MISCONDUCT BY BARROW PLANTATION MALE AND FEMALE COTTON PICKERS, 1840-1841

Number of Acts of Misconduct per Cotton Picker	Male	Female	Total
0	5	7	12
1	2	2	4
2	4	3	7
3–4	9	4	13
5–6	7	6	13
7–9	6	6	12
10+	3	2	5
Total Slaves	36	30	66

27

In all, the 66 cotton pickers engaged in no fewer than 181 disorderly acts during 1840-1841. The average per hand did not differ between men (4.3) and women (4.2). Men (86.2 percent) more commonly engaged in misconduct than women (77 percent), but the difference should not have greatly pleased Barrow. Over all, four in five cotton pickers engaged in one or more disorderly acts in 1840-1841. Once again, we do not include the twelve men and women who did not commit a detected disorderly act. Among those with disorderly records, four out of five committed three or more disorderly acts as shown in Table 4. As a group, a slightly higher percentage of women than men committed seven or more disorderly acts. Is it possible to describe these male and female slave cotton pickers as members of a well-disciplined, orderly, and efficient slave laboring class? To characterize them so distorts the historical record kept by the planter Barrow.

TABLE 4. FREQUENCY OF RECORDED ACTS OF MISCONDUCT AMONG MALE AND FEMALE COTTON PICKERS WHO COMMITTED ONE OR MORE ACTS OF MISCONDUCT, BARROW PLANTATION, 1840-1841

Number of Disorderly Acts	Percentage of Cotton Pickers Committing Disorderly Acts		
	Male	Female	Total
3 or More	80.6%	75.3%	79.7%
7 or More	29.0%	34.8%	31.5%

The Most Productive Cotton Pickers Were Whipped More Frequently and Were More Disorderly Than the Least Productive Cotton Pickers

In 1838 and 1842, lists also gave the amount of cotton picked each year by individual slaves, and much of social importance is learned by examining the relationships among the most productive cotton pickers, whippings, and acts of recorded misconduct during 1840-1841. Twelve men and twelve women were counted as Barrow's best field laborers. It is quite revealing to compare them to the least productive cotton pickers as illustrated in Table 5. The more productive cotton pickers — both the male and the female pickers but especially the females — were much more disorderly and were more frequently whipped than the less productive cotton pickers. Given their absolute and relative record of misconduct (nearly all of it is related to "inefficient" labor), is it possible to hint that these slave men and women had drunk deeply of the " 'Protestant' work ethic"? If the main thrust in the arguments of F + E is sound, the least productive workers should have been more disorderly and should have received more frequent whippings.

TABLE 5. ACTS OF MISCONDUCT AND WHIPPINGS COMPARED TO RANK OF COTTON PICKERS, BARROW PLANTATION, 1840-1841

	Males			
	Rank Among All Cotton Pickers		1840–1841	
Name	1838	1842	Disorderly Acts	Whippings
Atean	1	1	3	2
Ben	3	4	5	2
Dave B	2	2	12	8
Demps	8	6	6	2
Lewis	10	10	6	3
D. Nat	9	3	8	4
Randall	7	7	10	2
L. Tom	11	9	3	3
Levi	4	8	2	1
Dennis	..	5	8	2
Thornton	4(5)	..	1	0
Kish	4(6)	..	0	0
N			64	29
Highest Pick	622	520		
Lowest Pick	413	385		

	Females			
	Rank Among All Cotton Pickers		1840–1841	
Name	1838	1842	Disorderly Acts	Whippings
Betsey	1	3	5	2
Darcus	5	7	6	2
Fanny	10	6	6	2
Creasy	9	9	8	3
Hetty	4	8	2	1
L. Hannah	3	4	3	1
Luce	8	9	7	4
Oney	6	..	9	4
Patience	7	..	12	6
Lize	2	1	4	2
Milley	12	2	6	5
Sidney	11	5	0	0
N			68	32
Highest Pick	443	425		
Lowest Pick	273	300		

TABLE 5. CONTINUED

	Average Number of Disorderly Acts		Average Number of Whippings		Number of Slaves	
	Males	Females	Males	Females	Males	Females
Most Productive Pickers	5.3	5.7	2.4	2.7	12	12
Least Productive Pickers	3.7	3.1	1.9	1.1	24	18

Why the Barrow Cotton Pickers Had Not Internalized the " 'Protestant' Work Ethic"

That the Barrow cotton pickers had not internalized the " 'Protestant' work ethic" is further suggested by their ages and the moment in time for which a record exists of their behavior. The approximate ages of fourteen male and sixteen female cotton pickers in 1840 can be learned from the 1854 inventory. All except three of the males whipped were between the ages of 19 and 26. The others were older, the oldest among them aged 37. Betsey was 45, and another of the female cotton pickers was a 13-year-old, but nearly all of the other women whipped were between the ages of 15 and 26. The median age of cotton pickers whipped was nearly the same for men (23.8 years) and women (23.2 years). That means that these men and women had grandparents probably born in the 1760s and great-grandparents who probably were native Africans enslaved in the New World. These men and women were a few generations removed from initial enslavement. Nevertheless, three out of four among them had to be whipped — nearly always for labor inefficiency — during 1840-1841. Internalizing any new ethic (work or otherwise) is a social process and takes time. New attitudes toward work are not learned overnight. These same cotton pickers, moreover, were members of the last generation of adult Afro-American slaves. Upon emancipation, some were grandparents, and most were in their middle forties. Surely if any generation of enslaved Afro-Americans had internalized the work ethic prized by their owners, it had to be this one. It was not.

Barrow himself knew why. On April 16, 1840, he wrote in his diary: "am directing them to make a slow & sure lick in one place & to cut the full width of the hoe every time — unless reminded of it they would stand & make 4 or 5 licks in one place, tire themselves & do no work, have several grown ones that work harder & do less work than any in the field." He added disgustedly two days later: " — there never was a more rascally set of old negroes about any lot than this. Big Lucy Anica Center & cook Jane. the better you treat them the worse they are, Big Lucy the leader, corrupts every young negro in her power . . . gave my driver a few licks this morning, not knowing Who had done bad work."[30] There is much to learn from just these two diary entries. Barrow complained bitterly about the older slaves, the most "rascally set" he knew. And he regularly whipped the younger slaves during 1840-1841. If what F + E call the Protestant work ethic had been successfully internalized by the Barrow slaves, the values associated with it would have passed along from slave generation to slave generation. In this instance, that means from slave parents born in the late eighteenth or early nineteenth centuries to their children who lived into the Civil War. But, according to Barrow, the opposite happened. Too many of the "young" slaves listened to Big Lucy, and her message quite obviously differed from that emphasized by Barrow. Barrow, therefore, had an unusually difficult task and was kept busy "transforming" different generations of enslaved Afro-Americans. That fact may explain the frequency with which he used the whip. We have come a long way from the thoroughly misleading sentence that "the record shows that over the course of two years, a total of 160 whippings were administered, an average of 0.7 whippings per hand per year." That pseudostatistic fails to explain Barrow's behavior, the behavior of his cotton field hands, and the relative importance of physical punishment as a form of negative labor incentive.

Reviewing T/C, the historian David Rothman complains that F + E have made too much of the Barrow whippings: ". . . Fogel and Engerman offer a very weak analysis of physical punishments on the plantation. In part, this is a result of a paucity of quantitative data on whippings. One owner, Bennet Barrow did keep some records, and these are tabulated — an average of 0.7 whippings per hand took place each year. But Barrow was a very special sort of a planter, self-consciously dedicated to the proposition that the plantation should run as a factory. He fits the Fogel-Engerman model *too* well to stand as representative of the system."[31]

Rothman is right in calling the analysis "very weak" but wrong in suggesting that Barrow "fits the Fogel-Engerman model too well." Barrow, it has been seen and shall soon be seen again (because F + E return to this Louisiana cotton planter two more times), hardly fits the F + E model at all. That poses three different questions. Was Barrow untypical? Is the F + E model inadequate? And, most importantly, why did Barrow behave in the ways revealed by the data in these pages?

Why Barrow Whipped Slaves So Frequently
and Whether Barrow Was "Typical"

The third question, of course, is the most important. Unless Barrow's actions merely reflected a personal satisfaction in whipping slaves so fre-

[30] Davis, *Plantation Life,* pp. 191-193.
[31] David Rothman, "Slavery in a New Light," *New Leader,* 27 May 1974, pp. 8-9.

quently, we must look elsewhere than to his psychic needs or makeup to begin to comprehend his behavior. And the only place to start is with his slaves and their behavior. The whippings on his plantation make social sense primarily in relation to the misconduct among his slaves and to Barrow's conception of misconduct. The essential flaw in the F + E model is its failure to make a place in the historical process for slave behavior not directly determined by the policies and practices of their owners. Slaves "behave" in their model, but only in response to master-sponsored stimuli. They work hard when promised rewards or threatened with physical punishment. The Barrow slaves, of course, did not have to read their owner's diary or major in college algebra to know how frequently and why he used the whip. Ordinary vision and common sense made that clear. More than this, they surely had enough familiarity with Barrow and his whip to realize how their owner defined slave misconduct. And yet their acts of misconduct during 1840-1841 were by any measure numerous. Those acts of misconduct — mostly variants on the theme of not working hard enough — provoked their owner to use the whip. A model that fails to take into account the behavior of the slaves cannot explain the behavior of their owners.

Whether or not Barrow's response to the behavior of his cotton field hands was "typical" is a more difficult question to answer. Too little, for one thing, is yet known about the everyday behavior — especially in the fields — of slaves like those who lived on the Barrow place. More is known, of course, about Barrow himself. He was born in 1811, and, according to his biographer Davis, his "mode of living was that of a well-to-do planter." "A substantial and respected man in his community," observed Kenneth Stampp, "Barrow inherited lands and slaves from his father; he was in no sense a crude parvenu." (Stampp, incidentally, hardly cited the Barrow diary in *The Peculiar Institution*. Barrow is only mentioned twice in the index.) There are more substantial hints that Barrow was not unusual among Louisiana cotton planters. At least one planter nearby copied Barrow's plantation "rules." Bobby Jones points out that those rules, reprinted as an appendix in the Davis volume, were not original to Barrow. He had copied them verbatim from a "restrictive" system of plantation management advocated by the *Southern Agriculturalist* and then reprinted in the *Southern Cultivator* (March, 1846). His biographer, Davis, insists that in his "general outlook on the institution of slavery" Barrow was "typical of his time and section." Davis adds: "In general, Barrow treated his slaves better and took more time in the organization of his labor system than did many of the neighboring planters. He was in the planting business for the sole purpose of making money and evidently believed that a contented black would work far better than one who was dissatisfied with his surroundings." When a favored slave died, Barrow could say that "a more perfect negro never lived." But such sentiments should not be exaggerated. Barrow believed — according to his diary — that "negros are not Capable of self-government — want of discretion — judgement &." The historian Davis understood Barrow somewhat better than he understood the Barrow slaves. With the 1840-1841 record of slave misconduct before him, Davis nevertheless concluded: "On the whole the Negro was a tractable individual. Barrow's slaves gave him very little trouble. That they were not mean or vicious is evident; but that they often needed punishment for the breaking of plantation rules must be admitted."

We need waste little time with the tone of gentle apologetics that marred the abilities of the historian Davis. Despite this shortcoming, he had some insight into Barrow's management policies. "As a rule," observed Davis, punishments were "designed to be only severe enough to be conducive to good discipline." Brutal whippings were exceptional. "Barrow," Davis goes on, "was constantly devising ingenious punishments, for he realized that uncertainty was an important aid in keeping his gangs well in hand." The range of punishments — aside from whippings — has been indicated. Duckings followed brutal whippings. And, according to Davis, for the most "flagrant violations the Negroes were 'staked down.' This was apparently the old punishment of staking them to the ground on their backs, spread-eagle fashion. Periods of staking were usually short." But especially troublesome slaves were staked down for as long as between twelve and fifteen hours.

Barrow, nevertheless, also conformed in important ways to the managerial pattern emphasized by F + E. According to Davis, the slaves lived in "comfortable frame buildings." Their owner spent a "sizable" amount of money each year for clothing. Field hands ordinarily got four or five pounds of meat each week. The Barrow slaves enjoyed regular holiday celebrations and even dinners and dances. Their owner built a dance hall, but he also built a jail. In describing his conception of the plantation, Barrow used metaphors more appropriate to Yankee New England. "A plantation," he insisted, "might be considered as a piece of machinery, to operate successfully, all of its parts should be uniform and exact." That was an economic aspiration, not an economic or social reality. The slave Dave Bartley is a case in point. He was one of Barrow's best cotton pickers. At Christmas in 1839 he and the slave Atean were singled out for "their fine conduct." Each received a suit of clothes from Barrow. During 1840-1841, Dave Bartley committed more acts of misconduct and received more whippings than any other Barrow slave: twelve instances of misconduct and eight whippings were recorded. Only one other slave committed as many as twelve acts of misconduct. Her name was Patience. She was whipped six times. Neither Bartley nor Patience was "uniform and exact." That was their trouble. They were factors of production but did not exactly fit into Barrow's definition of the plantation as "a piece of machinery." That was so even though Dave Bartley had been given a suit of clothing by his owner.[32] Columbia University economist Peter Passell, who reviewed T/C in the *New York Times Book Review,* would have benefited from knowing Dave Bartley. The data in T/C describing the relatively decent treatment of enslaved Afro-Americans did not shock Passell. "All not very surprising," he said, "for a society that treated slaves as capital; good businessmen oil their machines."[33] Passell apparently does not know the difference between men and women like Dave Bartley and Patience and a steam engine or a cotton gin.

Negative Labor Incentives and the Ubiquitous Words More and Most in T/C

We are finished for the moment with Bennet Barrow and his slaves, but not yet with F + E on negative labor incentives. A brief paragraph follows the "summary" of the Barrow whippings to remind the reader once again that whipping was common in many places before the nineteenth century — even quoting from what is called "the Matthew's Bible," the English translation by John Rogers under the pseudonym Thomas Matthew. The next paragraph "generalizes" about whipping and contains ten sentences which indicate that none of the evidence used is "quantitative." The sentences are numbered *seriatum:*

[1] To attribute the continuation of whipping in the South to the maliciousness of masters is naïve. [2] Although *some* masters were brutal, even sadistic, *most* were not. [3] The *overwhelming majority* of the ex-slaves in the W.P.A. narratives who expressed themselves *on the issue* reported that their masters were *good men.* [4] *Such men* worried about the proper role of whipping in a system of punishment [*sic*] and rewards. [5] *Some* excluded it altogether. [6] *Most* accepted it, but recognized that to be effective whipping had to be used with restraint and in a coolly calculated manner. [7] Weston, *for example,* admonished his overseer not to impose punishment of any sort until twenty-four hours after the offense had been discovered. [8] William J. Minor, a sugar planter, instructed his managers "not [to] cut the skin when punishing, nor punish in a passion." [9] *Many* planters forbade the whipping of slaves except by them or in their presence. [10] *Others* limited the number of lashes that could be administered without their permission. [Italics added.][34]

Sentence 1 is left aside for the moment. The other nine sentences are a curious mode of argument in this work, mainly because the imprecision in language and the use of isolated examples (sentences 7 and 8) are styles of historical rhetoric and argument usually scorned by cliometricians when used

---

[32] Davis, *Plantation Life,* pp. 11, 37-41, 44-48, 52, 406-409; Kenneth M. Stampp, *The Peculiar Institution* (1956), pp. 186, 189.

[33] Passell, review of T/C, *New York Times Book Review,* 28 April 1974, p. 4.

[34] T/C, I, p. 146.

by noncliometricians. How typical were Weston and Minor?[35] What methods were used to establish their typicality? Sentences 2, 5, 6, 9, and 10 contain favored imprecise quantitative words such as *some* and *most* (2, 5, and 6), *many* (9), and *others* (10). It is surprising to see how often such ambiguous words are used. It is, of course, difficult to generalize without using words meant to describe the presence or absence of regularities, and such words are essential to the social and economic historian. But neither volume one nor volume two of T/C contains any evidence indicating how F + E uncovered such regularities in planter behavior. Sentences 3 and 4 — at least as written — do not bear at all on the question of planter patterns of punishment. The point under discussion is the regularity and frequency of slave punishment, not whether elderly former slaves, who were mostly between the ages of eight and twelve when the general emancipation occurred and, therefore, had probably never been beaten or whipped, felt their old owners to be "good" or "bad" men. Where, furthermore, is the evidence that the planters as a social class or group *"worried* about the *proper* role of whipping in a system of punishment and rewards" (italics added)? *Worry* has a fairly precise meaning, but *proper* is an ambiguous word. To worry means "to feel uneasy, or anxious; fret; torment oneself and suffer from disturbing thoughts." Did men like Bennet Barrow, William Minor, and Weston fret over the use of the whip and suffer disturbing thoughts? *Proper* has several meanings, and it is unclear which one is implied in this sentence. Do F + E mean that planters worried about how to adapt whipping to the purposes of enslavement? Do they mean that planters worried about conforming to established standards of behavior? Or do they mean that planters worried about whether or not whipping was right? These are quite different kinds of worries, and each has a social importance of its own.

Kenneth Stampp on Whipping and F + E on Kenneth Stampp

Sentence 1 concerns historiography. "To attribute the continuation of whipping in the South to the maliciousness of masters is naïve," insist F + E. No historians are mentioned, but this barbed sentence is aimed at so-called neo-abolitionist historians. Later in the first volume, the authors of T/C make it unnecessary to guess the target of their criticism: "[Kenneth] Stampp provided testimony that cruelty was indeed an ingrained feature of the treatment of slaves. . . . Cruelty, Stampp said, 'was endemic in all slaveholding communities'; even those 'who were concerned about the welfare of slaves found it difficult to draw a sharp line between acts of cruelty and such mea-

[35] It may have been that Minor did not want the skin cut because it lowered the value of a slave in the market. Who wanted to purchase troublesome property? Hardly a detached source, the *New York Tribune* (10 March 1853) reported that whipping scars cut the sale price of an adult male slave from $750–$800 down to $460.

sures of physical force as were an inextricable part of slavery.' For Stampp, cruelty arose not because of the malevolent nature of the slaveholders but because of the malevolent nature of the system. . . ."[36]

Stampp's arguments have not been fairly summarized. Here are Stampp's sentences from which F + E drew these extracts:

> Although cruelty was endemic in all slaveholding communities, it was always most common in newly settled regions. . . . [And then two paragraphs later] Southerners who were concerned about the welfare of slaves found it difficult to draw a sharp line between acts of cruelty and such measures of physical force as were an inextricable part of slavery. Since the line was necessarily arbitrary, slaveholders themselves disagreed about where it should be drawn. . . . But no master denied the propriety of giving a moderate whipping to a disobedient bondsman. . . . By [the] mid-nineteenth century. . . . [the whip] was seldom used upon any but slaves, because public opinion now considered it to be cruel. Why it was less cruel to whip a bondsman was a problem that troubled many sensitive masters. That they often had no choice as long as they owned slaves made their problem no easier to resolve.[37]

Stampp's explanation for the decline of whipping ("public opinion") is hardly satisfactory, but neither is the summary of Stampp's analysis as quoted by F + E. In fact, Stampp's analysis of whipping is as good as any we yet have and deserves to be read in full:

> . . . [T]he whip was the most common instrument of punishment — indeed, it was the emblem of the master's authority. Nearly every slaveholder used it, and few grown slaves escaped it entirely. . . . The majority seemed to think that the certainty, and not the severity, of physical "correction" was what made it effective. While no offense could go unpunished, the number of lashes should be in proportion to the nature of the offense and the character of the offender. The master should control his temper. . . . Many urged, therefore, that time be permitted to elapse between the misdeed and the flogging. . . .
>
> Planters who employed overseers often fixed the number of stripes they could inflict for each specific offense, or a maximum number whatever the offense. . . . The significance of these numbers depended in part upon the kind of whip that was used. The "rawhide," or "cowskin," was a savage instrument requiring only a few strokes to provide a chastisement that a slave would not soon forget. . . . Many slaveholders would not use the rawhide because it lacerated the skin. . . . How frequently a master resorted to the whip depended upon his

[36] T/C, I, pp. 229-230. The same sentence by Stampp is quoted a second time in T/C, II, p. 220. "Where Phillips characterized slaveholders as men of good will whose treatment of slaves was generally 'benevolent in intent and on the whole beneficial in effect,' Stampp responded: 'Cruelty was endemic in all slaveholding communities' and 'even those concerned about the welfare of slaves found it difficult to draw a sharp line between acts of cruelty and such measures of physical force as were an inextricable part of slavery.' " Once more, F + E have twisted the meaning of Stampp's argument.

[37] Stampp, *Peculiar Institution*, pp. 185-186.

temperament and his methods of management. . . . Physical cruelty, as these observations suggest, was always a possible consequence of the master's power to punish. Place an intemperate master over an ill-disposed slave, and the possibility became a reality.

Not that a substantial number of slaveholders deliberately adopted a policy of brutality. The great majority, in fact, preferred to use as little violence as possible. . . . The public and private records that do survive suggest that, although the average slaveholder was not the inhuman brute described by the abolitionists, acts of cruelty were not as exceptional as pro-slavery writers claimed.[38]

Stampp's illustrative evidence has not been included in this extract, but it strains the imagination to suggest that Stampp's quite balanced analysis can be characterized as representing little more than either crude neo-abolitionist bias or innocent naïveté. Stampp explicitly denied that "a substantial number of slaveholders deliberately adopted a policy of brutality," insisting that "the great majority, in fact, preferred to use as little violence as possible." Quite interestingly, Stampp emphasized that rational "economic" calculations often restrained the use of the whip. And the reasons given by this so-called neo-abolitionist historian hardly differed from those put forth two decades later by F + E.

F + E on the Economic Cost of Whipping, and James Hammond on the Social Utility of Whipping: The Inadequate Economic "Model"

The brief discussion of whipping in T/C is followed by a still briefer discussion of other slave punishments. F + E soundly remind readers that whipping as an instrument of labor discipline declined "with the rise of capitalism" when "impersonal and indirect sanctions were increasingly substituted for direct, personal ones." Hiring labor in the marketplace "provided managers . . . with a powerful new disciplinary weapon." "Workers who were lazy . . . or who otherwise shirked their duties could be fired — left to starve beyond the eyesight or expense of the employer." These summary sentences hardly differ from the classic indictments of early capitalism. "Interestingly enough," F + E add, "denial of food was rarely used to enforce discipline on slaves. For the illness and lethargy caused by malnutrition reduced the capacity of the slave to labor in the fields." The jailing of slaves is mentioned, but only to be dismissed as a common form of slave punishment. Nothing, however, in these findings is new. Stampp, for example, insisted that cases "of deliberate stinting of rations were fortunately few," and that hardly any slaveholders "built private jails on their premises" because "they knew that close confinement during a working day was a punishment of dubious

---

[38] *Ibid.*, pp. 174-181.

value."[39] F + E have not demolished yet another "myth" but simply confirmed (without adding new evidence) what is well known. Nevertheless, there is a need for more study about the relationship between control of the food supply, planter-sponsored labor incentives, and slave social behavior. Prolonged denial of food obviously causes malnutrition, just as prolonged overeating causes obesity. And that the "illness and lethargy caused by malnutrition" impair labor efficiency is self-evident. But the social issue is not whether owners denied slaves food; it has rather to do with how control of the food supply affected the life-chances and the behavior of slaves. The denial of a weekly meat ration on occasion did not cause illness and malnutrition, but it served by example to make clear that owners controlled the food supply. The presence of slave gardens where slaves often grew foodstuffs for family consumption does not alter the essential point. It simply makes it more complicated. Slaves did not own these garden plots, and such places could be taken from them. We need to study the relationship between control of the food supply, social dominance, and labor efficiency.

Much more is involved in slave punishments than an "economic" equation or an emphasis that does no more than stress the rational decisions of "economic man." F + E explain: "When the laborer owns his own human capital, forms of punishment which impair or diminish the value of that capital are borne exclusively by him. Under slavery, the master desired forms of punishment which, while they imposed costs on the slave, did so with minimum impairment to the human capital which the master owned. Whipping generally fulfilled these conditions." They write, "Whipping persisted in the South because the cost of substituting hunger [sic] and incarceration for the lash was greater for the slaveowner than for the northern employer of free labor."[40] So simple an "economic" explanation hardly does justice to the complex motivations that shaped planter behavior. "Remember," the articulate pro-slavery advocate James Henry Hammond insisted, "that on our estates we dispense with the whole machinery of public police and public courts of justice. Thus we try, decide, and execute the sentences, in thousands of cases, which in other countries would go into the courts." Hardly a detached observer, Hammond was anxious to minimize the harshness implicit in master-slave relationships. He wrote in answer to British critics of enslavement: "If a man steals a pig in England, he is transported — torn from wife, children, parents, and sent to the antipodes, infamous, and an outcast forever, though probably he took from the superabundance of his neighbor to save the lives of his famishing little ones. If one of our well-fed negroes, merely for the sake of fresh meat, steals a pig, he gets perhaps forty stripes. . . . Are our courts or yours the most humane? If Slavery were not in

[39] *Ibid.*, pp. 172, 289.
[40] T/C, I, p. 147.

question, you would doubtless say ours is mistaken lenity. Perhaps it often is; and slaves too lightly dealt with sometimes grow daring."

A South Carolina planter and lawyer who served in the United States Senate and felt both northern free laborers and southern plantation slaves "the very mudsills of society," Hammond had doubts about the social utility of whipping. "Stocks are rarely used by private individuals, and confinement still more seldom," said the planter, "though both are common punishments for whites, all the world over. I think they should be more frequently resorted to with slaves as substitutes for flogging, which I consider the most injurious and least efficacious mode of punishing them for serious offenses. It is not degrading, and unless excessive occasions little pain. You may be a little astonished, after all the flourishes that have been made about 'cart whips,' &c., when I say flogging is not the most degrading punishment in the world."[41] How do we fit Hammond's plea that stocks and jails be used more frequently than the whip into a model of planter behavior which measures the utility of diverse punishments only by their "cost" to the planter in "labor time"? Hammond suggests the limitations of so cost-conscious a model when he writes that whipping was insufficiently "degrading." We are back to the meaning of words and to the inadequacies of the central F + E model. To degrade, according to the *Oxford English Dictionary,* means to lower in "rank, position, reputation, [and] character." Why did Hammond feel whipping to be the least effective mode of punishing especially troublesome slaves? It seems clear that the whip — at least in Hammond's estimation — did not have its intended social effect. It failed to lower the troublesome slave in "rank, position, [and] reputation." Rank, position, and reputation among whom? Hammond and his fellow planters? Or the enslaved themselves? Hammond surely meant the enslaved. And if that is so, it is imperative that in measuring the utility of whipping we understand how the enslaved interpreted the act of being whipped. On the Barrow plantation, at least, whipping did not deter misconduct. Barrow himself built a private jail. And the South Carolinian Hammond proposed that jails and stocks be used more commonly than the whip. Was it because the enslaved felt incarceration to be more degrading than whipping? And if so, why? A narrow economic calculus cannot explain so important a social distinction.

Bennet Barrow's Perception of Inefficient Plantation Labor
and the Distortion of That Perception in T/C

We shall turn next to the treatment of incentives meant to reward slaves for efficient labor, but first we shall summarize briefly what has been learned about slave punishments. The single piece of numerical evidence (the Bar-

[41] "Letters on Slavery," *Pro-Slavery Argument* (1852), pp. 119-135.

row diary) tells the opposite of what F + E report in T/C. The supplementary evidence on punishment is slight at best, and the *general* details hardly differ from those emphasized in *The Peculiar Institution*. (The tone of the analysis, of course, is quite different.) The discussion of planter-sponsored rewards to encourage productive slave labor is hardly more satisfactory. Portions of the critical paragraph used by F + E to make the transition from negative to positive labor incentives have been printed earlier in these pages, but here I record the entire paragraph:

> While whipping was an integral part of the system of punishment and rewards, it was not the totality of the system. What planters wanted was not sullen and discontented slaves who did just enough to keep from getting whipped. They wanted devoted, hard-working, responsible slaves who identified their fortunes with the fortunes of their masters. Planters sought to imbue their slaves with a "Protestant" work ethic and to transform that ethic from a state of mind into a high level of production. "My negros have their name up in the neighborhood," wrote Bennet Barrow, "for making more than any one else & they think Whatever they do is better than any body Else." Such an attitude could not be beaten into slaves. It had to be elicited.[42]

Barrow entered that sentence in his diary on October 15, 1840, and it was extracted first by Davis in his essay and then by F + E.[43] By lifting the sentence from the full diary entry, Davis and then F + E completely distort its meaning. Barrow was not praising his slaves for identifying their fortunes with his fortunes. The full diary entry, together with the entries that preceded it, is as follows:[44]

October 1 Made all hands stop & trash cotten this morning. . . .
October 2 . . . Women trashing cotten men doing little of every thing, *not much of any thing*
October 5 . . . the trashyiest stuff I ever saw, some of my young Hands are doing verry Badly Ralph Wash E. Nat E. Jim Jim T. Henry Israel Harriet Sam&Maria Lewis & Randal
October 6 . . . bad news from the Cotten market
October 9 . . . never saw more cotten open to the Acre. & verry trashy . . .
October 11 . . . Gave the negros shoes. . . .
October 13 . . . I think my hands have Picked cotten worse this year than in several years picked it verry trashy & not better weights nor as good as *common*, intend Whipping them *straght*
October 15 Clear verry pleasant, Never have been more dissatisfied with my hands all Excepting 'Lize I [L.?] Hannah Jensey Atean & Margaret, am sattisfied the best plan is to give them every thing they require for their comfort and never that they will do

[42] T/C, I, p. 147.
[43] Davis, *Plantation Life*, p. 41.
[44] *Ibid.*, pp. 212-214.

without Whipping or some punishment. My negros have their name up in the neighborhood for making more than any one else & they think Whatever they do is better than any body Else.

These diary entries cannot be read as evidence that the Barrow slaves had become "devoted, hard-working, responsible slaves who identified their fortunes with the fortunes of their masters," or that Barrow had managed to "transform" the " 'Protestant' work ethic . . . from a state of mind into a high level of production." It may be possible to read the single sentence extracted in T/C that way, but not the full October 15 diary entry and surely not the full sequence of diary entries between the first and fifteenth of October. Read in the context of the full diary entry and in relation to recorded general whippings in 1837, 1838, twice in 1839, and again in 1840, as well as in relation to the frequency of punishment (whippings) during 1840-1841, it is quite clear that Barrow's single sentence meant to scorn the self-image that Barrow's slaves had of themselves and that others, including perhaps whites nearby, had of them. Barrow knew better; that is plainly and incontestably made known by the surrounding diary entries and by Barrow's behavior. A single sentence in the diary has been transformed in meaning to bolster a thin argument. The same rules of evidence, however, should apply to literary sources as to quantitative data. Barrow, of course, used positive labor incentives to elicit good work from his slave men and women, and Davis adequately summarizes them: "He devised many ways to increase their labors and to make them more contented; they were well fed and well housed; they received gifts of money at Christmas time; they were divided into rival gangs at cotton-picking time with the losing side giving dinners to the winners; and individuals sometimes raced down the cotton row. . . ."[45] But this summary of positive labor incentives in no way sustains the October fifteenth diary entry extracted so inaccurately by F + E. And that is because the full entry told that Barrow believed he had failed to elicit adequate productive work from his slaves. "The better you treat them," Barrow had written earlier that same year, "the worse they are." And why not? Barrow saw to it that the most productive slaves were better fed than the least productive slaves. But they were also the slaves whipped most frequently, and, when better fed, it was the least productive field hands who fed them.

45 *Ibid.*, p. 41.

Positive Labor Incentives
and Slave Work Habits

We have seen that the single piece of evidence used in T/C to deal with negative labor incentives (the Barrow whipping list) directly and in more ways than one contradicts the central theme of that book. The analysis turns now to F + E's treatment of positive labor incentives: their use by slaveowners, their importance relative to negative labor incentives, and the ways in which F + E use quantitative and literary data to show that a system of positive labor incentives encouraged enslaved Afro-Americans to internalize the Protestant work ethic. F + E wisely divide such positive incentives into three categories: "short-run" rewards, rewards "over periods of intermediate duration," and rewards of "a long-term nature, often requiring the lapse of a decade or more before they paid off." The third of these types of positive incentives is considered later in these pages. It is by far the most important, and F + E make a striking reassessment of the slave rural and urban occupational structures to describe it. We shall see that T/C adds nothing new to the conventional treatment of short-run and intermediate rewards and that the data used to construct slave occupational structures and to show that conventional scholars have given inadequate attention to the relatively "numerous" slaves who were neither field hands nor common laborers are based upon a misreading of conventional scholarship, the use of inaccurate sources, and a misuse of probate records. It shall, therefore, be seen that the opportunity for slaves to rise within the slave social hierarchy was much narrower than F + E argue, and that "achievement" based upon "mobility" opportunities played a negligible role as a positive labor incentive.

Similarities between Stampp and F + E on Short-Run Rewards

F + E add nothing to Kenneth Stampp's discussion of short-run incentives. Stampp wrote (and, once again, we leave out the illustrative evidence) :

The dollar may have been as important as the kind words. Some slaveholders apparently thought so; even though they had the power to coerce their workers to toil without compensation, they saw the wisdom of providing incentives for faithful service. . . . The rewards and incentives took numerous forms. Giving slaves a small plot of ground in which to cultivate their own crops during spare hours was one of the most popular. If this was not simply a means of forcing them to grow part of their essential food, as it sometimes was, it was an effective incentive. Bondsmen were thus able to add to the minimum diet provided them and to exchange the surplus for luxuries such as tobacco, sugar, coffee, and bits of finery. . . . Some masters permitted them to sell their goods in town, while others bought for their own use whatever their bondsmen produced. . . . A minority, however, thought it unwise to permit slaves to raise and sell produce. . . . Distributing gifts at the end of the year was a common practice. . . . Another form of incentive was to compensate slaves for work performed beyond what was normally expected of them, for example, for night and Sunday work. . . . Those who owned or hired skilled artisans frequently paid them for their labor above a specified minimum; factory owners paid their hands for overtime. . . . Cotton growers were resourceful in devising inducements for diligent toil at picking time. Some divided their pickers into competing teams; others promoted competition between individuals. . . . A few masters stimulated their laborers by making profit sharing agreements with them. . . . The promise of periodic relief from the labor routine was still another form of incentive. . . . Nearly every master observed a number of special holidays, the most common being Good Friday, Independence Day, "laying-by time," and Christmas. . . . Some went to considerable expense and took great pains to make the Christmas holiday pleasant. . . .[46]

I record next F + E's full discussion of "short-run" rewards:

Much of the managerial attention of planters was focused on the problem of motivating their hands. To achieve the desired response they developed a wide-ranging system of rewards. Some rewards were directed toward improving short-run performance. Included in this category were prizes for the individual or the gang with the best picking record on a given day or during a given week. The prizes were such items as clothing, tobacco, and whiskey; sometimes the prize was cash. Good immediate performance was also rewarded with unscheduled holidays or with trips to town on weekends. When slaves worked at times normally set aside for rest, they received extra pay — usually in cash and at the rate prevailing in the region for hired labor. Slaves who were performing well were permitted to work on their own account after normal hours at such tasks as making shingles or weaving baskets, articles which they could sell either to their masters or to farmers in the neighborhood.[47]

This paragraph does not improve upon Stampp except in suggesting that "planters . . . developed a wide-ranging system of rewards." But the para-

[46] Stampp, *Peculiar Institution*, pp. 164-170.
[47] T/C, I, p. 148.

graph itself merely illustrates some of the ways in which diverse planters sought to spur slave productivity. Such examples hardly show that planters developed ("caused to evolve," "brought into being," "generated") a system ("a coordinated body of methods or a complex scheme or plan of procedure") of positive labor incentives. We first need to know how many planters used such devices and then how regularly they were used. Then we can write of a "system." These are important matters to be explored in order to enlarge our understanding of the behavior of slaves and their owners. Once more, it is regularities that count. And there is no hint in T/C that the authors have examined planter practices in order to uncover such regularities.

Why Three Examples of Rewards "Over Periods of Intermediate Duration" Tell Nothing about Changes in Slave Productivity

F + E's treatment of intermediate positive labor incentives, furthermore, is quite flimsy and cannot be taken seriously. Three examples of intermediate incentives are described: a profit-sharing scheme by the Alabama planter William Jemison (the same example cited by Stampp in *The Peculiar Institution* [pp. 167-168]); the arrangements by which the Texas planter Julian L. Devereux marketed the crop that slaves grew on land allotted to them and then credited it to individual slave families, allowing them to draw cash or to have Devereux "purchase clothing, pots, pans, tobacco, or similar goods for them"; and, finally, year-end bonuses "given either in goods or cash" and "frequently quite substantial." The last of these three illustrations deserves attention. Once again, Bennet Barrow serves the purposes of F + E, but once again in curious ways. F + E write: "Bennet Barrow, for example, distributed gifts averaging between $15 and $20 per slave family in both 1839 and 1840. The amounts received by particular slaves were proportional to their performance. It should be noted that $20 was about a fifth of national per capita income in 1840. A bonus of the same relative magnitude today would be in the neighborhood of $1,000."[48] Unless F + E had access to materials not included in the Davis volume, these numbers are all wrong. There is no way to tell from that work how many slave families lived on the Barrow plantation in 1839 and 1840. The statement that gifts averaged "between $15 and $20 per slave family" is, therefore, another pseudostatistic. So, too, is the conversion of that bonus ($20, not $15) into 1974 dollars. Davis described the bonuses paid by Barrow: "[D]uring at least a part of his planting career, Barrow made substantial money gifts to his Negroes at holiday time. In 1838, he gave them $500 and sent them to town, and $700 each of the following years."[49] The diary itself records the 1838 and the 1840

48 *Ibid.*, pp. 148, 149.
49 Davis, *Plantation Life*, p. 52.

44

bonuses. The 1839 bonus is mentioned in an appendix. The Davis volume, however, records no other year-end bonuses between 1836 and 1845, a fact neglected by F + E but one which casts grave doubts on whether a system of short-run or intermediate positive incentives existed on the Barrow plantation.

Barrow's diary entries at the holiday season tell a different story from the one suggested by F + E:[50]

1836

Dec. 24   negros went to Town for Christmas

Dec. 26   House Jerry & Isreal chained during Christmas Jerry for general bad conduct — for a year and better — Isreal bad conduct during cotten picking season

Dec. 29   gave the negros a dinner

1837

Dec. 26   negros went to Town

Dec. 29   negros preparing for a dinner

Dec. 31   negros seemed to enjoy Christmas verry much ran two of Uncle Bats negros off last night — for making a disturbance — no pass — broke my sword Cane over one of their skulls

1838

Dec. 24   hands went to Town payed them last night over $500

Dec. 30   the negros behaved badly last night at their supper

1839

Dec. 23   negros went to Town to day Turnbulls Overseer Bailey caught Dennis yesterday

Dec. 24   intend exhibiting Dennis during Christmas on a scaffold in the middle of the Quarter & with a red Flannel Cap on

Dec. 25   negros appeared in fine spirits yesterday Let Darcas out of Jail — Dennis confined in Jail

Dec. 26   had quit a Dance yesterday — some of the old negros &c.

Dec. 28   negros preparing for a dinner

Dec. 29   negros had quit a fine supper last night

₁ ₃40

Dec. 24   Gave the negros money last night $700. all went to Town to day

Dec. 29   negros preparing for a Dinner

Jan.   3   Gave the negros a verry fine dinner yesterday evening at the House and afterwards inspected their manners in the Ballroom several acted very rude as usual. put them in Jail

1841

Dec. 22   Making up pants for men as Christmas presents

Dec. 26   *gave the negros articles* purchased for them in N. Orleans

[50] *Ibid.*, pp. 85, 104, 139, 175, 218-219, 247-248, 313-314. See p. 412 for evidence of the 1839 bonus.

1842

Dec. 28   Gave the negros as much of Evry thing to eat & *drink* during the Hollidays as they Wanted times so hard no able to give them any thing more

1843 and 1844

[No diary record of any celebration or gift-giving]

1845

Dec. 25   negros seem quite Lively

Dec. 29   getting tired of Hollidays, negros want too much, Human nature

Reading these entries together makes it rather difficult to suggest that Barrow's behavior indicates that he had developed a system of positive rewards meant to motivate the labor of his slaves. The diary entries as a group allow for the following generalization: The Christmas holiday at the Barrow plantation was celebrated in different ways between 1836 and 1845. Such celebrations occurred even though some troublesome slaves spent the holiday in chains or in jail and others were paraded in the quarters in insulting ways. Three times in this ten-year period it is recorded that Barrow rewarded his hands with Christmas cash payments. Barrow once purchased gifts for his slaves in New Orleans. Between 1836 and 1840 the slaves visited town at Christmas. That did not happen after 1840. In 1837, 1838, 1839, and 1840 the slaves prepared a holiday dinner for themselves, but in 1841 Barrow supplied them with food and drink. The last holiday recorded in his diary was the 1845 Christmas season. "Getting tired of Hollidays," Barrow then complained, "negros want too much, Human nature."

That is a fair rendering of the evidence. No pattern existed, and it is inappropriate to select from such evidence three cases of cash payments as characteristic types of intermediate-range labor incentives. It would be interesting to learn why Barrow failed to pay his slaves cash bonuses after 1840. Was it because business conditions had deteriorated and made cash short? That is hinted at in the 1842 entry. Or was it because Barrow's slaves had performed inefficiently by his standards? Why waste cash on workers who failed to respond positively to such stimuli?

Evidence illustrating planter-sponsored schemes to improve slave labor efficiency is of much importance, but the three examples cited by F + E neither support nor refute the central thesis in T/C concerning the positive results that followed the introduction of such schemes. Assuming that they were common, a mere listing still would not tell us anything about their effectiveness. Did slave productivity increase as a consequence of such schemes? That is a very different question from the level of slave productivity at a given moment. Nowhere in T/C are patterns of slave productivity compared to one another over time. F + E have not done more than Kenneth Stampp: they have given us examples of how slaveowners sought to improve labor efficiency by using carrots instead of sticks. It is hard to tell just what such "examples" mean. By way of introducing the Devereux "example," F + E write: "Masters also rewarded slaves who performed well with patches of land ranging up to a few acres for each family." It is well known that slaves over the entire South worked such patches of land. But were those bits of land given to slaves as rewards for efficient labor or stimuli to more efficient labor? F + E assume it happened for one of these reasons. No evidence sustains either or both connections. The slave garden patch has not yet had its historian. Suppose, for example, it turns out that plots went automatically to most heads of slave families and that this happened over two or three generations. "It was the *universal custom* in Georgia," explained Ralph Flanders in *Plantation Slavery in Georgia,* "to allow slaves the privilege of raising small crops of their own for which the master paid cash, or which could be exchanged at the storeroom for anything they chose to buy."[51] There is a great difference between a "universal custom" and a selective labor incentive. A custom is a habitual practice, nothing less than "the usual way of acting in given circumstances" — an established way of doing things. If it was allowed in this way, the garden patch hardly served as a positive labor incentive. That does not mean, of course, that such patches failed to create other satisfactions among the enslaved. (Interestingly, the former slave Solomon Northup described as a "custom" the practice of Louisiana owners "to allow the slave to retain whatever compensation he may obtain for services performed on Sundays." If viewed that way by slaves and their owners, this arrangement also hardly counts as a positive incentive.)[52]

Long-Term Positive Labor Incentives and the Urban and Rural Slave Occupational Structure: New and Important Evidence in T/C

"Long-term" rewards are the third and most important category of positive incentives; here — for the first time in their analysis of slave rewards and punishments — F + E use new quantitative data. So far their analysis has been based upon traditional "mini-data." In suggesting that long-term rewards were built into the developing slave economy, F + E shift to "maxi-data." But the new data — which allow F + E to construct slave urban and especially rural occupational distributions — are entirely unconvincing, which is unfortunate because much of the argument about the internalized slave work ethic and the success of planter-sponsored incentives in shaping that ethic rests upon these occupational distributions and no other evidence.

[51] R. B. Flanders, *Plantation Slavery in Georgia* (1933), p. 146 (italics added).
[52] Gilbert Osofsky, ed., *Puttin' On Ole Massa* (1969), p. 331.

F + E have greatly exaggerated the skill levels among urban and rural slaves. Erroneous assumptions, together with misused data, create in both distributions far too many slave artisans, drivers, and overseers and far too few slave laborers and field hands.

Readers should not misunderstand the pages which follow. It is of genuine importance to know roughly what percentage of slaves had such skills. It is of even greater importance to know if these percentages changed over time. An occupational structure is a most powerful clue for understanding a social structure or community. As a result, primarily, of the flawed analytic models used by most historians of enslavement, altogether too little is yet known about the rural and urban slave communities and how they changed over time. If data for such studies are found primarily in "maxi-sources" (census schedules, probate records, and so forth), they badly need to be studied to enlarge our understanding of how particular slave communities developed and changed over time. The sharp criticisms which follow should not be misconstrued. It is not that F + E have erred in using quantitative sources, but rather that such sources have been used erroneously and then used as supporting evidence for startlingly "new" but nevertheless shaky and sometimes even quite fantastical generalizations about slave belief and behavior. "The real question," F + E insist, "is whether quantitative methods have produced a more accurate and complete portrayal of slavery than was previously available."[53] That is only one of the "real" questions. It is just as appropriate first to ask whether quantitative sources and methods have been properly used in T/C to enlarge, if not alter, our understanding of slave society and of the enslaved themselves. That, after all, is the real message in T/C; we have misunderstood the economics of slavery and, therefore, misunderstood the slaves and especially the positive work ethic internalized by most ordinary slaves.

The Urban Slave Occupational Structure

Incomplete and Inaccurate Data on the Antebellum
Urban White Occupational Structure

How F + E treat the urban slave occupational structure — and especially the place held in it by the artisan — is looked at first. The authors have greatly inflated the importance of the urban slave artisan by taking at face value a very dubious and plainly incomplete 1848 Charleston, South Carolina, private census and then comparing its data to even more untrustworthy "statistics."[54] Most slaves, of course, did not live in cities, but it

---

[53] T/C, II, p. 19.

[54] J. L. Dawson and H. W. De Saussure, *Census of Charleston* (1848). De Saussure's name is incorrectly spelled in the T/C bibliography ("De Saussare").

remains essential to understand accurately their occupational status. The difficulty that plagues all historians, however, is that federal census enumerators failed to record the occupations of rural and urban slaves.[55] Other data, therefore, need to be used. But the 1850 and 1860 federal manuscript censuses contain detailed listings of occupations for southern whites and free blacks so that it is possible to reconstruct the occupational distributions of these two groups. Neither F + E nor Claudia Goldin, whose work is quoted at great length in T/C, apparently knows very much about the non-slave sectors of the southern urban labor force. Goldin's dissertation is cited at length in order to distinguish between demand elasticities for rural and urban slaves. Her technical competence is not at issue, but if the error that mars the following paragraph quoted by F + E is characteristic, there is good reason to question her conclusions: "Richmond stands out as the [southern] city with the most stable and large [sic] increases in demand for slaves. It is also the city with one of the smallest elasticities of demand. Richmond was the most industrial of all the urban areas, and *it was also not subject to much immigration.* Therefore, Richmond's slaves had few substitutes and they were, on average, a more skilled group than found in other cities" (italics added).[56]

We ignore the way in which Goldin, F + E, or anyone, for that matter, can "measure" the occupational distribution of urban slaves in Richmond or most other southern cities (when the federal census fails to list slaves by occupation) and concentrate instead on the assertion that Richmond was "not subject to much immigration." Anyone familiar with the free white and black occupations listed in the 1850 and 1860 manuscript censuses knows that this statement is factually erroneous. If the presence (or absence) of immigrant workers is essential to a study of relative urban slave demand

[55] Although it fails to list slave occupations and even slave names, the manuscript federal census apparently can perform wonders for some cliometric historians. F + E write: "Hiring was not a minor or inconsequential feature of slavery. Through the examination of data in the manuscript schedules of the U.S. census, it has been determined that about 31 percent of urban slave workers were on hire during 1860. In some cities, such as Richmond, the proportion was in excess of 50 percent. The proportion of slave rentals in rural areas was lower, generally running about 6 percent. For the slave labor force as a whole, then, about 7.5 percent were on hire at any moment of time. Since hire contracts rarely ran for more than a year, and many were for substantially shorter periods of time, the ratio of hire transactions to slaves was probably 15 or more percent. Thus hire transactions were probably over five times as frequent as sales" (T/C, I, p. 56). The reader searches in vain in volume two for some hint about how these percentages can be calculated from data which do no more than give the name of an owner and a slave's sex and age. And all he reads is: "Estimates of the incidence of hiring were constructed by Claudia Goldin. Communicated in a letter dated February 8, 1973" (T/C, II, p. 54). Are readers expected to take such "evidence" seriously? This type of "documentation" is an insult to commonplace scholarly canons.

[56] Goldin quoted in T/C, II, pp. 154-155.

49

"elasticities," that thesis is in serious trouble. The color and occupation of all free Richmond workers listed in the 1860 federal manuscript census show that skilled and unskilled immigrants were a very important component in Richmond's free labor force. Table 6 includes all free males listed as "laborers" and all free Richmond bakers, bricklayers, blacksmiths, coopers, machinists, painters, and shoemakers.[57] If just the free white workers are counted, it turns out that exactly half of the craftsmen and three out of four of the laborers were foreign-born. How can one write that Richmond was "not subject to much immigration"?

TABLE 6. COLOR AND PLACE OF BIRTH OF ALL FREE RICHMOND LABORERS AND ALL FREE ARTISANS IN SELECTED OCCUPATIONS, 1860

	Laborers	Selected Crafts
Free Blacks	12%	7%
Whites Born in the South	19%	39%
Whites Born in the North	4%	7%
Immigrant Whites	65%	47%
N	800	1,050

Slave "Managers" and the Misreading of Robert Starobin

F + E misread the findings and the arguments of the late Robert S. Starobin. In their estimates concerning the urban slave labor force, F + E find that "1.0 percent of male slaves . . . were managers," a suspect percentage. They draw, in part, upon the pioneering work of Starobin, who found some examples of slave managers in southern industrial firms.[58] The percentage is small, but still too large. F + E write: "Starobin argues that the ratio of one manager to 30 slaves prevailed in industry as on plantations. He also argues that white managers 'were scarce.' Accordingly, we assume that among firms using slaves, 72 percent of managers and foremen were slaves . . . and that there was one manager or foreman to every 30 unskilled hands other than domestics."[59]

Starobin did not write that "white managers 'were scarce.'" "Native white managers were scarce" is what he wrote. Starobin stressed the importance of the slave manager and foreman, but also emphasized that immigrant (and some northern) managers played important roles in southern industry. Any estimate, furthermore, which assumes "that there was one

[57] These data are gathered from the Richmond manuscript census (1860) and include *all* free white and black wage earners.

[58] Robert S. Starobin, *Industrial Slavery in the Old South* (1970), pp. 168-178.

[59] T/C, II, p. 41.

50

manager or foreman to every 30 unskilled hands other than domestics" greatly exaggerates the number of managers and foremen. "When more than thirty slaves were employed, personal supervision was difficult," noted Starobin, "since sales, supplies, and bookkeeping occupied the owner's time." That makes good sense. But before even the crudest estimate of urban slave managers and foremen can be made, it is necessary to know how many urban firms employed thirty or more slaves. F + E do not use so essential a measure. What if most unskilled hands labored in firms that had far fewer than thirty slave workers? Except possibly for Richmond, that surely was the case in most southern towns and cities, which means that the number of urban managers — black or white and slave or free — would have been very small.

Slave Artisans and the Incomplete 1848 Charleston Census

Whatever the number of managers and whatever their status or color, it is the urban artisans who are central to F + E's thesis concerning slave "rewards" and "mobility." F + E rely entirely for that estimate upon the 1848 Charleston census, one of the few sources that listed slaves by occupation. They write:

> Our estimate of the distribution of occupations in urban areas is based on the Charleston census of 1848. It shows that 22 percent of all male slaves over 10 were in crafts or semiskilled occupations. The indicated share of skilled workers among adult males would then be 27 percent.
> There is some possibility that the share of skilled persons in the [urban?] slave labor force was lower in Charleston than in the rest of southern cities. Wesley and Stavisky argue that blacks were 80 percent of all southern artisans during the antebellum era. In Charleston, however, blacks were only 44 percent of all craftsmen. It may be that in Charleston white artisans were particularly successful in limiting occupational opportunities for slaves.[60]

F + E are not the first to use the 1848 census. U. B. Phillips and Richard C. Wade used it earlier, but neither author misused the census. It is hard to know where to start in pointing out the errors in F + E's few sentences based on the Charleston census. I do not have the original Charleston listing and have worked instead from the chart that Phillips prepared in his 1907 essay "The Slave Labor Problem in the Charleston District."[61] The listed occupations and numbers which accompany them fix the percentage of artisans at about 15 percent instead of 22 percent, but that is a mere quibble. There are more serious difficulties in these sentences. The suggestion that slave artisans were less significant in Charleston than in "the rest of southern

[60] *Ibid.*, pp. 39-40.
[61] *Political Science Quarterly*, 22 (September 1907), pp. 416-439.

cities" rests on no evidence from other southern cities. That Charleston white artisans pressed to limit the occupations open to slaves is well known. But that happened in other southern cities, too. Wade, for example, cited an 1831 Savannah ordinance that said blacks could not be apprenticed to the "trade of Carpenter, Mason, Bricklayer, Barber, or any other Mechanical Art or Mystery." That ordinance was later amended to include cabinetmakers, painters, blacksmiths, tailors, coopers, and butchers.[62] It is not known how well that law was enforced, but there is a published Savannah 1848 census that apparently escaped the attention of F + E but was used in Wade's study.[63] F + E's argument that Charleston probably ("some possibility") had relatively fewer slave artisans than other southern cities would have been immeasurably stronger had they examined so essential a source. Instead of using such evidence, F + E rely upon Charles Wesley's estimate that "blacks were 80 percent of all southern artisans during the antebellum era."[64] No systematic evidence of any kind exists to support any estimate near that percentage. We shall soon see how far off it actually is. But the "80 percent" estimate allows F + E to assert that "blacks were *only* 44 percent of all [Charleston] craftsmen" (italics added). It *had* to be higher in other cities if only to make up for the obvious Charleston "deficiency."

Even more seriously, the 1848 Charleston census itself is a thoroughly dubious source, especially for comparative purposes. That census was far from complete, and it incorrectly counted male slaves and especially male free blacks and whites. That is known just by comparing it to the numbers in the published 1850 Charleston federal census. Only the number of slaves listed in 1848 approached the number reported in the 1850 federal census; the approximate undercount for free blacks (72 percent) and whites (79 percent) was extraordinarily high, so much so that Table 7 shows why the

TABLE 7. CHARLESTON CENSUS OF 1848 COMPARED TO 1850 PUBLISHED FEDERAL CENSUS LISTING ADULT MALES

Color and Status	Probable Number of Adult Males over 15 in 1850	Number of Males Listed in the 1848 Census	Approximate Percentage of Males Missing from the 1848 Census
Slaves	4,747	3,462	27%
Free Blacks	745	205	72%
Whites	5,631	1,170	79%

[62] Richard C. Wade, *Slavery in the Cities: The South, 1820-1860* (1964), pp. 273-275.

[63] Joseph Bancroft, *Census of the City of Savannah* (1848); Wade, *Slavery in the Cities,* pp. 32-33.

[64] Wesley did not mean that only slaves made up this 80 percent. F + E make that clear in another place: T/C, II, p. 196.

1848 Charleston census cannot be used to compare the relative importance of slave, free black and white artisans — or any other occupational groups, for that matter. Only so incomplete a census matched against the Wesley-Stavisky "estimate" could lead to the assertion that Charleston slaves and free blacks "were only 44 percent of all craftsmen." Even without a comparison to the published 1850 census, a document such as the 1848 Charleston census, which listed only nineteen free black laborers and just a single "superannuated" free black male, should have been viewed as totally suspect.[65] Instead, this single document allows F + E to generalize about the proportion of urban slave artisans in all antebellum cities. They insist that the Charleston artisans were relatively less important than slave artisans in other cities.

*How the Occupational Distribution among Free Black
and White Workers Shows That "44 Percent"
of Urban Male Artisans Could Not Have Been Blacks*

Another way — just as decisive but much more revealing — to see how misleading the 1848 Charleston census is results by examining the 1860 Charleston *manuscript* census listings of black and white free workers. Between 1850 and 1860, the Charleston male population changed: the free blacks remained fairly constant in number, and the whites increased by about 10 percent, but the slave population declined about 25 percent, as shown in Table 8. Although the 1860 manuscript census tells nothing about slave skills, it invaluably describes white and free black occupations. The skill distribution among all white and free black Charleston male workers

TABLE 8. CHARLESTON MALE POPULATION, 1850 AND 1860

Color and Status	1850	1860
Charleston White Males	10,238	11,714
Charleston Free Black Males	1,355	1,247
Charleston Slave Males	8,631	6,563

[65] See, for example, T/C, I, p. 38, in which F + E assert: "In several of the most important crafts of that city — including carpentry and masonry — slaves actually outnumbered the whites." That information draws entirely upon the misleading 1848 Charleston census. "Several," incidentally, means five. See also T/C, II, p. 234, where "several" becomes "many." Criticizing Stampp, F + E write: "Nor can one learn from Stampp's book that many southern crafts were dominated by slaves, that slaves may have even accounted for the majority of southern artisans."

in 1860 is indicated in Table 9:[66] two-thirds were artisans. If, as in 1848, "44 percent" of Charleston's artisans were blacks, there would have been about eleven hundred adult male slave artisans in 1860. That means that the absolute number of slave artisans would have increased by about 40 percent between 1848 and 1860 and that two out of five slaves in 1860 (as contrasted to about one in four in 1848) would have been artisans. And that would have happened even though the adult male slave population fell about 25 percent between 1850 and 1860. If 44 percent is a correct estimate, moreover, that means that more than half (about 56 percent) of all Charleston male workers in 1860, including the slaves, were skilled workers, a nearly absurd statistic.

Since fairly precise figures exist on the number of white and free black artisans in 1860, the 44 percent needs to be put aside. It is possible, however, to get a reasonable estimate of the relative importance of slave artisans as well as ordinary slave laborers in Charleston in 1860. We assume that the proportion of Charleston slave artisans to slave laborers remained constant between 1848 and 1860, but, in accordance with the drop in that city's slave population, their number fell by 25 percent. That allows for a rough comparison of the relative importance of slave laborers and artisans to white and free black laborers and artisans. Table 10 shows each group's relative importance. Overall, the free and slave Charleston workers were nearly evenly divided between skilled (45 percent) and unskilled (55 percent) workers, but the Charleston slaves had a radically different occupational composition from either the free black or the white workers. That difference is illustrated in Table 11. Only 15 percent of Charleston's slaves had skills, as contrasted to two-thirds of Charleston's white workers and three-fourths of Charleston's free blacks. It surely made a huge economic difference to be a white or a free black worker as opposed to a slave worker in antebellum Charleston. Any suggestion that urban slaves shared a common occupational structure with either free black workers or white workers or that slave artisans dominated the urban antebellum crafts is egregiously mistaken.

TABLE 9. OCCUPATIONAL STATUS OF WHITE AND FREE BLACK WORKERS, CHARLESTON, 1860

| Occupational Status | Number | Percentage | | |
		White	Free Black	Total
Unskilled Labor	1,109	34%	26%	32%
Artisans	2,323	66%	74%	68%
Total	3,432	2,894	538	100%

[66] This table is based upon a study of all free white and black workers in Charleston in 1860, as listed in the manuscript population census.

TABLE 10. OCCUPATIONAL STATUS OF SLAVES AND WHITE AND FREE BLACK WORKERS,
CHARLESTON, 1860

Occupational Status and Color	Charleston Skilled Workers		Charleston Unskilled Workers	
	Number	Percent	Number	Percent
Slaves (estimated)	391	14%	2,142	66%
Free Blacks	400	15%	138	4%
Whites	1,923	71%	971	30%
Total	2,714		3,251	

TABLE 11. OCCUPATIONAL DISTRIBUTION OF SKILLED AND UNSKILLED SLAVES, FREE BLACKS,
AND WHITES, CHARLESTON, 1860

Skill Level	Slaves	Free Blacks	Whites	All Workers
Skilled	15%	74%	68%	45%
Unskilled	85%	26%	32%	55%
Total	2,533(est.)	538	2,894	5,965

*Why It Is Wrong to Assert That the "Relatively Low-Skill Composition
of the Black Labor Force" Began Following Emancipation*

These are not mere disagreements over numbers: at issue, of course, is
the relative cost of enslavement to Afro-Americans and whether or not the
enslaved internalized the norms favored by their owners. It is hard to believe
that the white and free black working-class occupational structure — both
visible to Charleston slaves — created satisfactions among the enslaved and
spurred them to work harder. If the urban slave occupational structure did
not differ radically from that of southern free black and white workers, a
strong case might be made that enslavement — despite its harshness and
what F + E concede to be its immorality — created satisfactions among the
enslaved by permitting talented and energetic slaves to become skilled workers. That is precisely one of F + E's major arguments. Some slaves, of course,
became skilled workers. But the absolute number is important: it defines
the limits of "opportunity" at a given moment. And the relative number is
significant, too: if a particular labor market (Charleston, in this case) had
work for a given number of artisans and most were either white or free
black males, that fact is powerful evidence that enslavement, not a scarcity
of work and not "racism," limited opportunity. So far, slaves have been
contrasted to free workers, including free blacks. It also is useful to combine

the slaves and free blacks to get some indication of the occupational distribution within the antebellum black, not slave, community. That is indicated in Table 12. In their epilogue to volume one ("Implications for Our Time"), F + E insist that by setting the record straight on "the Economics of American Negro Slavery" they also have begun to put the post-emancipation decades in a more fitting historical perspective. They write:

> One of the worst consequences of the traditional interpretation of slavery is that it has diverted attention from the attack on the material conditions of black life that took place *during the decades following the end of the Civil War*. By exaggerating the severity of slavery, all that has come after it has been made to appear as an improvement over previous conditions. The relatively low levels of wages of freed blacks, *the relatively low-skill composition of the black labor force*,... these and other conditions of *the post–Civil War* decades have been explained largely as *the unfortunate inheritance of the era of slavery*.... Whatever blame there was for the unsatisfactory conditions of blacks after the Civil War thus rested with a class which no longer existed (the master class) or, unfortunately, with blacks themselves.
>
> During the last few years, the attention of cliometricians has begun to shift from the antebellum to the postbellum era. While the findings thus far are extremely tentative, the evidence that is beginning to accumulate suggests that *the attack on the material conditions of the life of blacks after the Civil War was not only more ferocious, but, in certain respects, more cruel than that which preceded it*.... The skill composition of the black labor force deteriorated. Blacks were squeezed out of some crafts in which they had been *heavily represented* during the slave era.... [Italics added.][67]

When compared to the occupations of black urban males in southern cities in 1880, the occupations of Charleston blacks in 1860 tell us that F + E — at least by this measure — are quite wrong. That is, unless one continues to figure with phantom statistics such as "22 percent," "27 percent," "44 percent," or "80 percent."

Certain general comments need to be made about F + E's conclusions before returning again to the 1860 Charleston blacks. First, F + E are making comparative judgments. The condition of southern Afro-Americans is

TABLE 12. ESTIMATED OCUPATIONAL DISTRIBUTION OF BLACK MALES, SLAVE AND FREE, CHARLESTON, 1860

Unskilled	74%
Skilled	26%
N	3,071

[67] T/C, I, pp. 260-261.

contrasted in two distinct time periods: before and after emancipation. Not a shred of evidence in T/C sustains even the "extremely tentative" conclusion that "the attack on the material conditions of the life of blacks after the Civil War was not only more ferocious, but, in certain respects, more cruel than that which preceded it." Second, what evidence tells that "the master class" disappeared ("no longer existed") after emancipation? F + E suggest that elites without roots in the antebellum slaveholding class came to power after 1865 and bear responsibility for the attack "on the material conditions of the life of blacks." That generalization is false. Third, the hint that it is the "cliometrician" who is changing our conception of the postbellum South and of the emancipated Afro-American is hardly the way to characterize the dozens of significant revisionist monographs on the postwar South and on the former slaves. Cliometricians deserve praise when they complete useful and even original work, but the revised views of the postbellum South and the emancipated Afro-American are not the result of any "cliometric revolution."

It is appropriate, finally, to mention that in their hasty and ill-drawn epilogue F + E improperly blame the material deterioration of the emancipated southern blacks directly on the behavior of antislavery critics. They insist:

Few of the antislavery critics had equality of opportunity for the races as the goal of their crusade. Since they conceived of blacks as members of an inferior race, equality of opportunity had little meaning to them. Most expected that freed Negroes would have to be constrained in various ways if an "orderly" society was to be maintained. . . .

What antislavery critics generally objected to was not the fact that slavery constrained the opportunities open to blacks, but the form which these constraints took. While physical force was unacceptable, legal restrictions were not. Thus many one-time crusaders against slavery sat idly by, or even collaborated in passing various laws which served to improve the economic position of whites at the expense of blacks. Licensure laws helped to squeeze blacks out of some crafts. Educational restrictions helped to exclude them from others. Meanwhile, taxation and fiscal policies were used to transfer income from blacks to whites, perhaps more effectively, certainly more elegantly, than had been possible under slavery.[68]

[68] *Ibid.*, p. 263. See also *ibid.*, p. 136, where F + E write: "Unfortunately, abolitionists and other antislavery writers were not free of racism merely because they carried the banner of a moral struggle. With their greater physical separation from blacks, these writers were often more gullible and more quick in their acceptance of certain racial stereotypes than slaveholders." No one needs to argue that antislavery writers were free of racism in order to see that F + E greatly distort them in comparison to Southern slaveholders. Where is the evidence that led them to this conclusion?

Antislavery critics were not without blemishes and deserve just as severe and detached an analysis as do the slaveowners. Many among them were racist, but there is really no serious evidence that they "collaborated" in passing licensure laws, fixing educational restrictions, and supporting taxation and fiscal policies that deprived the former slaves of "economic opportunity." The laws passed over the entire South in 1865 and 1866 limiting southern black mobility and opportunity were passed by southern whites. That story is well known and need not detain us. The central flaw in antislavery ideology was not its racial assumptions, but its belief that "equality of opportunity" — that is, the "free market" — would best serve the emancipated blacks and that no more was necessary than to impose the "free market" upon the conquered South.

Edward Everett Hale put it well. "The policy," he said in 1865 of those committed to transforming the South, and especially the formerly enslaved, "...has not been to make these people beggars. '*Aide-toi et Dieu t'aidera*' is their motto. The black people know they must support themselves, as they have always done." Hale calmed the worries of those concerned that Yankee benevolence promised dependence and regimentation. Such persons revealed "a general forgetfulness of the operation of the law of supply and demand under the regime of freedom." Hale explained: "Freedom is not bread and butter, it is not comfort, it is not houses and clothes, it is not a happy life, it is not a certain heaven. Some enthusiasts, seeing that the newly freed slaves do not yet possess these blessings seem disturbed, as if freedom were not secure. But freedom is simply the way to get these blessings. It is the right of choice by which the freedman selects one or another course, which he thinks best adapted to secure them. That is what the proclamation of freedom secured." Hale did not deny that such policies promised suffering, but went on: "Where is there not suffering in this world? We have never said that the black man's life should be raised above suffering. We have said that he should be free to choose between inevitable hardships. This promise we perform."[69]

It is appropriate to criticize this prescription for "black achievement," but that criticism has nothing to do with Hale's — or most other antislavery critics' — racist beliefs. It has much more to do with their naïve but deeply felt belief that only fixing rules which let the "free market" operate ("the law of supply and demand . . . under freedom") was needed to allow the former slaves to rise or fall in the great race for life. It was not that most antislavery critics rejected "equality of opportunity" for the blacks as the "goal of their crusade." It was rather that this was (and could only be)

[69] Edward Everett Hale, "Education of the Freedmen," *North American Review,* CI (October 1865), pp. 538, 542-543.

their single goal that so flawed mainstream antislavery prescriptions for the newly emancipated Afro-American.[70]

Let us return now to the Charleston 1860 black occupational structure and the striking proposition that the "relatively low-skill composition of the black labor force" has its origins in what "took place during the decades following the end of the Civil War." There is ample evidence from 1880 to test this proposition, to show it to be erroneous, and to indicate why the low-skill composition of the black labor force had its origins in slavery and nowhere else. Data on the 1880 Charleston black occupational structure have not yet been gathered, but the occupations of all adult Mobile and Richmond black males in 1880 are known and summarized in Table 13 together with a sample of northern white Paterson, New Jersey, male workers

[70] See the astute comments by David Rothman in his review of T/C, "Slavery in a New Light." "Make no mistake," Rothman wrote, "*Time on the Cross* does not sell slavery; it would be regrettable if it was so misunderstood. What it does is provide evidence that capitalism protected the slave, guaranteeing him a decent standard of living." Rothman complains that F + E have failed to give adequate weight to "racism" in their analysis. "Yet," he writes, "by omitting racism from their analysis, Fogel and Engerman give us little help with perhaps the most important question to emerge from their study: If capitalism protected the slave so well before the Civil War, why did it not protect the black equally after the Civil War?" Given the "evidence" in T/C which Rothman most gingerly accepts, he is, of course, right to insist that post-emancipation conditions cannot be explained by simply pointing "the finger at capitalism itself. At least, part of the answer must rest with racism." Rothman's logic cannot be flawed, but it rests entirely on F + E's argument that before 1865 "capitalism protected the slave, guaranteeing him a decent standard of living." It turns out that F + E do not present "compelling evidence" to sustain this thesis. The core of this argument rests upon data concerning slave treatment, not the treatment of emancipated blacks.

See also Nathan Glazer, "A New View of Slavery," *Commentary*, 58 (August 1974), pp. 68-72. Glazer, who did as much as any social scientist to popularize the Stanley Elkins model of slave socialization, finds it easy to transfer his loyalty from the slave Sambo to the slave Horatio Alger. He also draws significant inferences from F + E's sketchy epilogue: "The rehabilitation of the slave-owning South can only lead to the unveiling of a post–Civil War record in both South and North that reduced the Negro, in all measurable ways, *below* the level he had achieved under slavery. And as a matter of fact, this record is now being compiled by the same methods that were used to change our view of slavery." Like Rothman, Glazer assumes the accuracy of F + E's data describing the "condition" of enslaved Afro-Americans. It is premature to insist, as Glazer does, that "our view of slavery" has been changed. Glazer tells *Commentary* readers: "We are being warned there comes Herbert Gutman with his sobering story of the destruction of the black family in the post–Civil War North." That is not at all the "story" I tell. Glazer's informants have misled him. The outlines of that "story" were sketched in Herbert G. Gutman, "Le Phenomene Invisible," *Annales: Economies, Societies, Civilisations* (July-October 1972), pp. 1197-1218, and it is difficult to figure how any reader could have misinterpreted the article.

in 1880.[71] The distribution of skills within the Charleston black community (slave and free) in 1860 is also included. The Richmond black community in 1880 had different occupational "opportunities" from that in Charleston, but there is no reason to believe that the Charleston and Mobile black occupational distributions differed greatly. The occupational differences between the Richmond and Mobile blacks and the Paterson native whites and Irish are huge. The percentage of Irish artisans was at least three times greater and that of native white artisans at least four times greater than the percentage of either Richmond or Mobile artisans. To compare the white and black occupational structures in 1880 or earlier is only to notice the vast differences between them.

What then becomes important is an explanation for these differences, and it is here that the 1860 Charleston data have great importance. If a fictive "statistic" indicating an unusually high percentage of southern urban black (slave and free) artisans is accepted for 1860 or earlier, then the 1880 data indeed indicate a rapid deterioration in the urban black skill level. A more accurate estimate, however, suggests decline but hardly rapid deterioration. There is a difference. The causes for that decline remain unknown, but the antebellum Charleston free blacks, not the Charleston slaves, suffered most from the decline. This is so because even though slightly more than five times as many slaves as free blacks lived in Charleston in 1860, probably about half of Charleston's black artisans that year were free blacks. The southern urban occupational structure underwent significant changes in the decade and one-half following emancipation, but to suggest that the

TABLE 13. OCCUPATIONS OF BLACK ADULT MALES IN CHARLESTON, 1860, RICHMOND AND MOBILE, 1880, AND NATIVE WHITE AND IRISH MALES IN PATERSON, 1880, TWENTY AND OLDER

| Occupational Status | 1880 | | 1880 | | 1860 |
	Mobile, Ala.	Richmond, Va.	Paterson, N.J. Native Whites	Irish	Charleston, S.C. Free Blacks and Slaves
Unskilled	82%	80%	21%	43%	74% est.
Skilled	14%	15%	62%	45%	26% est.
High Status	4%	5%	17%	12%	unk.
Number	3,032	6,056	264	876	

[71] This evidence rests upon the reconstruction of the entire Richmond and Mobile black communities in 1880 as based upon the manuscript federal census. These are not mere "samples."

narrow occupational structure common to all Gilded Age southern urban black communities took its shape after emancipation is entirely misleading. That occupational structure had its roots in the urban slave occupational structure. In "suggesting" otherwise, F + E substitute one myth for another. That is not the way to begin rewriting Afro-American history (or any history for that matter).

THE RURAL SLAVE OCCUPATIONAL STRUCTURE

An Inappropriate Comparison between the Occupations of Slave Males in 1850 and All Males in 1870 (Tables B.5 and Figure 10)

F + E have also greatly exaggerated the number of skilled rural slaves, especially those working on plantations, a much more serious error than the misuse of the 1848 Charleston census. Most slaves, after all, did not live in cities. Different kinds of errors, however, have been committed in exaggerating the number of hands who did not work in the fields and who were not common laborers among the rural slaves, errors so severe that they make the entire analysis useless. The errors, incidentally, nearly all bias the evidence "upward" and increase greatly the percentage of slaves who were not field hands and not common laborers. These errors then become "evidence" in arguing that enslaved Afro-Americans benefited from the "mobility" opportunities accessible to rural blacks. Data on the slave rural occupational structure and on how it functioned in the larger incentive and reward system sponsored by profit-hungry owners are scattered throughout the two volumes of T/C but are combined here to do full justice to all the evidence and the arguments flowing from that evidence. The critical evidence is summarized in pages 38 to 43 of volume one, and these pages rest entirely on Table B.5 in volume two (page 40). The essential data in Table B.5, The Derivation of the Occupational Structure of Adult Male Slaves on Farms, are printed in Table 14. This table — one of the two or three most important in the entire study — appears in volume one in a different form, where it is used to compare the adult male occupational distribution among slaves and free persons. That comparison is made on page 39 in Figure 10, a bar chart entitled A Comparison between the Occupational Distribution of Adult Male Slaves (about [*sic*] 1850) and the Occupational Distribution of All Adult Males (in 1870).

It is assumed for the moment that the percentages in Table B.5 (Table 14) are accurate, and Figure 10 — the comparative bar chart — is examined first. (It shall be seen below that there is good reason to deny every percentage reported in Table B.5.) Figure 10 is summarized in Table 15. The

Slaves per Plantation	1 "Ordinary" Field Hands	2 Slave Drivers	3 Slave Overseers	4 Nonfield Craftsmen	5 Nonfield Semi- skilled	6 Assistant Drivers
1–10	84.6%	0.0%	0.0%	11.9%	3.5%	0.0%
51 or more	70.8%	12.2%	1.6%	11.9%	3.5%	0.0%
All Male Farm Hands	73.7%	6.5%	0.5%	11.9%	3.5%	3.9%

TABLE 15. A COMPARISON BETWEEN THE OCCUPATIONAL DISTRIBUTION OF ADULT MALE SLAVES (ABOUT 1850) AND THE OCCUPATIONAL DISTRIBUTION OF ALL ADULT MALES (IN 1870)

	Slaves (about 1850)	All Adult Males 1870
Managerial and Professional	7.0%	33.0%
Artisans and Craftsmen	11.9%	11.0%
Semiskilled	7.4%	7.0%
Laborers	73.7%	49.0%

data in Table 15 can be read in only one way. Although in "about 1850" adult male slaves were mostly laborers and had far less opportunity than free adult males in 1870 to become "managers and professionals," the percentage of adult slave male artisans and semiskilled workers hardly differed from the percentage of free males with roughly similar skills. Figure 10 allows F + E to challenge the "conventional wisdom":

While slavery clearly limited the opportunities of bondsmen to acquire skills [sic], the fact remains that over 25 percent of [slave] males were managers, professionals, craftsmen, and semiskilled workers. Thus, the common belief that all slaves were menial laborers is false. Rather than being one undifferentiated mass, slave society produced a complex social hierarchy which was closely related to the occupational pyramid. . . .

Neglect of the fact that more than one out of every five adult slaves held preferred occupational positions, which involved not only more interesting and less arduous labor but also yielded substantially higher real incomes, has encouraged still another oversight: that is, the failure to recognize the existence of a flexible and exceedingly effective incentive system that operated within the framework of slavery. The notion that slaveowners relied on the lash alone to promote discipline and efficiency is a highly misleading myth. In slave, as in free society, [sic] positive incentives, in the form of material rewards, were a powerful instrument of economic and social control. Although slavery restricted economic and social mobility for blacks, it did not eliminate it.[72]

We carefully examine Tables 14 and 15 and the arguments which follow from them. First, the comparison between the slave occupational distribution in "about 1850" and the 1870 adult male occupational distribution is utterly inappropriate. F + E themselves appear somewhat uncomfortable with their "comparison": "Ideally, we would have preferred to compare the occupational distribution of slaves in 1850 with whites in the same year. However, 1870 is the first year for which an occupational distribution of the labor force is sufficiently detailed to permit the breakdown into the 4 skill categories used in figure 10. Unfortunately, the data needed to separate the occupations of whites from blacks are not available for 1870. This limitation is not as serious as it might seem, since it is unlikely that the occupational distribution of white labor would have been much different from that of all labor in 1870."[73] Unconvincing and actually quite lame excuses for using the 1870 "data," they also are factually erroneous. Anyone familiar with the 1850 and 1860 federal manuscript censuses knows that occupational distributions are available for whites and free blacks. Some historians have used these detailed data — data which can be easily fitted into appropriate skill categories. One distribution — that for Charleston in 1860 — has been used in these pages. It is, furthermore, incorrect to suggest that "the occupational distribution of white labor" hardly differed "from that of all labor in 1870." Manuscript census schedules for that year (or, for that matter, for 1850, 1860, and 1880) offer decisive evidence in any southern rural or urban area that the occupational distributions of blacks and whites differed radically. That F + E assert the opposite suggests that such evidence has not been examined in preparing T/C. That, however, is hardly reason to tell readers that this evidence is either inadequately "detailed" or "not available." Comparisons between the white and black occupational structures are badly needed, but not between a distribution in 1870 and one in "about 1850" that counts only slaves. A useful comparison must hold the time factor constant. Important changes in the status of Afro-Americans, after all, took place between 1850 and 1870 which greatly impair any comparison using these two moments in time. The proper comparison is between slaves and nonslaves in either 1850 or 1860. And that comparison should be *regional* — not national. It will reveal nothing more than the vast occupational differences between slaves and nonslaves.

A small but not insignificant additional caveat about the "skill categories" F + E use for the 1870 occupational distributions is that historians compar-

[72] T/C, I, pp. 40-41.
[73] T/C, II, p. 37.

ing whites and blacks need much more subtle and complex occupational distinctions than those used in Table 15. The skill category "managerial and professional," for example, includes "landowning farmers." That is not an appropriate category; it homogenizes too many differences. The suggestion that "managers and professionals" were three times more common than "artisans and craftsmen" surely surprises anyone familiar with Gilded Age American society. If F + E are right, that will only be known after we are told how various occupations were assigned to these four skill levels. As it stands, the occupational categories used for the 1870 listing are of little analytic use. A Georgia black farmer and former slave who owned ten acres of land and J. Pierpont Morgan have been counted together in calculating that "33 percent" of adult males in 1870 who were either "managers" or "professionals."

Constructing a "Residual Percentage" to Determine the "Number" of Rural Slave Field Hands and Laborers

Figure 10 needs to be put aside, and so does Table B.5, which is so important to F + E's central thesis. The assertion that "over 25 percent" of slave males were "managers, professionals, craftsmen, and semiskilled workers" — a far-fetched percentage — is the essential statistic from which F + E write about "a flexible and exceedingly effective incentive system . . . within the framework of slavery." That percentage — and no other new empirical data in T/C — allows them to describe limited but nevertheless important slave "economic and social mobility." As shown in Table 14, F + E break down the rural slave male occupational structure into six very useful categories: (1) " 'ordinary' field hands," (2) slave drivers, (3) slave overseers, (4) nonfield craftsmen, (5) nonfield semiskilled, and (6) assistant drivers. Vexing questions exist about the percentages assigned each category. Overall, the percentages assigned to occupational categories 2 through 6 are greatly inflated. Column 1 — " 'ordinary' field hands," the most important occupational grouping (73.7 percent), is a residual percentage, calculated quite simply. Column 1 is the difference between the sum of columns 2 through 6 subtracted from 100 percent and, therefore, rests entirely on how the percentages in columns 2 through 6 have been derived. If, for example, the sum of columns 2 through 6 is 10 percent, it means that about 90 percent of rural male slaves were " 'ordinary' field hands." It is important, therefore, to examine closely how the percentages in columns 2 through 6 were assigned. Columns 4 ("nonfield craftsmen") and 5 ("nonfield semiskilled") — based upon a sample of probate records — are discussed below. Columns 2 (slave drivers), 3 (slave overseers), and 6 (slave assistant drivers) are not based upon any empirical evidence. They are merely speculative and inferential percentages. They depend upon assumptions, not evidence.

Estimating the Percentage of Slave Drivers on the Basis
of a Misused "Conventional Ratio"

Columns 2 and 6 are wrong: the percentage of adult male drivers (6.5 percent) and assistant drivers (3.9 percent) has been greatly exaggerated. F + E tell how they arrived at these estimates: "The probate records thus far processed do not provide an adequate basis for determining the proportion of slaves on each plantation who were drivers. Our estimate of the share of males over 10 who were drivers is based on the conventional ratio of one driver to every 30 slaves. This ratio was applied to all plantations with 30 or more slaves. On plantations with 11 to 30 slaves, fractional drivers were computed. . . . Since virtually all drivers were male, on plantations with 30 or more slaves, one out of 15, or 6.7 percent of all males, were drivers. . . ."[74] This percentage, however, is based upon an erroneous "conventional ratio." Citations to studies by Ralph Flanders, Lewis Gray, and William K. Scarborough allow F + E to fix that "conventional ratio." Flanders, however, fixed that ratio only for the Georgia rice plantations and only for the 1820s. ("In the twenties one driver to every thirty working hands was the customary division on the seacoast," wrote Flanders.[75] The task system of organizing labor was more common among rice than cotton planters, and it is too facile to assume that the gang system of labor — common on cotton plantations — had the same ratio of drivers as the task system. Flanders' observation, moreover, was not based upon a study of plantation records. He cited two published sources, one describing Georgia plantations in the 1850s by F. L. Olmsted.) F + E also refer the reader to Scarborough's 1966 study of the plantation overseer. Scarborough wrote: "In general, it is likely that in the rice, sugar, and cotton regions most planters employed an overseer when their total working field hands approached thirty. The figure in the tobacco and grain areas, where slaves were utilized on small farms, was probably closer to twenty. In making generalizations upon this point, it is important to distinguish between the total number of *slaves* and the total number of *field hands* — a distinction usually not made by earlier authorities" (italics in the original).[76]

In the pages F + E cited, Scarborough never mentioned slave drivers, but discussed the ratio of overseers to slaves. F + E apparently failed to see this rather important difference. Moreover, first Flanders and then Scarborough (much more decisively) pointed out that plantation and farm supervisory personnel, slaves among them, were related to the number of field hands (or "working slaves"), not to the total number of slaves. Scarborough pointedly criticized earlier historians for failing to make that dis-

---

74 *Ibid.*, pp. 38-39.

75 Flanders, *Plantation Slavery in Georgia*, p. 143.

76 W. K. Scarborough, *The Overseer: Plantation Management in the Old South* (1966), pp. 8-9.

tinction. F + E repeat the same error in setting "the conventional ratio of one driver to every 30 slaves," an error that greatly increases the estimated percentage of adult male slave drivers and assistant drivers. The magnitude of that error can be illustrated by a simple example. "If we define the adult labor force as those who are fifteen years of age or over," write F + E about large plantations, "drivers formed 12.2 percent of adult males on these large estates." For example, assume a plantation with 150 slaves, half of them females. Using F + E's estimates, 32 percent were not yet ten years old, and another 13 percent were between the ages of ten and fourteen. That leaves 44 adult males and 44 adult females. We assume that the plantation had no superannuated slaves, no artisans, no semiskilled workers, and no domestic servants. All males and females aged ten years and older labored as field hands. That, of course, greatly exaggerates the size of the group. We also assume that all females and males aged ten to fourteen counted as half hands. Even if the so-called conventional ratio (1:30) is used, this plantation had 2.4 drivers, which means that 5.5 percent — not 12.2 percent — of this plantation's adult males were drivers. The estimate by F + E is slightly more than twice too high. The difference between 12.2 percent and 5.5 percent — that is, 6.7 percent of all adult slave males — needs to be shifted from columns 2 and 6 to column 1, " 'ordinary' field hands," thus increasing F + E's residual column 1 (73.7 percent) by several percentage points. The percentages are small, but the numbers involved are quite large. If, for example, there were about 800,000 rural adult male slaves in 1850, the F + E estimate puts the number of drivers and assistant drivers at 83,000. The actual number is much closer to 41,600. Adult male slaves competed for far fewer slots as drivers and assistant drivers because there was less "room at the top."[77]

Estimating the Percentage of Slave Overseers on the Basis of Erroneous Assumptions Which Create a Large Class of Unemployed Southern White Overseers in 1860

According to F + E, slave overseers (column 3 of Table 14) account for only a tiny percentage of adult black males, 0.5 percent. But a conceptual error has inflated even that small but important percentage. It has long

[77] If the crude assumption in this example is dropped (that all adult men and women were field hands) and we assume that F + E's estimates on the percentage of artisans (11.9 percent), semiskilled hands (3.5 percent), and female field hands (80 percent of all adult women) are accurate and that about 5 percent of adult men and women were too old to do field labor, it turns out again, using the conventional 1:30 ratio, that the plantation had 1.95 drivers. The percentage of adult male slaves laboring as drivers and assistant drivers then goes down even further from 12.2 percent to 4.4 percent, a decline of nearly two-thirds. Assuming 800,000 adult male slaves, it drops from 83,000 to 35,200.

been known that some slaves labored as overseers just as some blacks owned slaves.[78] But if there were about 800,000 rural adult male slaves in 1850, "some," according to the F + E estimate, becomes four thousand slave overseers. That *is* a significant number. It, too, is far too large. Let us see why. Using the "Parker-Gallman sample" of cotton plantations, F + E find that surprisingly few had resident white overseers: "Among moderate-sized holdings (sixteen to fifty slaves) less than one out of every six plantations used a white overseer. On large slaveholdings (over fifty slaves) only one out of every four owners used white overseers. Even on estates with more than one hundred slaves, the proportion with white overseers was just 30 percent, and on many of these the planters were usually in residence."[79] F + E also report that on 75 percent of large cotton plantations without overseers "there were no sons or other males who could have assumed the duties of the overseer." An inference of some importance follows: "The conclusion indicated by these findings is startling: On a majority of the large plantations, the top nonownership management was black." We leave aside the shift in language from overseer to "top . . . management."[80]

Later, on the same page, F + E describe "a system" which produced "a high-quality *class* of slave managers" (italics added). If there were as many as four thousand slave overseers, it is appropriate to write about them as a class. But this statistic is just an inference. No empirical data exist to support it. David and Temin properly point out: "[Q]uite obviously, there are two unstated premises underlying the inference that the authors draw from these census observations: (1) they assume a large plantation could not be properly run without an overseer in addition to the resident owner, and (2) they suppose the large plantations must have been well run — because they were so efficient. Once the latter presumption is withdrawn, however, this piece of inference unravels along with the rest of the fabric of Fogel and Engerman's argument."[81] No hard evidence indicates the presence of "a high-quality class of slave managers," and F + E worry unnecessarily about why "so many scholars could have been so badly misled on this issue." In volume two, F + E write: "Some scholars have overestimated the number of free overseers employed in the slave sector because they assumed that all whites listed in the census as overseers worked on slave plantations. However, since the word 'overseer' is a synonym for 'supervisor,' it was used to describe managers in industry as well as in agriculture, on free farms as well as on slave farms, in the North as well as in the South."[82]

[78] See, for example, Robert Starobin, "Privileged Bondsmen and the Process of Accommodation: The Role of the Houseservants and Drivers as Seen in Their Own Letters," *Journal of Social History,* V (Fall 1971), pp. 59-65.

[79] T/C, I, pp. 200-201.

[80] *Ibid.*, p. 212.

[81] David and Temin, "Slavery: The Progressive Institution?"

[82] T/C, II, pp. 39, 151-152.

How many white overseers were listed in the 1860 federal census? No fewer than 37,883. If their residence patterns had not changed greatly since 1850, about 10 percent lived outside the South. That leaves about 34,000 free white southern overseers in 1860. If we assume (and this surely is greatly exaggerated) that one in three managed free southern farms, free southern factories, and slave southern factories, that still leaves about 22,000 white overseers available to supervise southern plantations. Is that a large or a small number? Once more, it depends. Scarborough's study helps answer this question. In the sugar, rice, and cotton regions, "most planters employed an overseer when the total number of working field hands approached thirty." In estimating the use of overseers, Scarborough insists, it is essential to "distinguish between the total number of *slaves* and the total number of *field hands*."

About how many slaves did a planter have to own to hire an overseer? That depends upon the ratio of slave field hands to slaves. About *fifty slaves* were needed to produce a residue of *thirty field hands*.[83] How many slave-owners in 1860 owned fifty or more slaves? About ten thousand. After making the above generous allowances, about twenty-two thousand free white plantation overseers lived in the South in 1860, more than twice the number needed to manage these large plantations. So far, no allowance has been made for slave overseers. It is now assumed that F + E are correct, but that two thousand (not four thousand, but enough to make for a "class") slaves labored as overseers. That would mean that eight thousand white overseers labored for the owners of fifty or more slaves. And what of the other fourteen thousand? Did they labor for owners of fewer than fifty slaves and, therefore, fewer than thirty field hands? Were many unemployed in 1860? Or had large numbers of whites misrepresented their occupations to the census enumerators? The inference that 0.5 percent of adult male slaves labored as overseers rests on F + E's assumption that "most" planters did not employ white overseers and, therefore, had to employ slave overseers. If that was so, what did most white overseers in the South do for a living in 1860? Rather than answer that question, we also need to put the 0.5 percent aside. The antebellum South had slave overseers, but their number was insignificant. They deserve study, but their place in the southern slave oc-

[83] This estimate is arrived at as follows: It is assumed that male and female slaves were equal in number, that 32 percent (the F + E estimate) were under ten years of age, that another 13 percent (the F + E estimate) were ten to fourteen years of age, that 5 percent were too old to work in the fields, that 80 percent of the remaining women (the F + E estimate) labored in the fields, and that 85 percent of the remaining males (the F + E estimate, making allowance for artisans, semiskilled workers, and servants) labored as field hands. On a fifty-slave plantation, that leaves about twenty-seven *full field hands*. I have counted women and youths ten to fourteen years as full field hands because, as shall soon be seen, the F + E estimate that 15.4 percent of adult male slaves labored as either artisans or semiskilled workers is far too high.

cupational structure and plantation managerial system needs to be measured more carefully first. It is not possible that "within the agricultural sector, about 7.0 percent of the [slave] men held managerial posts."[84] That percentage is much closer to 3.0 percent, and nearly all were drivers. There is no reason to ponder over why historians "have been so badly misled on this issue." There is no issue.

The Missing Rural Southern White and Free Black Artisan

Columns 4 (nonfield craftsmen) and 5 (nonfield semiskilled) of Table 14 are based upon much more substantial evidence than columns 2, 3, and 6 and come from a little-used source, probate records. The authors write: "The share of skilled and semiskilled laborers in nonfield occupations on plantations was determined from a sample of 33 estates, ranging in size from 3 to 98 slaves, retrieved from the probate records. This sample revealed that 15.4 percent of slaves over age 15 were engaged in such occupations. The percentage of skilled slaves was fairly constant over plantation size."[85] Most of such men were artisans (11.9 percent). F + E make much of this sample, but there are many difficulties associated with it. We save for the last the biases built into a sample of *artisans* drawn from probate records. "The fact is," F + E write, "that slaves . . . held a large share of the skilled jobs in the countryside."[86] That is not a fact. No one has yet studied the number of rural and village white and free black artisans in the antebellum South, so estimates of the relative importance of rural slave artisans remain speculative. If slave artisans were as common on plantations as F + E suggest, how, then, should we handle evidence which indicates that profit-hungry planters hired white artisans to do skilled plantation jobs? Bennet Barrow, for example, did not own a slave blacksmith. "There is no record," writes his biographer, "of a single major repair job being consigned to a slave."[87] J. C. Sitterson's study of the Bayou LaFourche McCollam plantation reveals that its owners hired carpenters and blacksmiths from the outside — even to build slave cabins.[88] There is, furthermore, some question about the quality of rural slave artisanal skills. Did a plantation carpenter or blacksmith share a common skill level with an urban slave carpenter or blacksmith? That is a subject which requires much careful study. In 1860, for example, the Charleston slave trader Louis DeSaussure advertised the sale of four "good carpenters": Stephen, Scipio, Jack, and Jacob. But Jacob was also described

[84] T/C, I, p. 39.
[85] T/C, II, p. 37.
[86] T/C, I, p. 38.
[87] Davis, *Plantation Life*, p. 35.
[88] J. C. Sitterson, "The McCollams: A Planter Family . . . ," *Journal of Southern History*, VI (August 1940), p. 350.

as a "plantation carpenter."[89] What did that distinction mean? There is, finally, some question about the occupations F + E include under the category "nonfield semiskilled": "teamsters, coachmen, gardeners, stewards, and house servants."[90] A slave gardener, for example, was usually an elderly male retired from field labor. Is semiskilled the appropriate skill level for such a person?

Estimating the Size of an Unknown Sample of Probate Records That Reveal the Distribution of Slave Artisans

The general and particular use of probate records by F + E as a source for estimating the percentage of slave artisans in the entire rural male population merits unusually close attention. The size of the sample is considered first: "33 estates, ranging in size from 3 to 98 slaves." That brief summary denies much to the reader: (1) the names of these estates, (2) their location, (3) the dates these probates were filed, (4) whether "3 to 98 slaves" means just adult males or all slaves, including women and children, and (5) the average size of these estates. If it is assumed that the average estate listed fifty slaves, 25 percent of them adult males, the entire sample included about 412 rural slave males, 50 of them "nonfield" craftsmen and 14 of them "nonfield" semiskilled workers.[91] Can percentages of slave skill distributions based upon so small a sample reveal very much? Is this sample — 50 rural artisans and 14 semiskilled slaves — adequate to indicate the diversity of occupations among rural slaves? I doubt it.

Contrasting Percentages of Black Artisans in a Rural Mississippi County (1880) and in Four Rural Virginia Counties (1865-1866)

The sample size is emphasized because the percentage of artisans found on these thirty-three estates far exceeds that found in other manuscript records examined by L. Rowland and by me. It is best to work backward with such data from 1880 to the late antebellum period. An occupational breakdown which includes all rural Adams County, Mississippi, adult black males in 1880 — nearly three thousand men — shows that 1 percent had artisan skills (Table 16).[92] Two-thirds of these few artisans were either carpenters or blacksmiths. It might be argued that this is an unfair comparison. It is possible that a large number of rural Adams County slave

[89] The advertisement is printed in Frederic Bancroft, *Slave Trading in the Old South* (1931).

[90] T/C, I, p. 39.

[91] I have multiplied 412 by F + E's estimates to get the approximate number of artisans (11.9 percent) and semiskilled workers (3.5 percent).

[92] These Adams County data are not a sample. They include all adult blacks listed in the pages of the 1880 federal manuscript census.

artisans quit that place upon emancipation. But if that happened, they did not move to nearby Natchez, because in 1880 that town had proportionately just as few black artisans as other southern towns. It also is possible that local white southern artisans drove the slave artisans from the rural Adams County market following emancipation. But if F + E are right and the slaves "held a large share of the skilled jobs in the countryside," that eviction would have been a superhuman task. In 1880 more than 90 percent of rural Adams County residents were blacks, and that county's rural law enforcement officers were mostly still blacks.

Data closer in time to enslavement reveal a different occupational distribution than in rural Adams County, but one that nevertheless shows a lower percentage of artisans than the F + E sample. Two military population censuses (Montgomery and York counties) and two Freedmen's Bureau marriage registers (Goochland and Louisa counties) indicate that far fewer Virginia slave males had artisanal skills than suggested by the probate sample (Table 17).[93] These data were collected in either 1865 or 1866. The range of skills among these former slaves was hardly wider than among the rural Adams County blacks a decade and one-half later. Just over 50 percent

TABLE 16. ADULT BLACK MALE OCCUPATIONAL DISTRIBUTION, RURAL ADAMS COUNTY, MISSISSIPPI, 1880

Occupation	Percentage
Farmer: Owns Land	6%
Tenant, Sharecropper, Farm Laborer	70%
Nonfarm Laborer	22%
Artisan	1%
High-status Occupation	1%
N	2,976

TABLE 17. ARTISANS AS A PERCENTAGE OF ALL ADULT BLACK MALES, VIRGINIA COUNTIES, 1865-1866

County	Number of Adult Males	Percentage of Artisans
Montgomery County Census	610	6.7%
York County Census	929	8.0%
Goochland County Marriage Register	719	8.3%
Louisa County Marriage Register	1,232	8.1%

[93] The 1865-1866 data draw from unpublished records in the Virginia Freedmen's Bureau records, Record Group 5, National Archives, and are further analyzed in my forthcoming study, chapter eight.

in all four counties were either carpenters or blacksmiths. These censuses and marriage registers were compiled too soon after emancipation to indicate that slave skills had deteriorated — for whatever reasons — as a consequence of emancipation. (The percentage of artisans in York, Goochland, and Louisa counties is somewhat higher than for the overall black population in 1865-1866 because artisans tended to be older men, and these three censuses or marriage registers had too great a number of older men among them to be typical.) F + E's error can be illustrated in yet another way. According to their overall estimate, 26.3 percent of adult male slaves had "privileged" occupations. We briefly examine such men in Copiah County, Mississippi. In 1860 there were 1,651 male slaves aged twenty and older living there, and according to F + E's estimates 434 should have had privileged slave occupational status. A Freedmen's Bureau labor register, probably gathered in 1866, gives the occupations of 388 Copiah black adult males. Unless either privileged former slaves had quit that place or a radical downgrading of rural black occupations had occurred by 1866, about 90 blacks should have listed privileged occupations. Six did. The percentage of former Copiah slaves with privileged occupations was 1.5 percent, not 26.3 percent. The Copiah registrants also gave their ages and as a group were significantly older than the adult male slaves listed in the 1860 federal manuscript census. According to F + E, artisans and other privileged former slaves tended to be older men. The percentage with privileged occupations in 1866, therefore, should have been even greater than 26.3 percent. But it was far lower — 1.5 percent — a foreman, a blacksmith, and four house servants.

The Occupations of 20,576 Union Army Kentucky Black Soldiers Contrasted with the F + E Estimates: A "Test" of the F + E "Thesis"

The fourth set of comparative statistics — and by far the most convincing — comes from Kentucky Union Army recruitment records and has been collected by Leslie Rowland as part of her continuing major study of Kentucky blacks during the Civil War. She generously has allowed me to use the statistics in this essay. The information is in Union Army Company Descriptive Rolls (or, when lacking, in Regimental Descriptive Rolls) filed in the National Archives in Record Group 94, Records of the Adjutant General's Office. These military records contain the most complete information yet available on slave occupations. By the Civil War's end, about half (a conservative estimate) of Kentucky's adult male slaves were in the Union Army. They came from all parts of the state. Rowland has examined records for 20,905 black Kentucky soldiers. Occupations are listed for all but 329 of these men (98.4 percent).[94] This evidence shows an opposite

[94] One hundred fourteen men did not have an occupation next to their names, and another 215 were simply described as "slaves."

distribution of slave skills from the one F + E constructed by sampling a few probate records.[95] Of the 20,576 men with listed occupations, all but 527 — that is, 97.4 percent — gave as their occupations "farmer" and "laborer." The occupational distribution, detailed in Table 18, also includes

TABLE 18. OCCUPATIONAL DISTRIBUTION OF KENTUCKY BLACK UNION ARMY SOLDIERS COMPARED TO THE OCCUPATIONAL STRUCTURE OF ADULT MALE SLAVES ON FARMS (TABLE B.5) IN T/C

Occupation	Kentucky Black Soldiers		F+E Percentage in T/C
	Number	Percentage	
Farmer and Laborer	20,049	97.44%	73.7%
Artisan	331	1.61%	11.9%
Servant	99	.48%	7.4%
Drayman, Wagoner, Teamster	86	.42%	
High Status*	11	.05%	7.0%
Total	20,576	100.00%	100.0%

* Among these eleven were five clergymen and three clerks.

[95] The rolls make no distinction between slaves and free blacks, but the majority listed were slaves. Regiments (and the companies therein) were used for those units known by Rowland to have been recruited primarily in Kentucky. The descriptive rolls do not give a place of residence, but Rowland assumed that recruitment at a Kentucky point indicated that the slave or free black had been a Kentucky resident in 1860. Because her work focuses on Kentucky blacks, Rowland correctly counted only volunteers and drafted men at Kentucky points. No substitutes, wherever they entered the army, were counted. To be acceptable as a substitute, a black had to be ineligible for the Kentucky draft. That meant he had to be under the age of twenty-one (seventeen to twenty years old) or from another state which had no draft (that is, a state in rebellion). Large numbers of substitutes were contraband blacks from the Confederate states, so no substitutes were counted in this tally. The resultant undercount of seventeen- to twenty-year-olds biases the occupational distribution of the *soldiers* upward. Men under twenty years old were less likely to have skills than men over twenty years of age. That means that the percentage of unskilled Kentucky soldiers was greater than that given in the table printed in this text.

When the final calculations appear in Rowland's completed work, they will be more refined, but the essential outline sketched in these pages should not change much.

I have tried without success to think of a reason why Kentucky slaves and free blacks would have misrepresented their occupations to Union Army officers. Some men may have inflated their skills in order to advance more rapidly in the military service, but there is no reason why a slave carpenter would have called himself a slave laborer. It is possible, however, that the recruitment and other officers carelessly listed black occupations.

Rowland examined records for the following regiments: U.S. Colored Infantry 100, 101, 107, 108, 109, 114, 115, 116, 117, 118, 119, 120, 121, 122, 123, 124, 125; U.S. Cavalry 4 and 5; and U.S. Heavy Artillery 4, 12, and 13. The records for all except four of these regiments appear complete.

for comparison the distribution drawn by F + E primarily from the sampled probate records. As elsewhere, Kentucky slave carpenters and blacksmiths predominated (three out of five) among the artisans. (Shoemakers made up the third most common craft, but only twenty-one shoemakers were listed.) The differences in these two occupational distributions are not slight. There is no possible way to reconcile these two sets of data.

It is possible, of course, that slaves with high skill levels — artisans and managers (drivers and overseers) — were underrepresented among those Kentucky blacks who took up arms against the Confederacy. Such men may have retained a loyalty to their owners, a reward their owners gained by allowing them to hold privileged slave status. But if that explains why nearly all black Kentucky soldiers were farmers and laborers, such evidence severely damages another proposition put forth in T/C:

> While the reward structure created much more room for upward mobility within the slave system than is usually supposed, the scope of opportunity should not be exaggerated. The highest levels of attainment were irrevocably foreclosed to slaves. The entrepreneurial talent obviously possessed by bondsmen such as Aham could not be used to catapult them into the stewardship [*sic*] of great businesses as long as they remained slaves.[96] No slave, regardless of his gifts, could aspire to political position. No man of letters — there were slaves who acquired considerable erudition — could ever hold an appointment in the faculty of a southern university as long as he was a bondsman. The entrepreneurial genius had to settle for lingering in the shadow of the master on whose protection he was dependent. The man of letters could go no further than the position of tutor to the children of a benevolent and enlightened planter. It was on the talented, the upper crust of slave society, that [the?] deprivations of the peculiar institution hung most heavy [*sic*]. This, perhaps, explains why it was that the first to flee to northern lines as Yankee advances corroded the Rebel positions were not the ordinary field hands, but the drivers and the artisans.[97]

F + E make a similar point in volume two. "Slavery," they suggest, "weighed most heavily on the talented."[98] F + E present no evidence that the "first

[96] "The highest annual figure we have been able to uncover for extra earnings by a field hand in a single year is $309. Aham, the Alabama slave whose sales of peaches, apples, and cotton yielded this sum, had accumulated enough capital over the years so that in 1860 he held notes on loans totaling over $2,400." This example, its origin never given, appears in the paragraph preceding the one quoted in this text.

[97] T/C, I, pp. 152-153.

[98] T/C, II, p. 118. The evidence cited is Theodore Hershberg's study of a small number of former slaves living in antebellum Philadelphia. It suggests that in 1838, and again in 1847, the former slaves had more wealth than those Philadelphia Afro-Americans born in the North. But Hershberg's study has one serious limitation in supporting this F + E argument. Nothing at all is known about the prior occupational status of these former slaves. What if most had been field hands and common slave laborers before making it to Philadelphia?

to flee to northern lines" were "the drivers and the artisans." There is none. And the occupations of Kentucky black soldiers — no matter how interpreted — severely damage one or another of the central themes that flow through T/C. If the Kentucky military occupational distribution is an accurate reflection of the Kentucky slave occupational distribution, that is good reason to doubt that slaves worked hard to rise within the slave occupational structure. It is known now how little room there was at the top. The "scope of opportunity" was indeed narrow. There was not much economic payoff in working hard. But if the Kentucky military occupational distribution underrepresented the more privileged slaves ("the drivers and the artisans") because they remained loyal to their masters and would not join the Union Army (the Emancipation Proclamation was issued before the time Kentucky blacks could join the army), then there is no way to argue that the "deprivations of the peculiar institution hung most heavy [*sic*]" on "the talented, the upper crust of slave society." If that was so, the "upper crust" should have been overrepresented in the military occupational structure. (Unless one is prepared to argue that joining the Union Army after 1863 was not an expression of profound discontent by an Afro-American slave.) F + E cannot have it both ways.

The Slave Artisan: Why Probate Records Are a Biased Source
for Estimating the Number of Antebellum Adult Slave Artisans

In good part, the serious discrepancy between the Kentucky occupational distribution and that constructed by F + E results from F + E's failure to take into account the upward age bias in probate listings of slave artisans. By themselves and without correction, probate records record too high a percentage of slave artisans in the general male population. That is so for two quite separate reasons. Once in each volume, F + E point out that as a group slave artisans tended to be older men.[99] That is illustrated in yet other sources as revealed in Table 19. Slave artisans differed in this respect from white Charleston and Mobile artisans in 1860. But probate records usually undercount younger adult slaves and, therefore, exaggerate the number of slave artisans. If most probate records are those of older men, their slaveholdings do not accurately reflect the age distribution of the slave population at large, because in building a plantation labor force such a man probably inherited or purchased a group of young slaves at the start of his career. These slaves grew older as their owner did. The age distortions in the probate records are illustrated by examining the ages of adult males on Henry Watson's Black Belt Alabama cotton plantation in 1843 and then in 1861 as well as the ages of adult males on the Cedar Vale plantation in

[99] T/C, I, pp. 149-153; II, pp. 117-118.

TABLE 19. PERCENTAGE OF ARTISANS UNDER THIRTY YEARS OF AGE

Place and Date	Number of Artisans	Percentage under 30
Blacks		
Montgomery County, Va., 1865-1866	37	30%
York County, Va., 1865-1866	76	8%
Goochland County, Va., 1866	71	13%
Louisa County, Va., 1866	109	28%
Whites		
Charleston, S.C., 1860	2,023	47%
Mobile, Ala., 1860	2,182	48%

Nansemond County, Virginia, in 1863 (the year that its owner died), as shown in Table 20. The bias in the probate record as a source for estimating artisan skills in the male slave population at large is seen by assuming that Watson died either in 1843 or in 1861. In 1843, one in four male Watson slaves was at least thirty years old. Twenty years later, nearly two in three Watson slaves were at least thirty years old. A probate record filed in 1843 would have contained too few artisans; one filed in 1861 would have contained too many artisans. Too few or too many, that is, to reveal accurately the percentage of artisans in the slave population at large. Unless the probate records examined by F + E included those of representative dead *young* planters, the bias in the age structure of male slaves listed significantly exaggerates the percentage of slave artisans listed in column 4 in Table 14 (T/C Table B.5). There is no way to tell the exact percentage of error, but I suspect the proper percentage is quite a bit lower than the 11.9 percent reported by F + E. A drop, say, to 7 percent shifts the nonartisans

TABLE 20. AGE DISTRIBUTION OF PLANTATION MALES FIFTEEN AND OLDER

Age	Watson Alabama Plantation		Cedar Vale Plantation
	1843	1861	1863
15–19	8%	18%	8%
20–29	67%	18%	17%
30–39	8%	27%	25%
40–49	17%	27%	42%
50+	0%	9%	8%
N	12	33	12
Adult Males as a Percentage of All Slaves	24%	29%	26%
Percentage of Adult Males 30 and Older	25%	63%	75%

to column 1 (" 'ordinary' field hands") along with the surplus slave "over-seers," "drivers," and "assistant drivers."

I cannot tell whether the age bias in probate records affected the estimated percentage of semiskilled slave workers, particularly house servants, but enough has been seen in the errors that inflated the percentages in columns 2, 3, 4, and 6 of Table 14 to realize that the actual percentage of ordinary field hands in the rural slave population in "about 1850" greatly exceeded 73.7 percent and was probably no less than 85 percent. In an adult male population of about 800,000, that shift in the residual percentage increases the number of field hands by at least 100,000 and severely weakens F + E's assertion that "slaves had the opportunity to rise within the social and economic hierarchy that existed under bondage."

The Key to T/C: Slave Occupational Opportunities and the Acceptance of Planter-Sponsored Labor Incentives by the Enslaved

What began as a discussion of F + E's analysis of slave rewards and punishments has shifted for these many pages to a detailed examination of their reconstruction of the slave occupational distribution. The reason for that detour needs to be emphasized. The single set of new quantitative materials used by F + E to argue that slaves accepted planter-sponsored positive labor incentives is Table B.5, the "adult male occupational distribution." It is this set of data — and no other — which allows F + E to tout their new "findings" about slave upward mobility. We need to return, therefore, to their discussion of the third category of rewards: those of "a long-term nature, often requiring a decade or more before they paid off." But in what follows, the reader should keep in mind the flimsy evidence used to construct the slave occupational structure. F + E correctly minimize "freedom through manumission" as a long-run reward. "The chance of achieving this reward," they admit, "was, of course, quite low." It would have been more accurate to write that the chance of achieving this reward was much greater in 1810 than in 1860. Manumission became more difficult as slavery grew older and became more institutionalized. Rather than stress manumission, F + E emphasize the opportunities slaves had to rise within the slave system: "Field hands could become artisans or drivers. Artisans could be allowed to move from the plantation to town where they would hire themselves out. Drivers could move up to the position of head driver or overseer. Climbing the economic ladder brought not only social status, and sometimes more freedom; it also had significant payoffs in better housing, better clothing, and cash bonuses."[100] There was, of course, always room at the top in slave society. But how much and whether one got there depended, in part, upon how many

[100] T/C, I, p. 149.

77

empty spots existed. Given the errors in F + E's slave occupational distribution, the metaphor of a slave "economic ladder" is badly chosen. A pole would be much more appropriate.

How Not to Study Slave Mobility: The Error in T/C

It needs also to be emphasized that the discussion of slave mobility in T/C is theoretically flawed and conceptually muddled. A simple occupational distribution ("about 1850"), whatever percentages are assigned to particular skill levels, tells nothing about upward or downward movement. Movement in either direction requires the passage of time. That is a basic point. Until there is evidence on the changing distribution of slave occupations — between, say, 1810 and 1850 — it is not possible to "infer" mobility patterns and resultant "payoffs." F + E, furthermore, do not clarify their discussion of slave "mobility" by the inferences based only upon the ages of artisans. What they write deserves to be quoted at some length to illustrate their confusion:

> Little attention has hitherto been paid to the manner in which planters selected the slaves who were to become the artisans and managers. In some cases boys were apprenticed to carpenters, blacksmiths, or some similar craftsmen when they were in their early teens, as was typically done with whites. For slaves, this appears to have been the exception rather than the rule. Analysis of occupational data derived from probate and plantation records reveals an unusual distribution of ages among slave artisans. Slaves in their twenties were substantially underrepresented, while slaves in their forties and fifties were overrepresented. This age pattern suggests that the selection of slaves for training in the crafts was frequently delayed until slaves reached their late twenties, or perhaps even into the [sic] thirties.
>
> Normally this would be an uneconomical policy, since the earlier an investment is made in occupational training, the more years there are to reap the returns on that investment. Slavery altered this pattern by shifting the authority to determine occupational investments from the parents to the masters. In free societies, kinship is usually the primary basis for determining which members of the new generation are trained in skilled occupations. But the slaveholder lacked the vested interests of a parent. He could, therefore, treat entry into the skilled occupations as a prize that was to be claimed by the most deserving, regardless of family background. The extra effort put forth by young field hands who competed for these jobs appears to have more than offset the loss in returns due to the curtailed period over which the occupational investment was amortized. We do not mean to suggest that kinship played no role in the intergenerational transfer of skills among slaves. We merely wish to stress that its role was significantly reduced as compared with free society.[101]

[101] *Ibid.,* pp. 149-150.

78

This argument in volume one is supported in volume two by a table (discussed below) and a quotation from "a plantation guide published in 1823 which advised slaveowners to choose artisans on the basis of previous performance," a work entitled *The Jamaica Planter's Guide* and published in London, England. F + E then pick up the argument put forth in volume one:

> Insofar as it precluded slaves from certain occupations, or greatly reduced the entry of slaves into certain occupations, slave society was more closed than free society. On the other hand, slave society appears to have been more open to the entry of any individual into the preferred occupations that were allowed to slaves; entry into these occupations appears to have depended less on kinship and more on performance than was the case in many free societies.
>
> To say that kinship played a weaker role in occupational mobility does not imply that it played no role. While a systematic count has not yet been undertaken, it appears that those who held preferred occupations were, to a disproportionate extent, the offspring of slaves who held such occupations.[102]

There is plain confusion in these few paragraphs. The reader learns that slave society was "more closed than free society" but "more open to the entry of any individual into the preferred occupations . . . allowed to slaves." More open than what? More open than free society? Hardly so. We have seen how few Charleston slaves had artisan skills. The Charleston free blacks were far fewer in number than the Charleston slaves, but Charleston had more free black than slave artisans in 1860. F + E, however, may mean that slave society was more open than abolitionist critics dared admit, but that is hardly a useful analytic point. This is 1975, not 1845. We need to know how open that society was. "More open" is not a useful concept. Nor is their discussion clarified by introducing "kinship" as the alternative source of skill opportunities. Kinship is greatly minimized in volume one as the source of slave skills in order to argue that owners treated skills as "prizes." In volume two, however, slaves "who held preferred occupations were, to a disproportionate extent, the offspring of slaves who held such occupations." It cannot be both ways. "What do you mean by that?" said the Caterpillar sternly. "Explain yourself!" "I can't explain myself, I'm afraid, sir," said Alice, "because I'm not myself, you see." "I don't see," said the Caterpillar. "I'm afraid I can't put it more clearly," Alice replied very politely.

Why Slave Artisans Tended to Be Older Men: An Alternate Explanation and Its Social Implications

Some of this confusion results from the fact that the probate records have once again misled F + E. That is clear if we look carefully at Table B.18

[102] T/C, II, p. 118.

in volume two (p. 118, and reproduced here as Table 21). Assuming that these data are drawn from the same sample (thirty-three estates) of probate records used to construct Table B.5 (Table 14, above), I have added an extra column indicating the *probable* number of artisans in each age group. There are two difficulties with this table. First of all, the estimated sample of artisans — fifty or so males in all — is hardly a satisfactory one. But even if the sample were ten or twenty times larger, that would not solve the error in the table. Columns 1 and 2 are not comparable. Column 1 is the age distribution of all adult slaves in 1860. In order for F + E's point to be established, Column 1 should give the age distribution of all adult slaves in the sampled probate records. The reason has been given before: compared to the overall adult male slave population, probate records contain a disproportionate percentage of older adult males, and slave artisans tended to be older men. To grasp the magnitude of this error, let us return briefly to F + E's estimate that 26.3 percent of adult male slaves had "privileged" occupations. If, as F + E insist, artisans tended to be older slaves because they had been "rewarded" for hard and loyal labor, it follows that other privileged slaves (overseers, drivers, and house servants) also probably tended to be older men. Let us examine Mississippi's male slaves in 1860 to see what that would mean. Of 117,706 male slaves aged twenty and older, about 31,000 would have been neither field hands nor common laborers. We assume the following. First, Mississippi male slaves aged seventy and older were superannuated and did not labor. Second, the age distribution among rural privileged slaves approximated that given for slave artisans in Table 21. If these are accurate assumptions, it turns out that *exactly half of all male Mississippi slaves aged forty to sixty-nine had privileged economic status in 1860.* Only a compound error could produce so wildly inaccu-

TABLE 21. A COMPARISON OF THE AGE DISTRIBUTION OF ADULT MALES WITH THE AGE DISTRIBUTION OF MALE ARTISANS

Age Group	Percentage of Males Age 15 and Over in Age Group	Percentage of Artisans in Age Group	Probable Number of Artisans in Probate Sample
15–19	20%	2%	1
20–29	33%	23%	11.5
30–39	20%	33%	16.5
40–49	13%	23%	11.5
50 or more	13%	19%	9.5
			50.0

Sources: Column 1: U.S. Bureau of Census, Eighth (1860), *Population of the United States* (1864), pp. 594-595.
Column 2: computed from the probate records.

rate a percentage, a percentage which means that a male slave who lived to be sixty years of age had one chance in two of rising in the slave occupational hierarchy. If that percentage describes aspects of the real world in which enslaved Afro-Americans lived, it is curious that the vast literature upholding slavery failed to emphasize this positive good. But such a "percentage" would have staggered the imaginations of even the most avid proslavery propagandists.

It nevertheless remains a fact — and one of much importance — that slave artisans as a group were older men. But was it because such jobs were distributed by owners as *prizes* to the "most deserving" young field hands for their "extra effort"? And was it that such positions went to men "regardless of family background"? Why, then, were those "who held preferred occupations ... to a disproportionate extent, the offspring of slaves who held such occupations"? An alternative explanation which reconciles the fact that most slave artisans were older men with the fact that younger slave artisans often had slave artisan fathers is possible. The explanation, however, requires that we put aside the crude and unproven assertion that artisan skills were prizes bestowed by owners upon hard-working field hands and also recognize the essential fact that enslavement *limited* opportunities for Afro-Americans to be artisans. Slave artisans did not compete in a free market. Owners determined the number of artisans needed for the efficient — profitable — use of the labor force they owned. A plantation, for example, needed *x* number of artisans to run efficiently. When a slave artisan died, a younger slave — a man in his late twenties or thirties — replaced the artisan. The new artisan, possibly the son of this dead craftsman, has mastered the requisite skills in his close association with his slave father. Whether a slave who became a recognized artisan in his early thirties found satisfaction ("a payoff") in that achievement is doubtful. Enslavement profoundly limited slave physical mobility, but slaves could see with their own eyes. If they lived in Charleston or Mobile in 1860 (or visited those towns), they would have seen that one out of every two white artisans was not yet thirty years old. Would that experience have tied them in more deeply to the slave system or revealed to them the enormous disadvantages imposed by enslavement?

Were Slaves Occupationally Better Off in 1860 Than Their Grandfathers Had Been in 1790?

Much remains to be studied about what happened to slaves — and to their skills — over time, and such study should not be deterred by the mangled analysis of slave mobility in T/C. But slave mobility has to be examined as much more than the mere consequence of "the mangerial attention of planters" to "the problem of motivating their hands." When sold from a farm or a small plantation to a larger unit of production, did a slave rise or fall occupationally — that is, did a slave experience upward or downward mobility? That change occurred often in the great expansion of the slave system following the War of 1812, and its effects on slave status and on slave self-image need careful study. And then there is the genuinely important process called "the transfer of intergenerational skills." Let us create an example: a slave carpenter living in Virginia in 1790 who was sold or moved with his family to Kentucky in the early 1800s. He and his descendants still lived there on the eve of the Civil War. By that time, the carpenter probably had as many as twenty grandsons. Were these young and middle-aged slave males mostly artisans, drivers, and overseers? According to F + E, three would have had such privileged jobs if they lived on farms, and six (29.2 percent) if they lived on very large plantations (with fifty-one or more slaves). But according to the Union Army enlistment records — lists that gave the occupations of at least half of Kentucky's adult male slaves in 1860 — only one of these men would have had the same or a higher skill as their eighteenth-century Virginia slave carpenter grandfather. Is this the "payoff" that encouraged hard work among ordinary antebellum slaves? Or is it the "payoff" that explains why so many unskilled, rural, and Protestant Kentucky blacks quit their owners and joined the Union Army?[103]

The Planter as Pioneer Personnel Manager and the Plantation as a "Modern" Factory: The Meaning of the Word Pre-Industrial

All of this evidence bears directly on the slave social character, and that is why it is so important. F + E do not shy away from translating numbers and percentages into beliefs and behavior. Slaveowners, and especially planters, busied themselves encouraging their slaves to work hard. And the incentives they supplied, mostly positive but occasionally negative, reshaped the culture of Afro-American slaves and, therefore, affected the aspirations (the beliefs and behavior) of ordinary slave men and women. Owners worked hard at this task: "No question was treated with more gravity than that of labor management. Planters recognized that this was the critical issue. Economic success rode or fell with it. No aspect of slave management

[103] If, by chance, F + E are right and owners distributed scarce artisan jobs to hardworking field hands who had "competed" for such prizes, other problems would have emerged. Artisan work was scarce on plantations, and only a handful of men in their late twenties and early thirties could be so rewarded. Is it difficult to imagine the disappointment felt by hard-working slaves when the scarce reward went to a fellow slave? And is it possible to argue that after such a disappointment these slaves remained "devoted, hard-working, responsible slaves who identified their fortunes with the fortunes of their masters?" Enslaved Afro-Americans had little formal education, but I very much doubt that they were so stupid.

was considered too trivial to be omitted from consideration or debate. Details of housing, diet, medical care, marriage, child rearing, holidays, incentives and punishments, alternate methods of organizing field labor . . . were all deemed worthy of debate." Planters differed among themselves about details, but agreed as a class that "the ultimate objective of slave management was the creation of a highly disciplined, highly specialized, and well-coordinated labor force. . . . On plantations, the hands were as rigidly organized as in a factory."[104] Planters surely worried greatly about slave labor, but to give the impression that they debated these matters regularly is to inflate that concern, at least if the pages of *DeBow's Review* are typical of publications directed to slaveowners. Between January, 1846, and December, 1860, 186 issues of that magazine appeared, and one or more articles dealing with the "material treatment" of slaves or with "labor management" appeared in only 21 (11.2 percent) of the issues. If such a "debate" occurred, it did not find its way into this well-known southern magazine.

Whatever the breadth of that "debate," F + E remain convinced that owner-sponsored incentives, together with relatively decent material treatment, had a transformational effect on the "quality" of slave labor: "Far from being 'ordinary peasants' unused to 'pre-industrial rhythms of work,' black plantation agriculturalists labored under a regimen that was more like a modern assembly line than was true of the routine in many of the factories of the antebellum era. It was often easier for factory workers to regulate the pace of machines to their accustomed rhythm than for the slaves to regulate the pace set by drivers. For much of antebellum manufacturing was still operated on the work patterns of the handicrafts. Division of labor was still at relatively low levels and interdependence of operations was still limited."[105] Slaves, of course, were not peasants and had distinctive slave work routines, but peasants and rural as well as most urban slaves — together with all artisans — were, in fact, accustomed to what F + E call "pre-industrial rhythms of work" because most slaves, many craftsmen, and all peasants did not work with machines. The concept "pre-industrial" is indeed a vague one, and its meaning varies from group to group and even changes over time. Nevertheless, it refers in general to work styles before the development of industrial technology and the use of steam as a source of power.

Field labor surely demanded regularities from slaves, but these were hardly the regularities identified with "a modern assembly line." They shared more in common with the regularities expected of a laborer on a sailing ship than in the Ford automobile factory. Industrialization did *not* create regular work rhythms; it changed them. It is asking entirely too much to visualize Uncle Tom working side by side with Charles Chaplin in *Modern Times*. The

[104] T/C, I, pp. 202-203.
[105] *Ibid.*, p. 208.

assertion that "much of antebellum manufacturing . . . operated on the work patterns of the handicrafts" is no more than the rhetoric associated with a lawyer's brief. Handicraft manufacturing was quite important in antebellum America, but modern factory production also made enormous strides before the Civil War. And except for the iron, other metal, and machine and tool industries, most large antebellum factories employed women and children, in part because the obstinate patterns of preindustrial work among male artisans made it difficult and costly to utilize the technology spawned by "modernization." Employers found it easier to develop labor-saving machinery that could be handled by women and children than to transform the settled work habits of craftsmen. The Lowell, Massachusetts, cotton mills come quickly to mind. Are F + E suggesting that the work rhythms on an Alabama cotton plantation had more in common with those of the Ford Motor Company than did the work rhythms in a Massachusetts textile mill? That seems so when they write: "Just as the great plantations were the first large, scientifically managed business enterprises, and as planters were the first group to engage in large-scale, scientific personnel management, so, too, black slaves were the first group of workers to be trained in the work rhythms which later became characteristic of industrial society."[106] But most slaves did not labor on machines. So if F + E are correct, it is necessary to put aside the conventional definition of industrialism: "an economic organization of society built largely on mechanized industry rather than agriculture, craftsmanship, or commerce."

Can the Historian Measure the Difference between Enslavement and "Quasi-Freedom"?

There is yet more exaggerated rhetoric in T/C. The "special quality of plantation labor," we learn, depended upon "the combination of the superior management of planters and the superior quality of black labor. In a certain sense, all, or nearly all, of the advantage is attributable to the high quality of slave labor, for the main thrust of management was directed at improving the quality of labor."[107] This emphasis on the "high quality" of slave labor helps to explain the harshness of F + E's attack on Kenneth Stampp's *The Peculiar Institution*. Stampp admitted the profitability of slavery (as did nearly all historians by the 1950s) but denied that it rested on either the "superior quality of black labor" or the relative satisfactions that emerged from the relatively decent material conditions of slave life. F + E, as has been seen, realize that their propositions about profitability and "efficiency" do not depend upon the material conditions of everyday slave life. Their exaggerated rhetoric together with their nearly eerie attack on Kenneth

106 *Ibid.*
107 *Ibid.*, pp. 209-210.

Stampp — a historian who dared "cast a stain on those [slaves] who strove to improve themselves within the system" — makes sense only when we realize how desperately important it is to the authors of T/C that we accept their central argument that the slaves — as a *class* — had internalized the work ethic urged upon them by their owners.

Some slaves — perhaps a significant number — did, and no sensible historian would deny that fact. In their insistence that the profitability of slavery and the "efficiency" of the plantation system did not rest upon the "material conditions" afforded the enslaved, F + E are left only with the beliefs and behavior of the enslaved. Stampp, however, insisted that the economic successes of the planters did not rest on a transformed and positive slave work ethic, and, therefore, he has to be severely criticized. The author of *The Peculiar Institution* failed to reject "the myth of the incompetence of slave labor."[108] The slaves, F + E write in summarizing Stampp's argument, "did not succumb; they resisted." Their resistance expressed itself in the "quality" of their everyday labor. It took a "subtle form." Stampp himself explained: "They were not reckless rebels who risked their lives for freedom. . . . [W]hen they could, they protested by shirking their duties, injuring the crops, feigning illness, and disrupting the routine. These acts were, in part, an unspectacular kind of 'day to day resistance to slavery.' " F + E vigorously dispute this point and depart here in a fundamental way from what they describe as the biased assumptions of Stampp and other so-called neo-abolitionist historians. Stampp erred mainly because "he overestimated the cruelty of the slave system" and, therefore, misunderstood the "superior quality of black labor." Stampp entirely misjudged the work habits of ordinary slaves. "The logic of his position," insist F + E, "made it difficult to acknowledge that ordinary slaves could be diligent workers, imbued like their masters with a Protestant ethic, or that, even though they longed for freedom, slaves could strive to develop and improve themselves in the only way that was open to them."[109]

[108] An attack on the historian Kenneth Stampp fills many pages of the second volume of T/C. No less than 36.7 percent of a seventy-nine-page historiographic essay is devoted to a criticism of *The Peculiar Institution*. No fewer than 11.7 percent of the pages in a volume subtitled *Evidence and Methods* detail this attack on Stampp's important book. F + E ask of Stampp: "What of black achievements under slavery? A world in which good work is synonymous with betrayal and in which evasion, deception, and sabotage are the objectives to which to aspire leaves scant room for black achievement. There were, of course [according to Stampp], those 'who lacked the qualities which produce rebels.' Such slaves 'had to seek personal gratification and the esteem of their fellows in less spectacular ways. They might find these things simply by doing their work uncommonly well.' But *The Peculiar Institution* did not emphasize these accomplishments, as though they were of a lower order. Stampp's scattered references to the high skill of slave artisans, for example, hardly add up to two full pages in a book of over 400 pages" (T/C, II, p. 225).

[109] T/C, I, pp. 231-232.

F + E carry their enthusiasm a bit too far and do so, in part, by exaggerating the economic opportunities available to slaves as contrasted to northern free blacks. They correctly point to the various legal and economic restrictions imposed upon free blacks by hostile northern white majorities, but draw from these restrictions an untenable conclusion: "For blacks during the antebellum era . . . freedom and slavery were not separated by a sharp dividing line. One gradually shaded into the other. To some blacks, especially among the talented whose opportunities were most constricted by slavery, even quasi-freedom was worth nearly any price — and they risked everything for it. But for the average slave, who in any case expected his lot to be that of a laborer, the costs of revolution, or even flight, were not worth the gains of quasi-freedom — except under special circumstances such as the separation of a man from his wife or parents from their children."[110]

There is no reason to idealize the material condition of the average northern free black. But to suggest that "for blacks" prior to the Civil War "freedom and slavery were not separated by a sharp dividing line" is a grotesque distortion of the history of antebellum Afro-Americans. At best, F + E might have written: "Our analysis of the material circumstance under which southern slaves and northern free blacks lived convinces *us* that freedom and slavery were not separated by a sharp dividing line." How blacks felt is quite another matter. Is there evidence, for example, that runaway slaves (many among them surely deeply disappointed by their encounters with northern society) returned to the South convinced that freedom ("quasi-freedom") "shaded" into slavery? And what evidence reveals that the "talented" fled? No one has yet studied the types of slaves who quit the South. The most that can be said is that those who fled lived nearest to "quasi-freedom." Family separation indeed sparked flight, but not to the North. Such runaways either trailed after departed kin or fled a new owner to hide near their former homes. Slaves who made it to the North, moreover, had no trouble realizing that their disadvantaged condition there nevertheless meant a fundamentally different life, and a better one, even though, as Moncure D. Conway, the former Virginia slaveholder turned abolitionist, put it in 1864, "they were in most of the Northern States a caste, a people by themselves." Conway had the good sense to realize that "this prejudice and these wrongs" were "the surplus fruit of Slavery itself."[111]

A New Myth Replaces an Old Myth

F + E are convinced that their data reveal the real ordinary slave. That slave was neither Kenneth Stampp's discontented but nonrevolutionary black

[110] *Ibid.,* p. 244.
[111] M. D. Conway, *Testimonies Concerning Slavery* (1864), pp. 98-99.

nor Stanley Elkins' "Sambo." Stampp and Elkins, along with most other historians of slavery, erred in accepting the "almost indestructible image of black incompetence."[112] "The Sambo syndrome or passive resistance images seem ... unbuttressed by evidence," writes the convert reviewer Passell in the *New York Times Book Review.* "Although obviously limited by their bondage," Passell writes, "slaves had a reasonable chance for economic mobility — one male in four rose above the status of common laborer."[113] Stampp was wrong. "Discovery [*sic*]," assert F + E, "of the relatively high average level of pecuniary payments to slaves not only calls into question the traditional interpretation of the incentive system, but also the traditional explanations for the relatively low incidence of rebellions on the part of the slaves."[114] Elkins was wrong, too. "No one could live," F + E write after summarizing the Elkins model of slave society, "under so brutal a machine without succumbing to it." The "typical plantation slave" was not Sambo: "docile but irresponsible, loyal but lazy, humble but chronically given to lying and stealing." These historians, among others, reveal the "power of ideology to obliterate reality." "The myth of black incompetence in American historiography," we are told, "is racism."[115] (Martin Duberman's response to this allegation is on target. "... [T]he accusation of 'racism,'" he writes in his review of T/C, "is ... double-edged: it makes just as much sense to apply the epithet to those who argue that blacks were so without internal resources, common sense, and self-respect that they would dutifully fulfill the role of worker heroes in a system designed to perpetuate their bondage.")[116] The "greatest achievements" of enslaved Afro-Americans, according to F + E, were not "such proficiencies" as "stealing, shirking responsibilities, and feigning illness." Nor were the enslaved "the pitiful victims of a system of slavery so repressive that it undermined their sense of family, their desire for achievement, their propensity for industry, their independence of judgment, and their capacity for self-reliance. ..."[117] And that was so because the *typical* plantation owner managed his enterprise well, prescribing for his slaves the proper dosage of positive and negative labor incentives. "Pecuniary rewards," after all, "were as integral a part of slavery as punishment."[118] The ordinary slave himself understood the value of these pecuniary rewards, because as he looked about him he could see that "so many" other slaves held "preferred occupational positions." Did they?

[112] T/C, I, pp. 223-232.
[113] Passell, review of T/C, *New York Times Book Review,* 28 April 1974, p. 4.
[114] T/C, I, p. 242.
[115] *Ibid.,* pp. 223-232.
[116] Duberman, review of T/C, *Village Voice,* 18 July 1974, p. 32.
[117] T/C, I, pp. 258-260.
[118] *Ibid.,* pp. 241-242.

The Slave Family, Slave Sexual Behavior, and Slave Sales

We shift attention sharply — from the slave work ethic and what shaped it — to the slave family, slave sexual behavior, and slave sales. What follows is *not* an analysis of the slave family, its origins, and its development. That is the subject of a forthcoming study of mine, one which examines some of the ways in which the adaptive capacities of generations of enslaved Afro-Americans encouraged and sustained the development of a distinctive family and kinship system among them while enslaved in Anglo-American society. That perspective — as we shall see — does not penetrate the pages of T/C. The questions its authors ask and the "model" they work from are quite different. Slave familial behavior and domestic arrangements — like slave work habits — are no more than a set of responses to rational planter (or owner) economic stimuli. The status of the slave family is essential to the central themes in T/C. It is well known that the family — slave or free — transmits values from generation to generation. But these values are determined elsewhere than within the family. The family, as the sociologist T. B. Bottomore reminds us, "is an agent, not a principal." Most enslaved Afro-Americans were socialized in families of their own. Because F + E insist that slave workers were highly efficient and productive laborers, they must argue that "the slave family" served as an "agent" for transmitting a version of the Protestant work ethic from one generation of slaves to another. For that to have occurred, it is also essential that enslaved Afro-Americans lived in *stable* families. But if slaves lived in stable families, that was so only because relatively few slave families were separated by owners for economic or other reasons. If slave families, after all, were broken up in large numbers, what reason would have existed for slave parents to socialize their children to work hard? (It is possible, of course, to argue that many slave parents worked hard to prevent the breakup of families and especially the sale of children. That argument, however, starts out with the assumption that slaves lived in unstable families!) F + E's whole argument about the stable slave family, as we shall see, rests entirely on dubious quantitative data meant to show a low incidence of *familial* and *marital* breakup by owners.

Essential Propositions in T/C on the Slave Family

F + E insist that planter "economic" needs and calculations, together with their moral beliefs, coincided to strengthen and sustain "*stable* slave families." Recent scholarship has caused historians to reexamine quite conventional views of the Afro-American slave family and to realize that the enslaved developed vital and affective familial and kin arrangements. F + E hastily ascribe these arrangements primarily to planter belief and behavior. Planters, they argue, found the slave family of "central importance" and "assigned three functions" to it. It served first as "the administrative unit" to distribute slave food and clothing and to provide shelter. It was also "an important instrument for maintaining labor discipline." Planters, therefore, kept busy "encouraging strong family attachments," hoping thereby to reduce "the danger that individual slaves would run away." And, finally, the slave family was "the main instrument for promoting the increase of the slave population." Economic interest fostered such attitudes and behavior. Although the southern civil law made no provisions for slave marriages, F + E insist that such marriages "were not only recognized but actively promoted under plantation codes." They add, "[T]he authority of the planter" differed from that of the northern manufacturer because it "extended not only to the conduct of business, but to the regulation of the family lives of slaves."

The operative and active explanatory concepts emphasized by F + E are the words *promoted* ("to help or encourage to exist or flourish"; "to aid in organizing") and *regulation* ("a rule or order proscribed by authority, as to regulate conduct"; "a governing direction or law"). There is no ambiguity in these words. Synonyms for *promote* include *abet, back, forward, advance, assist, help,* and *support.* And synonyms for *regulation* include *adjustment, control, direction, disposition,* and *management.* Prevailing social beliefs among the planters matched economic necessities: "We do not mean to suggest that planters viewed the slave family purely as a business investment. Victorian attitudes predominated in the planting class. The emphasis on strong, stable families, and on the limitation of sexual activity to the family, followed naturally from such attitudes. That morality and good business practice should coincide created neither surprise nor consternation among most planters." We encounter again the ubiquitous word *most* and ignore it for the moment. F + E repeat the same argument often to emphasize its importance. "[B]oth moral convictions and good business practice generally led planters to encourage the development of stable nuclear families," they write in another place. Not surprisingly, it follows that there were "relatively infrequent instances when economic forces led the planters to destroy, rather than to maintain slave families."[119] How F + E support these assertions — the data especially but also the arguments — is examined in what follows. "The burden of proof," after all, as David Fischer reminds us, "for any historical assertion, always rests upon its author. Not his critics, not his readers, not his graduate students, not the next generation. . . ."[120]

Vague Generalizations about the Slave Family in T/C
That Merit Little, If Any, Serious Discussion

T/C is filled with generalizations about the slave family and slave sexual behavior that are so lacking in documentation that they do not deserve serious discussion. Three examples follow.

Example One: F + E write: "Antebellum critics of slavery . . . assumed that because the law permitted slaveowners to ravish black women, the practice must have been extremely common. They also assumed that black women were, if not more licentious, at least more promiscuous than white women, and hence less likely to resist sexual advances by men, whether black or white."[121] These were not the core arguments made by most antislavery critics in discussing the "weaknesses" in the slave family. Their central argument had less to do with what the law permitted than with what the law did not allow. A powerful belief that marriage and the family — antislavery critics did not distinguish between the two — had their roots in the civil law and could not be sustained outside the law was at the core of the antislavery argument. It followed from this belief — and it applied to whites as well as to blacks and to free persons as well as to slaves — that enslaved Afro-Americans could sustain neither marriage nor the family. Promiscuity followed logically from the absence of legal restraint (that is, civil law) upon sexual behavior. It was primarily this conception of marriage, not racial beliefs, that sparked this particular criticism of slavery by most antislavery advocates.

Example Two: F + E write: "[I]t would be a mistake to assume that the black family was purely, or even predominantly, the creation of white masters. The exact interplay of external and internal forces in shaping the black family is still unknown. But there is considerable evidence that the nuclear form was not merely imposed on slaves. Slaves apparently abandoned the African family forms because they did not satisfy the needs of blacks who lived and worked under conditions and in a society much different from those which their ancestors experienced. The nuclear family took root among

[119] T/C, I, pp. 128-130, 143.
[120] David Hackett Fischer, *Historians' Fallacies* (1971), p. 91.
[121] T/C, I, p. 130.

blacks because it did satisfy those needs."[122] These are mere assertions and should not be taken seriously. There is no reason to dispute them here or elsewhere. F + E tell nothing about the process by which "African family forms" became Afro-American families as a consequence of the interaction between changing slave beliefs and planter objectives and needs. They assume that "Africans" did not know "the nuclear form," never define what they mean by "the nuclear form," and fail to make the most essential distinctions, such as the difference between a "nuclear family" and a "nuclear household."

Example Three: F + E write:

> That slave life pivoted around stable, nuclear families does not mean that the black family was merely a copy of the white family. No doubt the African heritage of blacks, as well as their particular socioeconomic circumstances, resulted in various characteristics which were, if not restricted to, at least more frequent among black than white families. For example, various bits of evidence suggest that wives tended to play a stronger role in black than in white families. Careful delineation of such special characteristics and the determination of their incidence is a task which has not yet been adequately essayed. The evidence already in hand, however, clearly invalidates many of the generalizations that now permeate history books.
>
> It is not true that, "the typical slave family was matriarchal in form" and that the "husband was at most his wife's assistant."[123]

These sentences are filled with nearly indescribable muddle. Their argument shifts, for example, from the "slave family" to the "black family." The two are not the same. They never define "the African heritage of blacks." What did that mean in 1720? 1770? 1840? 1860? We are never told how "various bits of evidence" as yet unstudied systematically can "clearly" invalidate "many of the generalizations that now permeate history books." Their point about the role of the "slave wife" is naïve. The issue disputed among historians of the slave family concerning male and female roles within the slave family has nothing at all to do with "various bits of evidence" which "suggest that wives tended to play a stronger role in black than in white families." It has rather to do with the relative strength of ties between the slave mother and her child as contrasted to ties between the slave wife and her husband. It has to do with the relative strength of consanguinal (blood) ties as contrasted with affinal (marriage) ties. And a comparison between these contrasting roles has much, much less to do with the nuclear form than it has to do with the relationships between slave families. Put simply, an assessment of the role of the adult slave woman depends first of all upon an analysis of her relationships with her spouse, her children, her parents,

[122] *Ibid.,* pp. 142-143.
[123] *Ibid.,* pp. 139-141.

and her adult brothers and sisters. The adult slave woman was not just "a wife." And before we generalize about her role as slave wife and compare that role to the role of the white wife, it is essential first to compare her role as slave wife to that as slave mother, slave daughter, and slave sister. That comparison involves a discussion of slave kinship systems and how they developed. But such a discussion has no place in this review-essay.

T/C Deals Mostly with Slave Marriages, Not with Slave Families

The concern here, then, is narrow: it is with F + E's evidence on "the slave family" and not much else. In their summary conclusion published in the prologue of T/C ("Slavery and the Cliometric Revolution"), F + E list as one of their ten "principal corrections" new findings on the "slave family": "The belief that slave-breeding, sexual exploitation, and promiscuity destroyed the black family is a myth. The family was the basic unit of social organization under slavery. It was to the economic interest of planters to encourage the stability of slave families and most of them did so. Most slave sales were either of whole families or of individuals who were at an age when it would have been normal for them to have left the family."[124] Evidence of varying kinds — some quantitative and some literary — supporting these conclusions is scattered throughout the two volumes of T/C and is brought together in the following pages. No serious student of the enslaved Afro-American family has argued in recent decades that enslavement "destroyed the black family." That is a myth. Instead, historians and social scientists have disputed with some vigor (and altogether too little evidence) about how Afro-American families (in their composition and in the roles played by different family members) were affected by enslavement.

Two essential points need to be made at the start. F + E intercede in this controversy, but not a shred of quantitative evidence in either volume of T/C shows that "most" planters "encourage[d] the stability of slave families." Even if F + E had substantial evidence indicating long slave marriages among large numbers of enslaved Afro-Americans (and they do not), such evidence, in itself, hardly proves that it was "to the economic interest of planters to encourage the stability of slave families" and that "most . . . did so." That evidence would merely pose problems for further study. Evidence of lengthy slave marriages, furthermore, is not evidence of "stable families." Nearly all the quantitative evidence used by F + E in discussing the slave "family" (and it mostly deals with sale) deals with slave marriages, not slave families. A significant difference exists between a family and a marriage. There is no social contradiction between a stable (or long-lasting) marriage and a broken family. When a young individual was sold from his

[124] *Ibid.*, p. 5.

or her slave family and thereby separated from parents and siblings, that sale counted as evidence of a broken slave family, not of a broken slave marriage. Because they deal nearly entirely with slave marriages, we examine in some detail the several serious errors that greatly weaken F + E's analysis of the breakup of slave marriages. It is important, however, to keep in mind during the discussion which follows just what is being analyzed. T/C tells very little about the slave family.

The Absence of Significant Evidence in T/C Concerning the Slave Family and Owner Attitudes and Behavior Toward It

In describing the attitudes of slaveowners toward slave marriage and the slave family as well as in explaining their intentions ("it was to the economic interest of planters . . ."), none of F + E's evidence in T/C is quantitative. It is, instead, conventional literary evidence — that used by noncliometric historians. And the mode of analysis itself is quite conventional, too. A few paragraphs drawn from volume one illustrate these points. I have italicized the pertinent words:

[*M*]*ost* planters shunned direct interference in the sexual practices of slaves, and attempted to influence fertility patterns through a system of positive economic incentives, incentives that are akin to those practiced by various governments today. The United States, for example, provides tax benefits for marriage and children; France has direct subsidies for childbearing; the Soviet Union combines subsidies with honorific awards — mothers of unusually large families become "Heroes of the Soviet Union." So too on the plantation. ["Heroes of Mississippi"?]

First and foremost, planters promoted family formation both through exhortation and through economic inducements. "Marriage is to be encouraged," wrote James H. Hammond to his overseer, "as it adds to the comfort, happiness and health of those entering upon it, besides insuring a greater increase." The economic inducements for marriage *generally* included a house, a private plot of land which the family could work on its own, and, *frequently,* a bounty either in cash or in household goods. The primary inducements for childbearing were the lighter work load and the special care given to expectant and new mothers. The fieldwork requirement of women after the fifth month of pregnancy was *generally* reduced by 40 or 50 percent. In the last month they were *frequently* taken off fieldwork altogether and assigned such light tasks as sewing or spinning. Nursing mothers were permitted to leave for work at a later hour than others and were also allowed three to four hours during the day for the feeding of their infants. There were, of course, more long-range benefits, too. Women who bore an unusually large number of children became "heroes of the plantation" and were relieved from all fieldwork.[125]

[125] *Ibid.,* pp. 84-85.

And later in the same volume:

> To promote the stability of slave families, planters *often* combined exhortations with a system of rewards and sanctions. The rewards included such subsidies as separate houses for married couples. . . . They *often* sought to make the marriage a solemn event by embedding it in a well-defined ritual. *Some* marriage ceremonies were performed in churches, *others* by the planter in the "big house." In either case, marriages were *often* accompanied by feasts and *sometimes* made the occasion for a general holiday. The sanctions were directed against adultery and divorce. For *many* planters, adultery was an offense which required whippings for the guilty parties. *Some* planters also used the threat of the whip to discourage divorce.[126]

In reading these sentences, it should be remembered that F + E are describing regularities: that is what words such as *most, generally, often,* and *frequently* mean.

It remains here as elsewhere a central task for the social historian to describe and then to explain as best he can regularities in social behavior. It is also important to explain how such historical evidence has been used to establish a regularity ("most," "generally," "often," and "frequently"). Not one of the suggested regularities described in the sentences reprinted above rests on evidence reported in either volume of T/C. The reader is not convinced, furthermore, that F + E are describing regularities in planter behavior when it is learned that only thirty sets of plantation manuscripts in just seven states have been studied. In 1860, after all, about ten thousand white families ("planters") owned fifty or more slaves. We shall consider planter "exhortation" and "inducements" meant to encourage fertility and "family formation" (the two are not the same) in another place. Let us focus here only on the slave marriage itself. What systematic evidence reveals that planters often made of a slave marriage "a solemn event by embedding it in a well-defined ritual"? What systematic evidence tells that planters often saw to it that slave marriages were accompanied by "feasts"? Some evidence exists. In 1866 and 1867 a District of Columbia clergyman remarried 875 former slave couples. All were asked who had first married them. Some could not remember. A small number said a clergyman. A yet larger number replied: "joined by permission of master" and "ceremony read by their master." Is this the "well-defined ritual" F + E refer to? Nearly half (48 percent) replied, "No marriage ceremony."[127] And then there is the matter of slave adultery and divorce. Isolated examples in plantation records indicate slave punishment (including whippings) by some owners on both accounts. It would strengthen F + E's arguments greatly if systematic evi-

---

[126] *Ibid.,* p. 128.

[127] This information is reported in Gutman, "Le Phenomene Invisible," pp. 1197-1218.

dence of such punishments supported their generalizations about the regularity of such planter behavior.

A rather casual use of certain literary evidence encourages this response. F + E, for example, admit that white owners and overseers had the legal power to abuse slave women but argue that the "economic" interests of planters checked that abuse: "Instructions from slaveowners to their overseers frequently gave recognition to this conflict. They contain explicit caveats against 'undue familiarity' which might undermine slave morale and discipline. 'Having connection with any of my female servants,' wrote a leading Louisiana planter, 'will most certainly be visited with a dismissal from my employment, and no excuse can or will be taken.' No set of instructions to overseers has been uncovered which explicitly or implicitly encouraged selective breeding or promiscuity."[128] We focus here merely on the last sentence. How would the logic that turns negative evidence into positive evidence deal with the following data? The data come from John Spencer Bassett's study of the plantation overseers employed on the Mississippi plantations owned by the family of James K. Polk. Hardly a detached student of slavery, Bassett believed that it was "the authority of the master that taught" the slave "to improve his ideas of morality" and that "in many ways slavery instilled" in Afro-Americans "the fundamentals of civilization." His examination of the letters overseers wrote their employers caused Bassett to conclude:

> There is not a reference to the marriage of slaves in all the 275 letters that have come into my hands. Within this long period (ca. 1833-ca. 1858) many such unions must have occurred on the plantation, but no overseer thought it worth his while to mention one. Also, there may have been divorces or separations of husband and wife. The letters contain no suggestion of such occurrences. The overseer wrote about the things that he thought the owner ought to know. He doubtless assumed that Polk had no concern with a negro marriage or a negro divorce. Runaways were more to the purpose. His letters, therefore, said nothing about a large area of conduct that was intimately connected with the life of the slaves.[129]

The same letters, incidentally, regularly reported the birth of slave children. Is one to conclude from these letters that Mississippi slaves on the Polk plantations never married and that all slave children were born out of wedlock? Despite his biases, Bassett had enough historical sense to realize the limitations of such evidence as a source for describing the life of the slaves. These points are not raised to pick unfairly at the quality of the evidence used by F + E in describing planter behavior. F + E themselves explicitly recognize the limitations of certain types of historical evidence:

[128] T/C, I, pp. 85-86.
[129] John Spencer Bassett, *The Southern Plantation Overseer,* pp. 21-22, 260-261.

Our aim has been to base our statements on evidence drawn from as high up in ... [the] hierarchy of reliability as possible. We have the least confidence in fragmentary evidence which is based on unverifiable impressions of individuals whose primary aim was the defense of an ideological position. Fragmentary evidence from objective sources, such as impressionistic reports of "detached" observers, may be more believable, but is still of a low order of reliability since it is usually not possible to submit such evidence to systematic statistical tests.

Data which can be subjected to systematic statistical tests ... are frequently more useful than fragmentary data.... We use fragmentary, impressionistic evidence in two ways: to illustrate and make more vivid results that have been established by more precise methods, and to fill in gaps in evidence where it has not been possible thus far to obtain systematic data.[130]

None of the data so far examined rank especially high in F + E's "hierarchy of reliability." T/C contains no systematic evidence that planters "promoted family formation both through exhortation and through economic inducements" to "influence fertility patterns." Nor does it contain any systematic evidence that planters "often combined exhortations with a system of rewards and sanctions" to "promote the stability of slave families." Instead, these important characterizations of planter behavior are supported by unsubstantiated generalizations or generalizations backed by isolated illustrations.

The Easy Assumption That Planters "Encouraged" Fertility By "Promoting Family Formation": Some Contrary Literary Evidence

Before considering in close detail the quantitative data used by F + E in their discussion of the slave family and slave marriage, some observations need to be made about the altogether too easy assumption in T/C that planters "attempted to influence fertility patterns through a system of positive economic incentives" and did so — "first and foremost" — by "promoting family formation." No necessary connection exists between fertility and "family formation." Historians did not have to await the publication of T/C to learn that slaveowners encouraged fertility among female slaves. The literary historical record — including the writings of planters themselves — is filled with evidence of that fact.[131] Enslavement, after all, meant much more than the use of human chattel as labor. It also required — after a time and especially after the abolition of the overseas slave trade — that the slave labor force reproduce itself. Few realized this requirement better than the slaveowners themselves. Their economic calculations regularly mixed the

---

[130] T/C, I, pp. 10-11.

[131] Unless otherwise noted, the evidence in the following nine paragraphs draws from my forthcoming study of the Afro-American family, chapter two.

production of wealth with the reproduction of labor. But the two are not the same.

"Efficient" slaveowners measured both in their entrepreneurial calculations. The planter W. H. Cook boasted publicly in 1858 that for six years he had been "trying to be a farmer." That meant breeding hogs and growing corn, peas, potatoes, pumpkins, and garden vegetables "to take care of and raise little negroes." The former Georgia planter John C. Reed, himself a Princeton graduate (1854), insisted in *The Brothers' War* (1905) that ". . . the greatest profit of all was what the master thought of and talked of all the day long — the natural increase of his slaves as he called it." According to Reed, "Really, the leading industry of the South was slave rearing. The profit was in keeping slaves healthy. This could be done at little expense in agriculture where even the light workers were made to support themselves. . . . This property," he boasted, "was not only self-supporting, but it was also the mostly rapidly self-reproducing that Tom, Dick, and Harry ever had in all history." Reed had hardly exaggerated. The very metaphors used by planters make this clear. Howell Cobb boasted that slave women multiplied "like rabbits." The *American Cotton Planter* told of the slave "girl" who could "breed like a cat." Then the U.S. secretary of the treasury and the president of the Georgia Cotton Planters' Association, Cobb insisted that for the planter the "largest source of prosperity is in the negroes he raises."

Owner indifference to the reproduction of the labor force would have been an act of economic insanity. The steady increase in the price of adult slaves would have fed this madness. Not surprisingly, therefore, planters and their spokesmen boasted of the reproductive capacities of enslaved women. Thomas Dew said that an owner's labor force doubled through natural increase every fifteen years. Howell Cobb made a similar estimate. Frederick Olmsted learned from Edmund Ruffin that a gang of slaves on a farm or a plantation increased four-fold over a thirty- or forty-year period. The historian Frederic Bancroft no doubt greatly exaggerated the volume of inter-regional slave sales but was quite right to insist that slaveowners "otherwise careless and spendthrift were eager to multiply their slaves," that over time such an investment "would rapidly augment like money at a high rate of compound interest," and that "slave-rearing was the surest, most remunerative, and most approved means of increasing agricultural capital." "Well treated and cared [for], and moderately worked," said the *American Cotton Planter* of the slaves, "their natural increase becomes a source of great profit to their owner. Whatever, therefore, tends to promote their health and render them prolific, is worthy of his attention."

Planters had every reason to encourage slave fecundity. Fanny Kemble noticed that "many indirect inducements [are] held out to reckless propagation, which has a sort of premium offered to it in consideration of less work and more food." A South Carolina slaveowner had no pangs of conscience in selling two girls who "had the objectionable habit of eating dirt . . . which, in his opinion, rendered them unprofitable as breeding women." Rewards to stimulate fecundity often served — to use Bancroft's words — as "virtual premiums." A Virginia woman remembered that her slaveowning uncle regularly gave a small pig to the slave mother of a newborn child. The South Carolina planter James Hammond felt it appropriate to give a slave mother a muslin or calico frock — but only when her newborn infant was thirteen months old. "The care of the expectant mother," insists William D. Postell in his *Health of Slaves on Southern Plantations*, "was the first concern of the planter." Postell found that "all the rules of plantation management clearly stated that pregnant women were to be particularly cared for. . . ." A pregnant woman on the Louisiana Prudhomme plantation worked in the general yard. The rice planter P. C. Weston had among his plantation rules one which read: "Women with six children alive at any one time are allowed all Saturday to themselves." The instructions to the overseer on the Yazoo-Mississippi Delta Green Valley cotton plantation did not include the word "family," but ordered that "the children must be very particularly attended to, for rearing them is not only a Duty, but also the most profitable part of plantation business." "The rules for plantation management and the reports of overseers demonstrate," concluded Bancroft, "that masters always wished to know about the number of actual and prospective infants." Accused by his Georgia employer John B. Lamar of abusing the slaves, the overseer Stancil Barwick denied the charge in 1855: "Now as regards the wimin loosing children, treaty lost one it is true. I never heard of her being in that way until she lost it. She was at the house all the time. I never made her do any work at all. She said to me in the last month that she did not know she was in that way her self untill she lost the child. As regards Louisine she was in the field it is true but she was workt as she please. I never said a word to her in any way at all untill she com to me in the field and said she was sick. I told her to go home. She started an on the way she miscarried. She was about five months gone. This is a true statement of case . . . a pon my word of honner. . . ." This overseer's defensive tone in dealing with terminated slave pregnancies prepares us for the fact that the Mississippi overseer on the absentee James K. Polk plantation regularly reported the birth of new infants but never once mentioned a slave marriage.

So far, nothing in the evidence reported contradicts F + E's insistence that slaveowners encouraged fertility among slave women. But such evidence does not show that slaveowners found in the "stable slave family" the "main instrument for promoting the increase of the slave population." According to F + E, slaveowners "believe[d] that fertility rates would be highest when the family was strongest."[132] Reproducing and rearing the slave labor force,

[132] T/C, I, p. 127.

however, required no more than the simple biological dyad, "mother and child." It hardly depended upon the presence of other dyadic ties, "husband and wife," "father and child." In itself, biological realities did not require that slaveowners encourage stable ("completed") slave families. A labor force that reproduced itself hardly required the "nuclear family" as its social base. Planter reckoning sometimes failed to include that social calculation. When the Yankee reporter Thomas W. Knox arrived in the Mississippi Valley in 1863 to cover the war and then to lease an abandoned plantation, he found a model plantation business ledger published in New Orleans which included blank spaces for "supplies . . . , lists of births and deaths (there were no blanks for marriages), time and amount of shipments of cotton, and for all the ordinary business of a plantation." The anonymous author of " 'Profits of Farming' — Facts and Figures" explained to readers of the *Southern Cultivator* in 1858:

> I would not be willing to be a manager, much less an owner, of any gang of negroes where there was no increase, and I doubt very much, even with the moving away, if Hancock county [Georgia?] does not show an increase. Why, sirs, negro population increases more rapidly than whites.
>
> I could name a dozen Planters who are worth $200,000 to $2,000,000 and who began with a few negroes and a small parcel of land, and if they ever owned bank stock the negroes made the money. I own a woman who cost me $400 when a girl, in 1827. Admit she made me nothing — only worth her victuals and clothing. She now has three children, worth over $3000 and have been field hands say three years; in that time making enough to pay their expenses before they were half hands, and then I have the profit of all half hands. She has only three boys and a girl out of a dozen; yet, with all her bad management, she has paid me ten per cent. interest, for her work was to be an average good, and I would not this night touch $700 for her. Her oldest boy is worth $1250 cash, and I can get it.

Another writer put it somewhat differently that same year in that same journal: "The statistics of the country show that our negro property increases at the rate of three per cent. per annum. This is a fact that cannot be denied or controverted. It is also a profit of three per cent. if there be no change in the price of such property and a greater gain if that kind of property rises in value. It is annual, and therefore, it is a gain which is compounding from year to year."

Such analysis has significant historical meaning for several reasons. The labor force was never described in familial terms: "a few negroes" and "our negro property." In their calculations, these authors never felt it necessary to mention the value of an adult slave male as either a husband or a father. An emphasis on the reproduction of the labor force which focused primarily on the slave woman as mother, not as wife or even as laborer, hardly had reason to discourage "fornication" — that is, sexual intercourse before or even outside of marriage. In his famed defense of Afro-American enslavement ("Harper's Memoir on Slavery"), Chancellor Harper pointed out that in a free society "the unmarried woman who becomes a mother is an outcast from society — and though sentimentalists lament the hardship of the case, it is just and necessarily so. She is cut off from the hope of useful and profitable employment, and driven by necessity to further vice. . . ." Harper's justification of enslavement rested in part upon the distinctive status it allowed "the unmarried woman who becomes a mother":

> She is not a less useful member of society than before. If shame be attached to her conduct, it is such shame as would be elsewhere felt for a venial impropriety. She has not impaired her means of support, not materially impaired her character, or lowered her station in society; she has done no great injury to herself, or any other human being. *Her offspring is not a burden but an acquisition to her owner;* his support is provided for, and he is brought up to usefulness; if the fruit of intercourse with a freeman, his condition is, perhaps, raised somewhat above that of his mother. Under these circumstances, with imperfect knowledge, tempted by the strongest of human passions — unrestrained by the motives which operate to restrain, but are so often found insufficient to restrain the conduct of females elsewhere, can it be a matter of surprise that she should so often yield to the temptation? Is not the evil less in itself, and in reference to society — much less in the sight of God and man? [Italics added.]

Men like Harper, of course, were not advocates of fornication. But that hardly mattered in the circumstances in which they found themselves. And the arguments of men like Harper give us reason to doubt that slaveowners "believe[d] that fertility rates would be highest when the family was strongest."

The encouragement of "stable" completed slave families by owners — that is, families with a husband and wife or a mother and father — rested on other considerations than just the reproduction of the labor force, reasons having more to do with the efficient production of staple crops and the steady performance of other unskilled and skilled adult male slave labor. If the slave woman counted mostly in the calculations of slaveowners as the critical factor in the reproduction of the labor force, the slave male counted mostly as the critical factor in the production of commodities. A single adult male might be the father of children by more than one woman, but — and using a favored cliometrician phrase, "other things being equal" — two prime male hands planted and worked more cotton, tobacco, and rice than one prime male hand. Fanciful economic theory was not essential to such a calculation. Efficient slave labor required labor discipline, and if completed slave families, including a husband or a father, were not essential to the reproduction of the labor force, such familial units had important functions related to the maintenance of that discipline. That was especially so because the enslaved themselves had internalized powerful familial sensibilities. This emphasis in no way means to minimize the fact that Christian slaveowners also often had "non-economic" reasons for sponsoring slave families. It is stressed to emphasize the social fact that slaves living in their familial units — and especially the greatly prized adult male slaves — were more amenable to positive and negative labor incentives that exploited *their* familial obligations and sensibilities. More, that is, than slave males detached from such human networks. Monetary rewards based on family labor (such as a "garden plot" and incentive payments for "extra" work) neatly balanced the threat, if not the reality, implicit in the possible sale of slave kin. It is quite possible, therefore, that the threatened breakup of slave families or kin networks — the sale of a spouse and especially the sale of a grown child — served as the most powerful of all labor incentives meant to encourage efficient production.

In an essay entitled "Duties of Christian Masters," the southern Baptist divine Holland Nimmons McTyeire insisted that "every Southern plantation is an *imperium in imperio*" and that slaveowners had reason to encourage marriage "with all the forms of consent, postponement, preparation, and solemn consummation. . . . Let the institution be magnified," said McTyeire of slave marriage: "Servants ought, as far as possible, to be divided into families, and thus there is the opportunity for family government. . . . Why not gratify the *home feeling* of the servant? Local as well [as] family associations, thus cast about him, are strong yet pleasing cords binding him to his master. His welfare is so involved in the order of things, that he would not for any consideration have it disturbed. He is made happier and safer, put beyond discontent, or the temptation to rebellion and abduction; for he gains nothing in comparison with what he loses. His comforts cannot be removed with him, and he will stay with them." A cotton plantation overseer who managed an enterprise near Natchez put it this way to Frederick Olmsted: "As soon as he saw that one [slave] was gone he put the dogs on, and if rain had not just fallen, they would soon find him. Sometimes, though, they would outwit the dogs, but if they did they almost always kept in the neighborhood, because they did not like to go where they could not sometimes get back and see their families, and he would soon get wind of where they had been; they would come round their quarters to see their families and to get food, and as soon as he knew it, he would find their tracks and put the dogs on again." Labor discipline based upon the familial beliefs of the enslaved was a powerful instrument in shaping plantation life.

Slaveowners anxious to encourage slave fecundity had good reason to reward productive slave mothers, and slaveowners anxious to maintain labor discipline had good reason to reward productive slave fathers. But they were *not* the same reasons, and that is why it is erroneous to assert that slaves lived in *stable* families. The maintenance of a slave marriage over time depended fundamentally upon the capacity of a slave wife to become a slave mother. And the maintenance of a whole slave family over time depended fundamentally upon the capacity of a slave father to work hard and to get his children to conform to planter expectations. Planters, not slave parents, measured the capacity of slave parents and their children to conform to planter expectations. A *minimal* rate of family breakup by sale or for other involuntary reasons taught all slaves the essential cost of their enslavement. No greater power allowed slaveowners to reproduce a labor force and to produce a marketable commodity than the right to sell a *single* slave. And that social fact — and no other — may explain why slave women multiplied like "cats" and "rabbits" and why slave men worked "hard" in the fields. But that right did not explain why slave wives and husbands loved and protected each other and their children. All that right did was to define the precarious conditions within which such expression thrived.

Let us put aside such "traditional" evidence — it is meant merely to dispute F + E's easy connection between planter-promoted high slave fertility and planter-promoted "stable" slave families — and examine the quantitative data in T/C dealing with the relationship between slave sales and slave marriage. "We feel confident," an unidentified white South Carolinian wrote in *Fraser's Magazine* sometime in the 1850s, "that, if statistics could be had to throw light upon this subject, we should find that there is less separation of families among the negroes than occurs with almost any other class of people."[133] Contemporaries like that writer greatly disputed the impact of slave sales on the slave family, and it has remained a subject of much controversy among historians since that time. By examining hitherto neglected evidence, F + E rekindle that long-standing controversy. Their findings boldly challenge the "conventional" interpretation that interregional slave migration, and especially the interregional slave trade, greatly damaged the slave family. But before historians begin disputing the "meaning" of these new data, it is important to see if they have been properly analyzed and if the assumptions and arguments that accompany them are accurate.

F + E on Interregional Slave Migration and Sale and the Slave Family: The Argument

In all quantitative studies, some data are always more important than other data, and among the most important but flawed sets of percentages in T/C are those dealing with the effects of interregional slave redistribution on the slave family. According to F + E, 835,000 slaves were moved from the Upper South ("exporting" states) to the Lower South ("importing" states) between 1790 and 1860, a flow of Afro-American men, women, and

[133] Quoted in Harriet Beecher Stowe, *Key to Uncle Tom's Cabin* (1854), p. 258.

children explained by the spectacular increase in the world demand for cotton and by improved transportation networks. Virginia, Maryland, and North and South Carolina supplied 85 percent of these migrants, and Alabama, Mississippi, Louisiana, and Texas received 75 percent of all Upper South slaves. This flow to the Lower South was uneven, so three times as many were moved between 1825 and 1860 as between 1790 and 1825. That means that between 1830 and 1860 about 575,000 enslaved blacks were shipped from the Upper to the Lower South. A hint as to the magnitude of this flow is suggested by the fact that 565,529 persons lived in Philadelphia — the nation's second largest city — in 1860. The interregional flow of enslaved Afro-Americans, especially between 1830 and 1860, counts as one of the great forced migrations in world history, and its social consequences among the enslaved remain central to any serious reexamination of their condition and their behavior.

F + E give that flow needed attention. It has been widely assumed among historians that sale — and especially sale managed by interregional slave traders — facilitated the transfer of "most" Upper South slaves to the booming plantation regions of the Lower South. F + E, however, question the importance of that trade and ask instead, "did most slaves take the interregional journey together with their owners as part of a movement in which whole plantations migrated to the West?" Their findings cause F + E to challenge the argument that sale explained most interregional slave movement. "Available evidence," they state, "indicates that about 84 percent of the slaves engaged in the westward movement migrated with their owners."[134] This estimate — it means that "only" 127,000 slaves were sold in the interregional trade between 1810 and 1860, about 2,500 per year — is one of F + E's half-dozen most significant new "findings." Despite its clear importance, F + E surprisingly do not offer a shred of evidence (or even argument) in either volume of T/C which tells how they arrived at the statistic "84 percent." We must accept on faith the fact that most slaves made it to the Deep South by accompanying migrant owners and that only about one in six were sold into the Deep South. The importance of this unsubstantiated percentage to F + E's entire argument about the slave family cannot be exaggerated. It serves as the numerical underpinning for their criticism of "the contention that the interregional slave migration resulted in the widespread division of marriages, with husbands wrung from wives and children from both." (In this sentence, incidentally, F + E again confuse a slave marriage with a slave family.)

Let us assume that compelling and authoritative evidence exists to sustain the "84 percent" statistic and proceed with F + E's argument. Sales, they conclude, accounted for 16 percent (1.00 − .84 = .16) of the total inter-

---

[134] T/C, I, pp. 47, 48.

regional movement of slaves. Study of New Orleans slave sales invoices —
an important source considered below — convinces F + E that "more than
84 percent of all sales over the age of fourteen involved unmarried individuals" and that about "13 percent, or less, of interregional sales resulted
in the destruction of slave marriages." F + E do not deny that "the interregional slave trade resulted in the destruction of *some* slave marriages."
That "is beyond dispute. What is at issue is the extent of the phenomenon."
And their estimate of the importance of interregional sales, together with
the New Orleans slave sales records, causes them to "sharply contradict the
popular view that the destruction of slave marriages was at least a frequent,
if not universal, consequence of the slave trade." That and even more erroneous conclusions are based upon a simple computation: "[I]t is likely that
13 percent, or less, of interregional sales resulted in the destruction of marriages. And since sales were only 16 percent of total interregional movement,
it is probable that about 2 percent [$.16 \times .13 = .02$] of the marriages of slaves
involved in the westward trek were destroyed by the process of migration."
Two percent is small — sufficiently small, that is, to encourage F + E to go
on: "Nor is it by any means clear that the destabilizing effects of the westward
migration on marriages was [*sic*] significantly greater among blacks than it
was among whites." Later in the same pages, readers learn that this "evidence" shows that "slave owners were averse to breaking up black families."
The data, of course, fail to "tell us about the reasons for their reluctance."
F + E blame "earlier historians" who "became overly preoccupied with
dramatic and poignant but relatively isolated instances of the destruction of
black marriages" and, therefore, "failed to grasp the extremely important
role that the master class assigned to the family institution."[135] This finding
and the percentages accompanying it already have filtered into the popular
media. Gannett press readers learned that "they estimate the family breakup
rate in slave trading at 2 to 8 percent, and conclude that for the vast majority of black American slaves, marriage and the family were strong, per-
manent institutions."[136]

*Why Interregional Migration with an Owner Could Break Up Many
Slave Families and Marriages: A Key Error in T/C*

Unless much additional evidence exists, these conclusions are ill-founded.
We need to put aside $0.16 \times 0.13 = 0.0208$ and the denial that "the destabilizing effects of westward migration on marriages was significantly greater

[135] *Ibid.*, pp. 49, 52.
[136] Linda Hansen, "A New Picture of Slavery: Achievement under Adversity,"
Journal News (Nyack, N.Y.), 10 May 1974, p. 11A.

among blacks than it was among whites." The argument rests upon a thoroughly inaccurate assumption. Let us accept F + E's "finding" that 84 percent of slaves engaged in the "westward [sic] movement" migrated with their owners. Is this evidence that slaves moving with their owners failed to experience the breakup of either a family or a marriage? That depends. F + E assume that all members of particular Upper South slave families involved in the great migration belonged to the same owner. That assumption is essential to their argument that 701,400 of the 835,000 slaves involved in the migration moved in family units with their owners. Put differently, slave husbands and wives among these 701,400 migrants, according to F + E, did not experience marital breakup. Their owners just moved them from, say, Virginia to Mississippi. F + E's subsequent analysis of the impact of the interregional redistribution of the slave population on the slave family, therefore, gives no attention to the marital and familial arrangements of no fewer than eight out of ten migrant slaves. F + E instead assume that only 133,600 slave men, women, and children could have had their family status altered by interregional transfer (not just sale). But F + E tell nothing about the relationship between slave marriage and family and patterns of slave ownership among Upper South slaves before and during the great migration. No evidence sustains their assumption that in most slave families all members — and especially the husband and wife — belonged to the same owner. That is the essential precondition for accepting their entire argument.

The only available data indicating the relationship between slaveownership and the Upper South slave family — and they were published before the appearance of T/C — come from an 1866 military census of former slaves living in Princess Anne County, Virginia.[137] These blacks gave the names of their owners in 1863, information which allows us to learn about the relationship between ownership and slave family structure. In two out of three families that had in them either a husband and wife; a husband, wife, and their children; or a father and his children, at least two members of the slave family had different owners. Most commonly, and not surprisingly, the husband or father had a different owner from the wife, mother, and children. The Princess Anne census is dated 1866, but that late date does not invalidate its use in pointing to the erroneous assumption in T/C. F + E themselves indicate that the flow of slaves from the Upper to the Lower South was three times greater between 1825 and 1860 than between 1790 and 1825. The Princess Anne County data tell that unless a spouse was purchased by a migrating owner, Upper South slave families were frequently broken just by the movement of an owner with his resident slaves to the Lower South. No sale had to be involved. It is that simple. In itself, sale is a thoroughly inade-

[137] Reported in Gutman, "Le Phenomene Invisible," pp. 1197-1218.

quate measure of the ways in which interregional migration broke up slave marriages and slave families.

Scant evidence yet exists indicating that before migration owners purchased slaves to keep families together, and it is contradictory. "In my neighborhood," said a South Carolina planter of the pre-1835 decades, "every planter agreed that, if he has a negro married to a negro woman and he wishes to get rid of the negro or quit the vicinity, he will either offer the slave to the proprietor of the negro woman, or will himself purchase the latter; in this case, the price is regulated by the other planters."[138] An advertisement in the *Augusta Chronicle and Sentinel* in 1859 explained that a local Georgian planned to sell his farm and real estate as well as several house servants. He was moving to Cherokee, Georgia. "They are negroes of excellent character," said the notice of these house servants; "and as the object of the owner in selling, is to avoid the necessity of separating husbands and wives, they will not be sold out of the city or its immediate neighborhood."[139] Some of this man's slaves had spouses who belonged to other whites in or near Augusta, and he obviously respected their unions. But the former Pittsylvania County, Virginia, slave Lorenzo Ivy recollected a quite opposite experience from the one this advertisement reported. He felt his first owner "bout de meanes' white man livin' " but went on: "Dere was only one good thing he ever did, an' I don't reckon he 'tended to do that. He sole our family to my father's Master, George H. Gilman. Ole Marsa caught de 'cotton fever.' Ev'ybody was dyin' to git down South an' raise cotton to sell. So dat ole man separated families right an' lef'. He took two of my ants an' lef' der husban's up here, an' he separated seven husban's an' wives. One 'oman had twelve chillun. Yes sir! Separated 'em all an' took 'em wid him to Georgy and Alabama."[140]

The separation of Ivy's two aunts from their husbands and of seven more "husban's an' wives" would never have been recorded in an interregional sales record. Before F + E estimated the percentages of slave marriages broken by interregional migration, they should have figured out what percentage of the 701,400 "migrant" slaves who accompanied their owners to the Deep South were adult slaves, what percentage had spouses belonging to other owners, and what percentage of migrating owners purchased such spouses to keep slave families together. A smaller percentage of Upper South slaves than has been assumed made it to the Deep South by being sold in the interregional slave trade. That much seems clear. But the effects of interregional migration on the slave family cannot be measured simply by revising the importance of interregional sales. Sales were not the only way

[138] Arthur Calhoun, *Social History of the American Family*, II, p. 268.
[139] Bancroft, *Slave Trading in the Old South*, pp. 217-218.
[140] Work Projects Administration, *The Negro in Virginia* (1940), p. 173.

106

in which slave marriages and slave families were broken. And 701,400 unstudied migrants is hardly an insignificant number of enslaved men, women, and children.

Much remains to be studied about the impact of forced interregional migration upon slave marriages and slave families — and especially in the three decades preceding the Civil War. We need particularly to give attention to the ways in which the enslaved themselves dealt with that massive social upheaval. But such study cannot assume that quantitative data have shown that "about 2 percent of the marriages of slaves involved in the westward trek were destroyed by the process of migration." We have seen why that is an unfounded and baseless percentage. And there is just as good a reason to reject the assertion that it is by no means "clear that the destabilizing effects of the westward migration on marriages was significantly greater among blacks than it was among whites." That is a ridiculous comparison, failing to take account of the rather obvious differences between voluntary and involuntary physical movement. The Princess Anne County census, of course, has its limitations. It remains the only known source which allows us to measure the prevalence of marriages between slave adults belonging to different owners. Additional evidence is needed on such marriages — and especially among Upper South slaves. It would appear that marriage between slaves belonging to different owners occurred most commonly among adult male or female slaves belonging to a farmer or a small planter. That was not the only precondition for inter-owner slave marriages. In selecting marital partners, slaves rarely if ever married close blood relatives. Evidence of slave exogamy is common among slaves over the entire South and is found among late eighteenth- as well as nineteenth-century enslaved Afro-Americans.[141] The size of units of slave ownership, together with the prevalence of exogamous marital taboos among the enslaved, greatly encouraged inter-owner slave marriages.[142] And these facts mean that when an owner migrated and took his slaves with him, slave marriages and slave families were shattered. Evidence of this kind tells us why F + E's assumption that migration with an owner did not break up slave families is so glaring an error.

[141] Exogamous slave marital beliefs and practices as contrasted to endogamous slaveowner marital beliefs and practices are examined in my forthcoming study of the slave family, chapters two and three.

[142] In an interview with the French historians Francois Furet and Emmanuel Le Roy Ladurie published in *Le Nouvel Observateur* (9 September 1974), Fogel explained that I had "reconstructed [slave] kinship networks over several generations." That is true. "He's discovered," Fogel went on, "a predominantly European type of family structure with, for example, an extensive taboo on marriages between cousins." That is *not* true. Slave marital taboos were not copies of European taboos. Their taboos, in fact, were exactly the opposite of those of large owners.

A Poorly-Described Source

In disputing the "traditional" argument that the interregional slave trade greatly damaged the integrity of slave *marriages,* F + E find their strongest evidence in data recorded in the New Orleans slave sale invoices between 1804 and 1862. A number of difficulties, however, limit the ways in which this source can and has been used and make the inferences drawn from it in T/C nearly whimsical. The size of the initial data base from which a sample of "approximately 5,000 slave sales" has come is never revealed. Richard C. Wade examined some of these same sources and found more than 4,440 invoices in 1830 and "over 3,000 . . . in the last ante-bellum year." Wade said "the figures fluctuated annually."[143] If about 2,000 such transactions occurred each year, that means that F + E have sampled about 4.3 percent of the total data, an adequate sample. It is important, however, to know whether this sample covered the entire period because of the changing size of the New Orleans slave population between 1820 and 1860 as indicated in Table 22.

A sample drawn primarily from the years 1820-1839 (years when the New Orleans slave population greatly increased) promises to record more interregional sales than a sample that draws primarily from the years 1840 to 1860 (years when the resident slave population greatly declined). The latter twenty-year period, of course, is the more important one. The domestic slave trade was at its height in those decades. Unless large numbers of Upper South slaves were shipped first to New Orleans and then sold into the interior sugar and cotton plantations, it is quite possible that a sample based on just the two last decades contains serious biases. The first and most important finding indicated by F + E, for example, is that an unusually large percentage of slaves traded in New Orleans belonged to Louisiana owners at the time of sale and that a smaller but still significant percentage had other Deep South owners: "The New Orleans data indicate that only 25 percent of the slaves sold there were from the exporting states. Approximately 68 percent of the slaves marketed in the Crescent City were owned by residents of Louisiana. The other 7 percent belonged to owners who lived in western

TABLE 22. New Orleans Slave Population, 1820-1860

Year	Male Slaves	Female Slaves	Total Slaves
1820	2,709	4,646	7,355
1840	9,795	13,653	23,448
1860	5,382	8,003	13,385

[143] Wade, *Slavery in the Cities,* pp. 199, 314.

states which were, like Louisiana, net importers of slaves."[144] That conclusion would lose much of its meaning if the F + E sample drew mostly on the 1840-1860 period, when the New Orleans slave population dropped significantly.

There are several other questions concerning this vaguely described sample. It is assumed that in their demographic analysis of the slaves involved in interregional sales, F + E did not include slaves involved in local sales. If they were included, the entire analysis becomes flawed because local sales might have involved different sorts of slaves than those involved in interregional sales. If "local sales" — that is, sales between sellers and buyers who both had Louisiana or other Deep South residences — are excluded, that cuts the sample from 5,000 to 1,250 (5,000 × .25 = 1,250). But the residence of a New Orleans seller is a bit more complicated than F + E indicate. New Orleans, as is well known, had a large number of resident interregional slave traders. When such a resident Louisiana trader sold slaves purchased in the Upper South (or the exporting states), were these sales counted by F + E as local or as interregional sales? If F + E counted them as local sales — sales involving Louisiana residents — they greatly undercounted the number of Upper South slaves in their sample of 5,000. It is possible, of course, that there were insignificant demographic differences between slaves involved in local and interregional sales, but that cannot be known until there are separate profiles of each group. F + E make no such analysis. F + E, finally, fail to break down their sample by sex. That, too, is unfortunate because their analysis entirely ignores the males sold. If, for example, only one-third of the slaves shipped from the exporting states were females, that would mean that the "sample" examined is neither "approximately 5,000" nor 1,250, but closer to 416.[145] That would also mean that the "potential" slave mothers (and I accept — for the moment — F + E's erroneous conclusion that slave women had a first child when aged "22.5") in the entire sample were about 185 women. But this is mere speculation based upon F + E's failure to supply adequate information. I assume — for the purpose of analysis — that all of the "corrections" described in this paragraph were made, and that half of the slaves sampled in these invoices were females. Their distribution by age would, therefore, be as given in Table 23.

[144] T/C, I, p. 53.
[145] According to Wade, "urban slavery increasingly contained an imbalance between male and female Negroes" because after 1820 owners in increasing numbers "began to sell their younger males to planters, especially in the cane and cotton country." In 1860, there were 67.5 male slaves for every 100 female slaves in New Orleans. Analyzed properly, the New Orleans slave sale invoices might tell us much about the way in which sale by age and sex affected the urban slave sex ratio and thereby affected the urban slave family. (Wade, *Slavery in the Cities,* pp. 23, 330.)

Age Group	Estimated Percentage	Estimated Number of Females
0–12	9.3%	58
13–24	65.0%	406
25+	25.7%	161
N	100.0%	625

F + E's Major "Finding"

F + E find in this evidence a way to estimate the frequency with which a slave marriage might be broken by interregional sale. Before that estimate is examined in close detail, their conclusion is recorded:

Data contained in sales records in New Orleans, by far the largest market in the interregional trade, sharply contradict the popular view that the destruction of slave marriages was at least a frequent, if not a universal, consequence of the slave trade. These records, which cover thousands of transactions during the years from 1804 to 1862, indicate that more than 84 percent of all sales over the age of fourteen involved unmarried individuals. Of those who were or had been married, 6 percent were sold with their mates; and probably at least one quarter of the remainder were widowed or voluntarily separated. Hence it is likely that 13 percent, or less, of interregional sales resulted in the destruction of marriages. And since sales were only 16 percent of the total interregional movement, it is probable that about 2 percent of the marriages of slaves involved in the westward trek were destroyed by the process of migration.[146]

I have shown earlier that the statement that "sales were only 16 percent of the total interregional movement" is not backed by any supporting data. Let us now examine the 13 percent. It is not difficult to arrive at that percentage:

(1) 625 female slaves of all ages were included in the sample. Of that number, 567 (90.7 percent) were at least thirteen years old.

(2) Among the 567 females thirteen years and older, 16 percent — or 91 females — were or ever had been married ($567 \times .16 = 91$).

(3) Among the 91 married or ever married, 6 percent — or 5 females — were sold in the New Orleans market with their husbands ($91 \times .06 = 5$).

(4) Among the remaining 86 females ($91 - 5 = 86$), "probably at least one quarter ... were widowed or voluntarily separated." Let us assume that 25 percent had been widowed or had separated voluntarily prior to sale. That leaves 65 females ($86 \times .75 = 65$).

[146] T/C, I, p. 49.

(5) F + E then divide the remaining number of adult *women* by the total number of *females* in the sample to arrive at an estimate of the percentage of *female slaves* whose marriages *could have been broken* by interregional sale ($65 \div 625 = .104$). The estimated percentage in this illustration is 10.4 percent; F + E's calculation fixes the percentage at "13 percent or less." The percentage point difference is insignificant.

(6) F + E then multiply 13 percent by 16 percent and arrive at 2.08 percent.

That percentage (2 percent) upholds their argument that only a small number of "the marriages of slaves involved in the westward trek were destroyed by the process of migration."

Has the Right Question Been Asked?

There are difficulties with these data. It is assumed (for the moment) that the assumptions essential to these computations are accurate. The 13 percent measures the maximum percentage of possible marriages broken among all female slaves sold in the interregional trade. Is it the correct measure? Is it appropriate to stack "married" and "ever-married" women against all females listed in slave sale invoices, which include young female children? That measure promises to produce a quite low percentage. It is much more helpful to know how many slave women were of marriageable age, how many were married before their sale, how many were sold in the New Orleans transactions with or without their spouses to new owners, how many were widowed before sale, and how many were voluntarily separated before sale — and that may be impossible to tell from these data. After making such estimates, it would be appropriate to study only women of marriageable age. That would record the maximum percentage of possible marriages broken among all marriageable female slaves sold in the interregional trade, not all females. F + E assert (no evidence sustains this assertion) that the "average age of a woman at first marriage was 20."[147] It was, as shall be seen, much closer to eighteen. If most slave women married at about eighteen, that means that in this sample of 625 females, 397 could have been married at the time of sale.[148] According to F + E, 6 percent (24) were sold with their spouses. That leaves 373 women, of whom, again following the F + E estimates, 25 percent (93) had been widowed or had voluntarily separated from a spouse before sale into the New Orleans market. That leaves 280 females.

[147] T/C, II, pp. 114-115.
[148] This estimate is arrived at as follows. I subtracted the number of females under thirteen from 625 ($625 - 58 = 567$). Then I assumed that females thirteen to twenty-four years of age were distributed evenly in each year and also deducted those females thirteen to seventeen years of age.

It could be argued as follows: Among the 397 adult slave women of marriageable age (eighteen or older) in the sample of the New Orleans slave sale invoices examined between 1804 and 1862, 6 percent were sold with their mates. About a quarter of those remaining had been widowed or voluntarily separated from their spouses before sale. The number married and living with spouses prior to their sale to New Orleans among the remaining 280 is unknown. But if all had been married, that means that *71 percent* of married adult women involved in the interregional slave trade were separated from a spouse $(280 \div 397 = .71)$. If half of the 280 marriageable women had been married before sale, that drops the percentage of disrupted slave marriages among those sold in the interregional market from 71 percent to "only" about 35 percent $(140 \div 397 = .35)$.

Imagine then reading this "conclusion": Data contained in the sales records in New Orleans, by far the largest market in the interregional trade, sharply contradict the popular view that the destruction of slave marriages was at least a frequent, if not a universal, consequence of the slave trade. In the sample examined, about 397 women were of marriageable age. After accounting for those sold with spouses or widowed and voluntarily separated from a husband before sale (117 women), it turns out that some amount between 35 percent and 71 percent of women of marriageable age involved in interregional sales were separated involuntarily from their husbands by that business transaction. That percentage, of course, depends upon how many of these 280 women were married before their sale.

There are vast differences in the meanings of these percentages. These differences depend upon what number is divided into what other number and also upon a fairly accurate way of *estimating* how many slave women in the New Orleans market had been married *prior* to their sale.

Who Would Buy Childless, Single, and Older Slave Women?

If we translate the estimated percentages assigned by F + E to these New Orleans females into real numbers, a pattern emerges that poses teasing questions and that, in fact, makes neither economic nor social sense. According to F + E, the New Orleans sales records "indicate that more than 84 percent of all sales over the age of fourteen involved unmarried individuals." Using the percentages suggested in Figure 14, the estimated age distribution of females fifteen and older is shown in Table 24.

According to F + E's analysis, only 81 of these 509 females were or had been married at the time of sale $(509 \times .16 = 81)$. Let us assume that none of the females between the ages of fifteen and twenty-four had ever been married before their sale. (That is, of course, a dubious assumption. F + E themselves tell in another place that "in the slave population as a whole

Age	Number of Females (est.)
15–24	348 (406 − 58 = 348)
25+	161
Total	509

about half of the women aged twenty to twenty-four had one or more children.")[149] That means that the 81 married or ever married women were all at least twenty-five years old at the time of sale. But F + E's sample included 161 women at least twenty-five years old. And that means that half of the mature slave women sold in the New Orleans market had never married! It also means that 16 percent of females fifteen years old and older in the slave market were women at least twenty-five years old who had never married and, according to F + E's conception of the slave family, probably had been barren of children (81 ÷ 509 = .16).

Ordinary common sense casts grave doubt on that curious percentage. What were so many older single women doing in the New Orleans slave market? And who would have purchased them? If F + E are correct in insisting that few slave women had a first child before marriage or any children outside of marriage, is it possible that single women twenty-five years of age and older attracted purchasers anxious to reproduce their expanding labor force? Did a demand exist for older single slave women as field laborers? It is difficult to figure out why these women would have been attractive to purchasers of slaves needed for labor on the expanding Lower South cotton and sugar plantations. Instead of speculating on these and similar questions, it is more fruitful to examine how F + E arrived at dubious percentages which, in turn, pose unreal historical questions.

How F + E "Estimate" the Percentage of Slave "Marriages"
Broken by Interregional Sale

F + E find the New Orleans slave invoices the occasion to use a flawed procedure meant to make an "estimate of the proportion of female slaves . . . forcibly separated from their husbands." It is a quite simple one. They compute the percentage of women (in different age groups) with one or more children first among the women listed in the New Orleans sales records and then among women "in the slave population as a whole." The two per-

[149] T/C, II, p. 49.

centages are then compared. Here is the argument: "For example, in the slave population as a whole, about half of the women aged 20-24 had one or more children. . . . However, among the slaves traded in New Orleans, less than 20 percent of women aged 20-24 had one or more children. Since women with infants or young children were virtually always traded together with their offspring, the 'shortage' of women with children in the New Orleans sales indicates that traders were not indifferent to whether women were married, but strongly preferred unmarried women."[150]

An impressive mathematical model that runs for nearly two pages accompanies this analysis.[151] The accuracy of the model is not at issue here — that is for others more expert in such work to examine — but how the estimated numerical values are assigned to the crucial symbols M, M', U, U', α_1, and α_2 can be carefully evaluated by noncliometricians. Here is what these symbols mean:

U' = number of childless females from selling states sold in New Orleans
M' = number of females with child from selling states sold in New Orleans
U = number of childless females in the selling states before sale
M = number of females with child in the selling states before sale
α_1 = proportion of the number of childless females from the selling states bought in New Orleans
α_2 = proportion of the number of females with child from the selling states bought by New Orleans.[152]

The entire procedure, therefore, rests upon how accurately F + E determine the number of childless females (U') and females with child (M') from the selling states sold in New Orleans and the number of childless females (U) and females with child (M) in the selling states before sale. The crucial — that is F + E's word — comparison is between M' and M. Such a comparison causes F + E to conclude: "From these figures it can be seen that slaveholders were *six times* ($\alpha_1/\alpha_2 = 6.1$) more likely to buy an unmarried woman than a married woman. In other words, although the number of married women in the East potentially available for sale (in the age category 20-24) was slightly larger than the number of single women, New Orleans traders bought six single women for every married woman that they purchased. Clearly such a strong preference for unmarried women indicates the influence of powerful economic and social forces which militated against the disruption of families."[153] The careful reader will notice two points: one is peevish, and the other is pivotal. In their conclusions,

150 *Ibid.*
151 *Ibid.*, pp. 49-51.
152 *Ibid.*, p. 38.
153 *Ibid.*, pp. 51-52.

F + E switch the argument from "the proportion of female slaves . . . forcibly separated from their husbands" to the "forces which militated against the disruption of families." The two are not the same. Their comparison — here and elsewhere — tells nothing about the "disruption of families." It only tries to measure the breakup of marriages. Once more, they have confused "marriage" and the "family." Second, it is clear that this forceful argument depends entirely upon a correct estimate of the values of M, M', U, and U'.

How the Assumptions Made by F + E Greatly Undercount the Number of Married Slave Women Sold in the New Orleans Slave Market

How F + E figured the value of U' and M' is examined first. These estimates are based entirely upon the New Orleans data, but the slave sale invoices contain a severe limitation: they do not describe the prior marital status of women (or men) in the New Orleans slave market. The only demographic data indicated for all slaves sold are their age and sex. For a small number — those slaves sold in "complete families" (F + E, incidentally, do not define what they mean by "complete families." Does it mean only a husband, wife, and their children? Or does it include a husband and a wife, a mother and her children, and even a father and his children? These latter groups are not "complete families.") — the sale invoices apparently indicate familial relationships. How, then, does one estimate prior marital status for most slaves from just their age and sex? F + E explain their ingenious use of this source:

> The New Orleans slave invoices contain no direct statements regarding the marital status of slaves, except when slaves were sold in complete families. In particular, they contain no statements regarding whether or not slaves sold without husbands (or wives) were separated from their spouses as a consequence of being traded. Even if the New Orleans invoices did contain statements regarding previous marital status, such information could hardly be considered reliable. Not only would economic (and possibly moral) considerations have led to false reporting, but we would not be willing to assume that the only valid slave marriages were those recognized by slaveowners or white officials who accepted the behavioral norms of slaveholders.
>
> We consider as slave marriages all unions that the slaves involved intended, or expected, to be "stable" (for our purposes, this term need not be defined), regardless of what view others may have had of these unions. For the purpose of estimating the breakup rate, we take as evidence of such intent, the existence of a child. In other words, we consider every case of a slave woman who is sold with a child but without a husband to be a broken marriage. Since some women with children did not intend to have stable unions with the fathers, this assumption tends to exaggerate the degree to which the slave trade destroyed

marriages. However, because we are attempting to show that the breakup rate was low, it is appropriate that we choose a criterion of marriage that biases the result against the case we are trying to make.[154]

Here is what F + E have done: the single measure of a slave woman with a prior marriage broken by sale is the presence of a child and the absence of a husband. That is the only evidence. Let us assume that twenty women aged thirty to thirty-four turn up in the invoices; two have been sold with their spouses and children; two others have been sold only with their children; the remaining sixteen have been sold alone. The breakup rate is estimated as shown in Table 25. According to this procedure, 10 percent of women aged thirty to thirty-four had been separated from a spouse by sale $(2 \div 20 = .10)$. But that is because F + E consider only the presence of a child as evidence of a prior slave marriage. This is the erroneous method by which U' and M' have been estimated. It guarantees a low breakup percentage.

Estimating marriages prior to sale in the New Orleans market in this way greatly underestimates the number of slave marriages broken by sale. Let us see how by creating several archetypal examples:

(1) The slaves John and Mary were married but childless. Prior to their purchase by an interregional trader, they lived in Virginia. John and Mary were sold to different Louisiana buyers. Mary would count as a single woman in the F + E estimate. But her marriage had, in fact, been broken by sale.

(2) The slave woman Tenah and her children lived with a North Carolina owner prior to sale. Her husband, Sam, belonged to a different owner. Tenah and her children were sold to an interregional trader. Her husband remained with his North Carolina owner. At the time of sale, Tenah was forty-five years old, and her two children were aged sixteen and eighteen. Tenah was sold separately from her children. Tenah would count as a single

TABLE 25. NUMBER OF WOMEN AGED THIRTY TO THIRTY-FOUR IN THE NEW ORLEANS SLAVE SALE INVOICES AND THEIR MARITAL STATUS

Marital Status	Number
Sold in "Complete" Families	2
Women with Children but without Husbands	2
Women Alone (or "Single")	16
Total Women Aged 30 to 34	20

[154] *Ibid.*, pp. 48-49.

woman in the F + E estimate. But her marriage had, in fact, been broken by sale.

(3) The slaves Harriet and John were married and belonged to a Kentucky owner. So did their three children. The three children died. John and Harriet were sold to separate Louisiana purchasers. Harriet would count as a single woman in the F + E estimate. But her marriage had, in fact, been broken by sale.

There are yet other reasons why this estimate greatly undercounts previous slave marriages broken by sale. F + E assert that "women with infants or young children were virtually always traded with their offspring." Virtually always? No evidence in T/C sustains this important generalization. In 1836, at the height of the interregional slave trade, Ethan Allen Andrews, a Yale College graduate who had spent some years teaching in the South, published *Slavery and the Domestic Slave Trade*. Andrews had returned to the South in 1835 to investigate that trade in Maryland, the District of Columbia, and Virginia. He described behavior quite different from that indicated by F + E. "The southwestern trader," said Andrews, "wants only those slaves who will be immediately serviceable upon the cotton and sugar plantations. Young children, therefore, are for his purposes of no value." Interstate traders often found young children "an encumbrance." A visit among a boatload of slaves headed for the Deep South convinced the former schoolteacher that "frequently . . . they sell the mother while they keep her children." Andrews told of one Virginia trader accused of "sending off a number of mothers without their little children, whom he had purchased with them. He had separated them, because the children were of no value in the market to which the mothers were sent." "It is difficult," Andrews admitted, ". . . in such reports to separate truth from falsehood."[155]

Historians share that difficulty with Andrews, but that is not a reason for such evidence to be ignored. It may, in fact, have happened, as F + E suggest, that most infant children were sold with their mothers. But what about older children, children aged, say, ten or twelve? Frederic Bancroft figured that "as a rule, the dividing line between children that were worth more with their mothers and those that were worth more without them was at about eight years of age." Bancroft insisted, furthermore, that "when women of 35 or 40" were sold in slave markets "without any children or only with those of tender age, it was almost certain that there had been separations."[156] Is it possible that some of the young children sold in the New Orleans slave market — 9.3 percent of the F + E sample was made up of

---

[155] Ethan Allen Andrews, *Slavery and the Domestic Slave Trade* (1836), pp. 49-50, 105-106, 146, 149, 165.

[156] Bancroft, *Slave Trading in the Old South,* pp. 197, 202.

117

children under the age of thirteen — were sold separately from their mothers so that F + E counted their mothers as single women? F + E are correct in figuring that some of the older women without children in the New Orleans slave market had been widowed or had separated voluntarily from a spouse before their sale. But these calculations are not answers to Bancroft's argument. What about the woman aged thirty-five or forty and sold alone in New Orleans?

It might, of course, be argued that Andrews was a biased contemporary observer and that Bancroft was a biased twentieth-century "neo-abolitionist" historian. And it might even be argued that the examples cited above rarely occurred. These may be accurate criticisms, but such assertions do not confront the essential fact that a document which usually records only the sex and age of a person cannot reveal much, if anything, about that person's prior marital status. The essential data needed to estimate precisely the number of slave marriages broken by interregional (or local) sale are lacking. Harriet Beecher Stowe understood the limitations of such evidence. In the *Key to Uncle Tom's Cabin,* she reprinted an advertisement placed by the trader Thomas G. James:

> He has just arrived from Virginia with a very likely lot of Field Men and Women; also House Servants, three Cooks, and a Carpenter. Call and see.
> A fine Buggy Horse, a Saddle Horse, and a Carryall, on hand, and for sale.
>
> THOMAS G. JAMES.

James listed the occupations of the slaves, but that information is just as useless to the student of slave marriage as a mere listing of sex and age. Stowe commented: "And had no families been separated to form the assortment? We hear of a lot of field men and women. Where are their children? We hear of a lot of house-servants — of 'three cooks' and 'one carpenter,' as well as a 'fine buggy horse.' Had these unfortunate cooks and carpenters no relations? Each one of these individuals has his own ties; besides being cooks, carpenters, and house-servants, they are also fathers, mothers, husbands, wives; but what of that? They must be selected — it is an *assortment* that is wanted."[157] Stowe may have been a sentimentalist, but she had a good point. Data are useful for some purposes but not for other purposes.

An Example Meant to Illustrate What Cannot Be Learned from Such a Source about Slave Marriages

How F + E seriously erred in their use of the New Orleans slave sale invoices and in assigning values to U' and M' can be learned by examining

[157] Stowe, *Key to Uncle Tom's Cabin,* p. 269.

a single document which contains data similar to those recorded in the New Orleans slave sale invoices. It is an advertisement placed by Tardy & Co., a Mobile, Alabama, slave-trading firm, in the *Mobile Register* on January 5, 1859.[158] The advertisement announces the public auction for cash of between sixty and seventy slaves owned by the estate of John Darrington. Only forty-six are listed. Their ages are given and their sex ("negro man," "negro boy," "negro woman," and "negro child"). The full list is shown in Table 26. Let us assume that an interregional slave trader purchased these men, women, and children, that they ended up in the New Orleans market, and that all were listed in the sale invoices. Only the females concern us. F + E, after all, do not examine the previous marriages of male slaves. (How can they? Unless males were sold in "complete families," none had children listed with them.) Table 27 illustrates the way that the Darrington slave females would be listed according to F + E's assumptions. Let us keep in mind the importance of U' and M' to F + E's argument: these are the only numbers ("estimates") used to figure "the proportion of female slaves ... forcibly separated from their husbands." And U' and M' do not profess to

TABLE 26. SLAVES OF THE DARRINGTON ESTATE SOLD IN MOBILE, JANUARY 5, 1859

Males		Females	
Doctor	22	Elmira	15
Octo	19	Molly	18
Nonen	16	Peggy	18
Fortune	32	Dolly	16
Adam	30	Emily	14
Peter Fox	35	Hesper	22
Jim	45	Eliza	8
Allee	30	Abby	10
Hannibal	25	Fanny	50
Sampson	45	Ellen	14
Marlow	50	Lindy	45
Fortune	60	Mary Ann	45
Edwin	8	Kate	16
Ned Ball	65	Louisa	10
George	14	Mary Ball	40
Alfred	12	Jane	19
Albert	12	Margaret	not given
Barney	24	Betty	40 and with her four children
Tom	60	Tener	28 and with her four children

[158] *Mobile Register,* 5 January 1859, printed in Bancroft, *Slave Trading in the Old South,* advertisement opposite page 300.

119

TABLE 27. AGE DISTRIBUTION OF WOMEN IN THE DARRINGTON SLAVE SALE AND THEIR MARITAL STATUS

Age of Darrington Slave Females	Number	Number Ever Married	Number of Childless Females Sold in New Orleans = U'	Number of Females with Child Sold in New Orleans = M'
0–12	3	0		
13–24	9	0	9	0
25+	6	2	4	2
Unknown	1			

estimate previous marriages, but only women in the New Orleans market with children.

Only Betty and Tener, Darrington slaves, had children listed with them. Does that mean that Fanny, Lindy, Mary Ann, and Mary Ball — all at least forty years old at the time of sale — were widowed women? Voluntarily separated wives? Or slave spinsters? Hardly! And what about the children listed? Betty and Tener each had four unnamed children. The following young slaves sold were between the ages of ten and sixteen: Elmira, Peggy, Dolly, Emily, Abby, Ellen, Kate, Louisa, Nonen, George, Alfred, and Albert. Were they born on the plantation? If not, they had been purchased into the plantation. That means, incidentally, that families had been broken by Darrington to build his labor force. If they were born on the plantation, who were their mothers? Was Lindy one of them? And, if so, who was Lindy's husband? Was he dead in 1860? Or was she separated from him? None of these questions — and countless others dealing with the slave family and with slave marriage — can be answered from just this evidence. How many possible marriages, for example, existed among these slaves? Nine of the women and fourteen of the men were eighteen years old or older at the time of sale. Let us assume that the women were not separated or widowed and that all had spouses on the plantation in 1860. That makes nine marriages. Were the four other "surplus" males unmarried? What if three had spouses living on a farm or a plantation nearby? That would raise the number of marriages to twelve. How many marriages were broken by sale? We are playing the game of numbers, but it is not a mere exercise. The inadequacy of the Darrington listing is being illustrated. And so, too, is the inadequacy of the New Orleans slave sales invoices being described. A woman with a child and without a husband in the New Orleans sales invoices cannot measure slave marriages broken by sale. It is that simple, and it is, therefore, necessary to put aside M' and U'.

*Can Anything Be Learned from the Manuscript Census
about Childless and Child-Bearing Slave Women?*

That leaves us with M, U, α_1, and α_2. But since α_1 and α_2 depend for their accuracy on M' and U', α_1 and α_2 need also to be discarded. What about M and U? M symbolizes "the number of females with child in the selling states before sale," and U symbolizes "the number of childless females in the selling states before sale." F + E correctly explain that these estimates cannot be gotten directly from the New Orleans invoices but add: "They can, however, be estimated by combining information contained in the probate records with information contained in the census." A page later, however, it is pointed out that M and U have been "estimated from census data," not from "information contained in the probate records [combined] with information contained in the census."[159] Despite this confusion, it is assumed here that M and U were estimated from census data. These data must be the manuscript slave census schedules. Just how such estimates were made is never described in T/C. The manuscript slave census schedules, in fact, are even more obscure on matters about the slave family and slave marriage than the New Orleans invoices and the Mobile advertisement. The census usually listed slaves by their age and sex. In 1850 or 1860, the slaves belonging to a particular owner might be listed as shown in Table 28.

How can one possibly estimate marital and family connections from such a listing? And how, especially, is it possible to use the slave manuscript census to separate out by specific age groupings women with children from childless women? That, after all, is what M and U symbolize. Although some probate

TABLE 28. EXAMPLE OF A MANUSCRIPT SLAVE CENSUS SCHEDULE

Sex	Age	Sex	Age
Male	60	Female	18
Male	44	Female	15
Male	23	Male	8
Male	35	Male	6
Male	17	Male	5
Male	19	Male	3
Male	16	Female	11
Male	81	Female	10
Female	58	Female	8
Female	45	Female	5
Female	40	Female	1
Female	31	Female	1
Female	23		

[159] T/C, II, pp. 50-51.

records listed slaves in family groupings, there also are seemingly insurmountable difficulties, as illustrated below,[160] in using those data to reveal such important matters as the age of slave women at marriage. Our concern here is just with M and U.

Have the Authors of T/C Found in This Source Evidence That Interregional Sale Broke Up Relatively Few Slave Marriages?

The New Orleans slave sale invoices remain an unusually valuable source. No doubt much can be learned from them about the age and the sex of slaves sold in the interregional and local slave trade. But it is quite doubtful that these data can help in analyzing the relationship between the slave trade and slave marriages. We need first an accurate measure of the marital status of particular slaves at the time of sale and of overall slave marital patterns against which such sales can be measured. F + E correctly suggest the need to examine the relationship between $M + U$ and $M' + U'$. Their own examination of M, U, M', and U', however, is so defective in its essential assumptions that it casts doubt on these main symbols, the lesser symbols that depend upon their accuracy (α_1, α_2, M_a, M_d, M'_d, B_1, B_2, W, X, and Z), such precise percentages as "84 percent," "6 percent," and "13 percent," such imprecise measures as "at least one quarter," the assertion that "slaveholders were six times more likely to buy an unmarried woman than a married one," and especially the conclusion that "about 2 percent of the marriages of slaves involved in the westward trek were destroyed by the process of migration." The relationship between slave sale and slave marriage — as well as the relationship between slave sale and the slave family — remains open. That

---

[160] F + E realize that their use of a present child as the measure of a "stable" slave marriage has limitations. It fails to account for "some women without children [who] were married but had not been married long enough to bear children." Probate records, they insist, allow them to adjust for the weakness. "Probate records," they write, "indicate that among married women 20–24, approximately 10.2 percent were married during the previous year" (*ibid.*, p. 52). Probate records, of course, are an invaluable source. They indicate a person's economic status at the time of his death. Slaves sometimes listed in "family" groups are included. How is it possible to tell from such a record when slaves married and even to report that one in ten slave women 20–24 years of age had married "during the previous year"? Is there a connection between the decision of slaves to marry and the death of an owner? F + E later reveal that the "average age of a [slave] woman at first marriage was 20 and . . . the average age of her groom was 24" (*ibid.*, p. 115). That information is not given in the slave manuscript census schedules and appears very infrequently in manuscript plantation records. I suspect that it, too, comes from the ubiquitous "probate records," but that is unclear. F + E could explain how these "averages" were computed. The age at which most slave men and women married is too important to be obscured by the absence of the pertinent evidence.

much, at least, is clear from a careful examination of the ways in which F + E have misused the New Orleans slave sale invoices. Their examination of that source does not refute or even modify one of the major arguments in Frederic Bancroft's *Slave Trading in the Old South*. Bancroft exaggerated the volume of the interstate slave trade, but his essential point, as we shall see, remains unchallenged.

F + E insist that Bancroft and other historians dealing with the slave trade used mainly "the accounts of firsthand observers," contemporaries who "lacked the hard data needed to actually determine the scope and nature of this trade" and who therefore "could only convey their impressions." Historians like Bancroft chose "between . . . conflicting and contradictory tracts," and the "conventional view of the slave trade" was "fashioned" by historians who "uniformly rejected the impressions of southern writers as apologetics and accepted the views of northern or European critics as accurate."[161] Some of these historians, F + E admit, knew of the existence of the New Orleans data, but failed to use that information. "If historians have not previously exploited the New Orleans data," F + E explain, "it is . . . because the volume of data was so massive that it could not be assailed successfully by scholars untrained in modern statistical methods."[162] Such methods are useful but not essential to exploiting these and other quantitative data. Such methods, moreover, have not been used by F + E to confront Bancroft's essential point. We discount the volume of local and interregional sales. "The fact," Bancroft insisted, "that . . . all but a small percentage of the slaves had for sale were 'single,' or young mothers with children, and that the slaves in the markets, unless in gangs from estates, were almost exclusively of the same kind" is "conclusive evidence that it was common to divide families."[163] Until there is a more accurate analysis of the New Orleans slave sale invoices, the evidence in that source does no more than confirm Bancroft's conclusion that it was "common to divide families." Bancroft, however, dealt with "families," not with "marriages." And F + E never consider the impact of slave sales on the slave family. Any child sold from its parents — including unmarried teenagers with living parents — counts as evidence of the breakup of a slave family. If one accepts the vitality of the slave family, there is no other way to read such evidence.

---

[161] It is tempting to ask why F + E list only the evidence of "southern writers . . . [and] northern or European critics." What about the evidence left by former slaves and contemporary free blacks? That temptation is encouraged by F + E's complaint that in *The Peculiar Institution* Kenneth Stampp failed to "emphasize the work of Negro writers," citing "members of the Negro school [*sic*] . . . only 24 times" (*ibid.*, pp. 233-234).

[162] T/C, I, pp. 51-52.

[163] Bancroft, *Slave Trading in the Old South*, p. 199.

Was a Slave Sold on Average Every 3.6 Minutes between 1820 and 1860?

Using only their own data, there are abundant and compelling reasons to dismiss F + E's assertion that the "economic forces" which led "planters [more properly slaveowners] to destroy rather than to maintain slave families" were "relatively infrequent" and that "the emphasis put on the sanctity of the slave family by many planters, and the legal status given to the slave family under plantation law, cannot be lightly dismissed."[164] An accurate reading of their data — a reading that involves just a different but quite simple computation — reveals that *about two million slaves (men, women, and children) were sold in local, interstate, and interregional markets between 1820 and 1860, and that of this number perhaps as many as 260,000 were married men and women and another 186,000 were children under the age of thirteen.* If we assume that slave sales did not occur on Sundays and holidays and that such selling went on for ten hours on working days, a slave was sold on average every 3.6 minutes between 1820 and 1860. The way in which F + E misinterpreted their own data and thereby greatly underestimated the magnitude of slave sales and consequent family breakups needs to be examined in close detail. We therefore ignore the inexplicable fact that F + E neglected to examine Mississippi and Louisiana wartime marriage registers kept by the Union Army, sources in which thousands of Deep South slaves told whether an earlier slave marriage had been broken by sale (or force). That evidence would have allowed them to test and perhaps modify their assertions that slavery had a benign effect on the Afro-American slave family because owners found it essential to "promote the stability of slave families" in order to better administer plantations, maintain "labor discipline," and promote "the increase of the slave population."[165] F + E knew of these sources because their extensive bibliography includes references to two recent publications that made explicit use of these wartime slave marriage registers.[166]

The Importance of William Calderhead's Study of Maryland Slave Sales between 1830 and 1840 and How It Has Been Trivialized

F + E share problems with other historians of the slave family: they do not know how many slaves were married and they do not know how many slaves were sold. None of the "masses" of data they examined — probate records, slave sale invoices, and manuscript census data — reveal informa-

---

[164] T/C, I, pp. 128-129, 143.
[165] *Ibid.*, pp. 127-128.
[166] T/C, II, pp. 250, 257, items 21 and 165.

tion about these two important social facts. In T/C, the authors rely entirely on just a single source — New Orleans slave sale invoices between 1804 and 1862 — to examine the relationship between slave sales and slave marriages. In addition, they assume the correctness of the findings in William Calderhead's recent study of Maryland slave sales between 1830 and 1840 and use Calderhead's general findings to bolster their pickings in the New Orleans invoices.[167]

Calderhead's study *is* of great importance. It is the first and only study to examine in detail local slave sales in a way that allows us to estimate what percentage of a particular slave population was sold. Proper use of Calderhead's findings, however, casts total doubt on F + E's arguments about the slave family. Their summary of Calderhead's estimates, moreover, allows us to see that what the wartime Mississippi marriage registers recorded — the fact that in one of three marriages registered in which one or both partners were at least forty years old an earlier marriage had been broken by force (or sale) — was not a wild exaggeration. F + E summarize Calderhead's findings: "A study of slave trading in Maryland over the decade from 1830 to 1840 revealed that total sales (local and interstate) amounted to 1.92 percent of the slave population each year. If that ratio is projected to the national level, total slave sales over the period 1820-1860 averaged about fifty thousand per year." Their projection is accurate, but their interpretation of it is entirely unsatisfactory. "In other words," the very next sentence in T/C reads, "on average, only one slaveholder out of every twenty-two sold a slave in any given year, and roughly one third of these were estates of deceased persons."[168] This average tells about slaveholders, not about slaves. The sentence more properly should have read: In other words, given that total sales (local and interregional) averaged about fifty thousand per year, approximately *two million* slaves were sold between 1820 and 1860, a figure arrived at by multiplying fifty thousand slaves per year by forty years. The estimate, incidentally, that about fifty thousand slaves were sold a year is somewhat lower than a casual estimate made in antebellum America that "60 to 80 thousand humans beings" were "yearly . . . sold in the market." A statistician did not make that estimate. It was made instead by Harriet Beecher Stowe![169]

F + E apparently did not find in Calderhead's important work a way to estimate the total number of slaves sold in all markets, and without such an estimate we cannot begin to examine seriously the relationship between slave

[167] William Calderhead, "How Extensive Was the Border State Slave Trade? A New Look," *Civil War History,* XVIII (March 1972), pp. 42-55.

[168] T/C, I, p. 53.

[169] Stowe, *Key to Uncle Tom's Cabin,* p. 298.

sales and the slave family. Calderhead's 1.92 percent sale rate per year projected to the national level assumes great significance when we examine the overall slave population between 1820 and 1860, as shown in Table 29. Using F + E's projection of Calderhead's estimate, we can write: In a slave population that increased from 1,538,022 in 1820 to 3,953,760 in 1860, approximately two million slaves were sold. That estimate — surely too large — turns writers like Frederic Bancroft and Kenneth Stampp, whom F + E scorn as "neoabolitionists," into apologists for slavery. Even Frederick Douglass and William Lloyd Garrison never hinted at so large a volume of slave sales between 1820 and 1860. It is probable that Calderhead's estimate is high for the entire South. Maryland may have been exceptional in that 1.92 percent of its slaves were sold each year. Let us, therefore, assume that only 1 percent of slaves were sold each year over the entire South. This allows us to take into account the differences between exporting and importing states. But cutting the percentage sold by half still means that no fewer than one million slaves were sold between 1820 and 1860. If that is evidence supporting the assertion that slaveholders as a social class sponsored stable slave families for sound economic reasons, then the word *evidence* has taken on a strange new meaning.

How Does the Historian Figure the "Marriage Breakup Rate"
and Then Measure the Social Importance of That Rate
Among Enslaved Afro-Americans and Their Families?

What of "broken slave marriages"? F + E never tell us how many slave marriages were broken up. They cannot because they do not know how many slaves were married. Instead, they estimate a "marriage breakup rate," using as their data only the New Orleans slave sale invoices. They write: "If it is assumed that the marriage breakup rate was the same in all slave sales as in the interregional trade, the New Orleans data can be used to provide a tentative estimate of the proportion of slave marriages destroyed through all slave sales." That can be done, apparently, without knowing either the

TABLE 29. UNITED STATES SLAVE POPULATION, 1820-1860

Year	Total Number of Slaves
1820	1,538,022
1830	2,009,043
1840	2,487,355
1850	3,204,313
1860	3,953,760

number of slaves married or the number of slaves sold. Let us follow their brief argument: "Calderhead estimates that 1.92 percent of slaves were sold each year in Maryland. If, as in the interregional trade, 13 percent of these sales involved the destruction of marriage, approximately 0.25 percent (1.92 × 0.13 = 0.25) of slave marriages were broken through trade each year."[170] Once more, I suspect, the wrong numbers have been multiplied. If Calderhead is correct, and if the distribution between married and single slaves reported by F + E from the New Orleans slave sale invoices is typical, it follows that 6,500 married slaves were sold each year between 1820 and 1860 and that no fewer than 260,000 married slaves were sold between 1820 and 1860 (50,000 × .13 × 40 = 260,000). This figure, of course, does not tell how many slave marriages were broken by sale: it simply records the estimated number of married slaves sold over this forty-year period.

A series of estimates — starting out with 5.8 percent as the "probability that a marriage would be broken by trade rather than death" and adding to that "probability" Calderhead's estimates on the number of marriages broken through estate divisions and gift transfers (another 2.8 percent) — allows F + E to conclude that "roughly 8.6 percent of all slave marriages were destroyed through economic transactions in slaves."[171] What does this percentage mean in the absence of knowledge about how many slave marriages existed? If, for example, 2 million slave marriages took place between 1820 and 1860, it follows that only 172,000 slave marriages were "destroyed through economic transactions" (that is 172,000 more than occurred among nonslaves). If we assume that each couple so separated had 10 blood relatives nearby and 20 intimate slave friends, that means that each year 4,300 marriages were broken by sale affecting no fewer than 8,600 husbands and wives and 129,000 blood kin and friends. It rarely happened that slave marriages were broken more than once, so we can assume that each year 4,300 different marriages were broken by sale. That means that between 1820 and 1860 more than 5 million persons — all slaves — directly or indirectly experienced the psychological and social crisis that accompanied the breakup of a slave marriage by sale (8,600 + 129,000 × 40 = 5,504,000). If we assume that only 1 million slave marriages occurred between 1820 and 1860 and apply the 8.6 percent to that number, those affected directly or indirectly by these breakups merely total 2,752,000 men, women, and children. Social estimates of this kind — not narrow and meaningless "percentages" — tell why the fear of breaking up a slave marriage was a much more powerful "incentive" to "productive labor" than the many fringe benefits exaggerated in importance by the authors of T/C and discussed earlier in these pages.

[170] T/C, II, p. 115.
[171] *Ibid.*, p. 116.

127

Let us examine the social meaning of the breakup of a slave marriage by sale somewhat differently by making the following assumptions:

1. Calderhead's estimates are far too large for the entire South. We cut them by half so that only 25,000 slave sales occurred each year.

2. We assume that about one million slave marriages occurred between 1820 and 1860.

3. We assume that F + E are correct in their "estimate" that 8.6 percent of slave marriages were broken involuntarily by the decisions of owners. Such decisions involved sale, gift, estate division, and hire. On "average," that means that each year about 2,150 slave marriages were broken for involuntary reasons rooted in ownership.

4. We assume further that these involuntary breakups were distributed evenly over the entire South.

In 1860, slaves were owned in about one thousand southern counties. That means, then, that each year in each county just two slave marriages were ended involuntarily. Is this a large number or a small number? That, of course, depends. And the importance of this number depends entirely upon the real social world of slave kin and non-kin networks within which these two marriage breakups took place. Let us, therefore, make the following additional assumptions:

1. Each marriage that ended involved a slave husband and wife who between them had ten consanguinal and affinal kin nearby — children, parents, older siblings, and aunts and uncles.

2. Together the couple had ten non-kin slave acquaintances — slave friends and neighbors. These persons learned of the broken marriage.

3. When moved a distance (any distance — it hardly matters), the husband and wife each described the breakup of their marriage to five different slave adults.

Thirty persons — in addition to the couple involved — learned of the breakup of this single marriage. Is the breakup of two slave marriages a year per county between 1820 and 1860 (*only* 86,000 slave marriages in all over that forty-year period) a small number?

But imagine reading the following: On average, about two slave marriages a year were broken involuntarily by owners in each southern county between 1820 and 1860. About 86,000 slave marriages were ended by sale, gift transfer, estate division, and hire. On average, however, each of these couples had ten consanguinal and affinal kin and ten close slave friends and neighbors. After separation, moreover, each adult involved described the breakup to five separate adult slaves whom they came to know. That means that 2,752,000 slaves learned directly and indirectly of the breakup of these

86,000 slave marriages (2,150 marriages × 2 partners × 10 relatives × 10 friends × 10 new friends = 2,752,000 slaves). Is it possible to argue that the breakup of "only 86,000 slave marriages" between 1820 and 1860 is evidence that enslaved Afro-Americans lived in *stable* nuclear families?[172] I doubt that the large number of slaves affected by these few involuntary breakups of slave marriages would have offered an affirmative answer.

More needs to be said about the relationship between "8.6 percent" and what the Mississippi and Louisiana blacks reported in registering their marriages in 1864 and 1865. F + E tell us that 75 percent of slaves who were moved from the exporting to the importing states ended up in Alabama, Mississippi, Louisiana, and Texas. When we consider the number of slave marriages broken by owners who moved their slaves with them to the Lower South and thereby broke up a marriage between slaves belonging to different owners and add to this number the estimates worked out by Calderhead as well as the data derived by F + E from the New Orleans slave invoices, we begin to understand why the Mississippi and Louisiana blacks differed so greatly in *their* estimates of marriages broken by force (or sale) from F + E. Table 30 illustrates the difference. Given our current state of knowledge, Calderhead's overall estimates, and the meager data base from which F + E work, there is every reason to insist that these blacks reported the percentage of slave marriages broken by an "economic transaction" far more accurately than "cliometricians" working with computers more than a century later.

---

[172] In the interview with the French historians Furet and Ladurie, Fogel explained what "stable" means: "We estimate that at least two percent of the marriages were split up by interstate slave trading. If local trading is included, the figure rises to eight percent. Naturally, this high figure more than justifies a blanket moral condemnation of this practice. But statistically speaking, the percentage is not high enough to have precluded the development of a large number of stable families. Another way of considering these data is to say that ninety-two percent of the marriages were not split up by slave trading. Thus, we can see how even though slave trading constituted a threat to the family, it did not make the existence of stable marriages an impossibility" (*Le Nouvel Observateur,* 9 September 1974).

The example cited in the text — whatever the percentage of slave marriages broken by sale — tells why it is inappropriate to describe unbroken slave marriages as "stable." The point in dispute is not "8 percent" versus "92 percent" but the effect on the enslaved of "*x* percent" of involuntarily broken marriages. A "small" percentage of such dissolutions had a large effect on the entire slave community. That is what the example in the text is meant to suggest.

The attentive reader, I hope, will also notice that Fogel has, once more, confused slave marriages with slave families.

In the same interview Fogel also insists that the slaves "developed a very stable family life." "Very" stable?

TABLE 30. COMPARISON OF MARRIAGES BROKEN BY FORCE OR SALE

Observer	Percentage of Marriages Broken by Force	Number of Marriages Broken by Force as a Ratio of All Marriages
Fogel and Engerman	8.6%	1 of 11.6 marriages
All Mississippi and Louisiana slaves aged 30 and older registering marriages in 1864-1865[173]	22.7%	1 of 4.4 marriages

An Undercount of the Numbers of Children Sold

There are similar questions about F + E's estimates concerning the sale of slave children — boys and girls not yet thirteen. By ignoring the numbers sold in *local* markets, as contrasted to interregional markets, F + E entirely misjudge the magnitude of such sales. Their own estimates, together with Calderhead's study, make this clear. A sample drawn from the New Orleans slave sale records reveals to F + E that "only 9.3 percent of the New Orleans sales were of children under thirteen." They conclude: "Projected to the national level, this implies that the total interregional sales of children amounted to just 234 per annum. This small number of child sales could easily have been explained by orphans, as U. B. Phillips and other southern historians have claimed. Because of the high death rates of the time, approximately 15.9 percent of children under thirteen were orphans. Thus there were approximately 190,000 orphans in the age category 0–12 in 1850. The interregional sale of just 1 of every 810 orphans would account for the full extent of the trade in children."[174] F + E have trivialized the number of children sold. Using Calderhead's estimate that 1.92 percent of slaves were sold each year (about 50,000), and assuming that the New Orleans records accurately measured the percentage of slave children under thirteen as a percentage of all slaves sold (they were surely too low), we learn that 4,650 children were sold each year, and that about 186,000 children under the age of thirteen were sold between 1820 and 1860 (50,000 × 0.093 × 40 = 186,000). It does not surprise us to learn that "U. B. Phillips and other

---

[173] A full analysis of the Mississippi and Louisiana wartime marriage registers appears in my forthcoming study, chapter eight. But a preliminary analysis was published in Gutman, "Le Phenomene Invisible," pp. 1197-1218, so these findings (so different from what F + E uncovered in the New Orleans slave records) were available to F + E before the publication of T/C. It is surprising that F + E failed to consider this quantitative data in dealing with the impact of sale on slave marriages. Some of the same registers were also used by John Blassingame, *The Slave Community: Plantation Life in the Antebellum South* (1972), pp. 89-92, especially the table on page 90. Blassingame's analysis, I should add, is quite different from mine.

[174] T/C, I, pp. 49-50.

southern historians" failed to make so simple a computation. These data were not accessible to them. But it is surprising that F + E failed to make so simple a computation. One does not need a computer to multiply 50,000 × 40 × 9.3 percent. (There is, incidentally, reason to question F + E's high percentage of orphaned slave children in 1850. If they are right, there should have been a huge number of orphans in the early post-emancipation South. All contemporary observers, however, were shocked by their actual limited number. Large numbers of these so-called orphans were absorbed into slave kinship groupings larger than the immediate family. That is a subject, however, which cannot detain us here.)

Is Purchase into a Productive Plantation a More Important Measure of the Relationship between "Sale" and the Slave Family Than Sale from Such a Place?

We are not yet finished with slave sales. In another place, F + E write:

> That slaves were generally purchased for use, rather than speculation, is clearly revealed by the extremely low sales rates of ongoing plantations. Not only was a purchased slave rarely resold, but slaves born on such estates were rarely put on the market. These conclusions have emerged from the analysis of the birth, purchase, and sales records of nineteen plantations with a total population of thirty-nine hundred slaves. Over a period of ninety years ending in 1865, a mere seven slaves were sold from these plantations. Of these, six were born on their plantations and one was purchased. Since a total of thirty-three hundred slaves were born on these nineteen plantations during the years in question, the ratio of sales to births was a mere 0.2 percent. On these plantations, at least, the breeding of slaves for sale in the market simply was not practiced.[175]

A perfectly accurate set of observations, nothing more can be inferred from them than that few sales took place on "ongoing plantations." But the reader should be told that this is hardly an adequate sample of plantation behavior. In 1860 the entire South had about 42,600 units of ownership, mostly plantations, involving twenty or more slaves. This sample represents no more than 0.0004 percent of all such plantations; that is, one out of two hundred fifty. More than this, the measure of sales on productive plantations is not by sale from such a place but purchase into such a place, and *not* purchase over a ninety-year period. Purchases often involving the breakup of slave families counted greatly in the early history of an agricultural enterprise that became a plantation. Estimates "over a period of ninety years" minimize the ways in which the destruction of slave families permitted the initial construction of large business enterprises. More than this, the fact that such breakups occurred in the early years of an enterprise meant that they served as im-

[175] *Ibid.*, p. 54.

131

portant examples of the power slaveholders had over families for later generations of slaves, further evidence that the relationship between the power to break up families and labor efficiency cannot be measured by simply estimating "breakups."

Why Sale Is an Inadequate Measure of the Stability of the Slave Family: Estate Division and Gift Transfer as Studied by Stampp, Jones, Phifer, and Mohr

The discussion of the *causes* for slave sales by F + E contains much confusion and even some misrepresentation. After discounting the "notion that speculative purchases and sales of slaves were common among southern planters," they ask: "How then did most slave sales originate?" Calderhead's study, they report, "indicated that approximately one half of all sales were the consequences of the breakup of the estates of deceased planters whose heirs were unable or unwilling to continue the family business. There is little evidence regarding the circumstances which attended the balance of the sales."[176] The effects of such divisions on the slave family are entirely ignored by F + E. They themselves have not examined inheritance patterns in particular local settings to see how frequently slave families were broken. Instead, they flay Kenneth Stampp's work:

> Stampp argues that wills show an overwhelming conflict between masters' interests in slaves as property and the integrity of slave families. He suggests that as a consequence of nine of the wills, slave families were broken up and that only in the tenth case was the entire plantation retained intact. Stampp's conclusions are not based on the actual disposition of the slaves but on such assumptions as the following: the division of eight slaves among three children, "in equal portions, share and share alike," necessarily "made the sale of all or part of these slaves inevitable." Stampp gives no report of whether such a sale in fact took place, and if it did, whether it resulted in the breakup of the slave families. Nor does Stampp indicate whether his sample ratio of nine to one is to be taken as indicative of the population parameter. He never explicitly discusses how his sample of wills was drawn or its representativeness, although the conclusion that he reaches strongly implies that the sample was indeed representative. . . .[177]

Stampp, perhaps, did not examine many wills, but it is entirely unbecoming of F + E to criticize Stampp because he failed to tell how his sample of wills was drawn and did not discuss its representativeness. The authors of T/C themselves never discuss how their sample was drawn from either the New Orleans slave invoices or the probate records. Nowhere can the reader

---

[176] *Ibid.*, pp. 54-55.
[177] T/C, II, p. 232.

132

learn the size of the sample. Nor is this all. Early in volume two, readers learn that "major bodies of data" have been "collected by the cliometricians." Those bodies of data are listed. Among them is item 11: "Slave demography and plantation life," for which is given "geographic area and number of observations: 30 plantations from Alabama, Georgia, Louisiana, Mississippi, North Carolina, and Texas."[178] Not a single one of these plantations is ever identified by name in either volume of the study, making it difficult for other students of slavery to examine those records and thereby scrutinize F + E's findings and arguments. This omission is especially surprising since so much stress is placed upon the integrity of data. Stampp listed his sources, however "limited" they were.

It is even less becoming to condemn Stampp so harshly because F + E themselves have given no attention to the findings of other students of slavery who have systematically examined how inheritance and estate division affected the slave family. Without exception, their findings run against the assertions of F + E. These are not obscure works. One of them (Jones) is cited in the bibliography in T/C. Another was published in *Phylon* in 1972 but is not cited in that "exhaustive" bibliography (Mohr). Neither is the third (Phifer), which first appeared in the *Journal of Southern History* and then was reprinted in the widely used first edition of Allen Weinstein and Frank Gatell, eds., *American Negro Slavery*.

Let us examine these works briefly to see the kind of evidence that has been neglected. Bobby Frank Jones, for example, concluded in his still unpublished but nevertheless important and quite original study "A Cultural Middle Passage: Slave Marriage and Family in the Antebellum South" (1965):

[T]he threat of separation cast a pall over the entire institution. . . . Once they had been designated as chattel property, slaves inevitably became involved in any litigation of which their master or his estate might be a part. As a businessman, the slaveholder incurred debts, took risks in the market, and stood liable to financial reverses the same as a man engaged in any other industry. Inconveniences normally arise when an employer is no longer able to retain those economically dependent upon him, and in this sense, any man who has another in his hire is in a position to affect the lives and futures of many families other than his own. The slave family was in a radically different position from an average employee. As a part of the slaveholder's capital which could be seized to satisfy debts, the family not only was inconvenienced when business crises occurred, but it risked disintegration. The risk also applied to divisions of estates when slaveholders died. Inevitable death sooner or later removed the protection of even the most benevolent master, and slaves could expect under these circumstances that family ties would be disregarded by neutral administrators. Financial difficulties and estate divisions account for the en-

[178] *Ibid.*, p. 24.

trance of more bondsmen into the slave trade than all other reasons combined. ... In order to realize the highest market price, or to divide an estate equally, slaves could be sold separately, or parceled among heirs, without regard to age. Since family groups sold for less than individuals, husbands were frequently separated from wives, and parents from children. Even when "divided out," which appears to have been more acceptable to slaves because they would belong to a group of relatives and would be able to maintain contact with their families, there was no assurance that an heir would not put a child into the slave trade as an "orphan." ... Some slaveholders showed concern for family groups when these situations arose, but the efforts of one North Carolinian seem feeble considering what had already transpired. Concerning the disposition of an estate, Thomas Turner wrote:

"I shall advertise to sell them separately, and then all together; with right reserved in myself to choose which set of bidders shall be the purchaser. I shall so advertise because in the first place the law will require that they be sold separately, and in the next place because I wish to sell them all to one person so as not to separate Mother & children; hoping that some person (yourself for instance,) will give one dollar more for the whole than the aggregate amount of the separate sales. —

The negroes are as follows — :

1 Hannah the mother aged about 36 to 40
2 Wilson a boy aged about 10 to 11
3 John a boy aged about 8 to 9
4 A girl aged 5 to 6
5 A girl aged 3 to 4
6 A girl aged 1 to 2

These negroes are healthy. Here are 5 of 11 children the woman has had; the other 6 having been sold; not one of whom ... is dead. They are also on the side of father and mother of excellent temper and character. The woman has had but one husband; he but one wife; they have always lived peaceably together, and were never separated until Decm. 1840."

Here was a case where a slave child one year old faced with the possibility of sale and separation from a family it would never know. But these crazy quilt separations are characteristic of estate divisions — children and parents scattered all over a county or a state.[179]

That letter was dated 1841, but the actions it implied were not new. Family separation resulting from estate division had a long history. An early illustration of the breakup of slave families by the death of their owner is found in the will and the inventory of the seventeenth-century Virginia planter William Fitzhugh. The will was dated 1701. Fitzhugh owned fifty-one slaves at the time of his death and divided them nearly equally among his wife and his four sons. Will and Black Peggy, together with a son, went to Fitz-

[179] Bobby Frank Jones, "A Cultural Middle Passage," pp. 189-193.

hugh's widow, but two other sons went separately to John and Henry Fitzhugh. Two of Mulatto Sarah's sons were given to John Fitzhugh, but she and her daughter went to George Fitzhugh. Hannah and a daughter went to Fitzhugh's widow, but Fitzhugh willed three other of Hannah's children to John Fitzhugh.[180]

Jones did not systematically examine local wills in particular slaveowning communities, but Clarence L. Mohr and Edwin W. Phifer did, and their separate studies neatly balance each other. Mohr examined Ogelthorpe County, Georgia, a staple-producing cotton county in which seven out of ten slaves were owned in units of twenty or more slaves. Phifer, on the other hand, studied Burke County in western North Carolina, a place where in 1860 only 60 of 921 slaveholding families owned ten or more slaves and where staple production was hardly known. Mohr says of the Georgia Black Belt slaveowners: "Available evidence indicates that most Ogelthorpe blacks were bought and sold on a purely pragmatic basis, with little or no regard for family ties. . . . The author bases this statement upon an examination of county will books for the antebellum period. While slaves were sometimes willed to a single individual or allowed to choose their new owners, they were most often treated simply as a portion of the chattel property in an estate and disposed of accordingly."[181]

Phifer analyzes three types of slave transfer: sale, hiring, and inheritance. "Slave sale or slave trading," he writes, " 'slave mongering,' has generally been considered the most odious of the three. Yet it is certainly altogether possible that often hiring or inheritance transfer created the greater hardship and grief for the slaves." Compared to land sales, Burke County slave sales were quite infrequent. Court records of deeds and bills of sale "reveal approximately twenty land transactions to every slave transaction." Phifer then adds: "Fragmentation of slave families was in fact inevitable, particularly in the transfer of slaves by inheritance. Wills were principally concerned with equitable distribution of property to rightful heirs, and administrators of estates were compelled by law to manage the affairs of the deceased in a manner which would produce the greatest revenue. Auction sales at the courthouse door — a necessary part of the institution — were unaffected by sentimental considerations. Individual slaves went to the highest bidder." Estate divisions that resulted directly or indirectly in the sale of slaves counted in any overall estimate of slave sales.[182]

[180] Richard B. Davis, ed., *William Fitzhugh and His Chesapeake World, 1676-1701* (1963), pp. 377-379, 382.

[181] Clarence L. Mohr, "Slavery in Ogelthorpe County, Georgia, 1773-1865," *Phylon,* 33 (Spring 1972), p. 12.

[182] Edwin W. Phifer, "Slavery in Microcosm: Burke County, North Carolina," *Journal of Southern History,* XXVIII (May 1962), pp. 137-160.

But estate divisions did not always result in sale. The absence of sale, however, did not mean the maintenance of the "integrity of the slave family." And in any estimates of involuntary slave family breakup, it is essential to consider the numbers of families broken up by inheritance but without sale being involved. "Transfer by inheritance," Phifer writes, "although of necessity usually impersonal, was sometimes relieved of its harshness by the provisions of testator, most of whom tried to see that a mother and her smaller children were kept together." After giving several such examples, Phifer significantly adds: "In a general way, it may be said that the small slaveholder more commonly made special provisions in his will for his slaves than did the large slaveholder with multiple heirs, whose will was usually more impersonal in order to make it more easily administered."[183] This last point is one of unusual importance. If further study shows that Phifer's distinction between large and small slaveholders holds up for other southern places, it needs to be underscored that after 1830 most slaves lived on large units of ownership, and that if ongoing plantations rarely sold slaves, as F + E suggest, slaves on such places felt the danger of family breakup much more regularly on the death of an owner than slaves owned in smaller numbers. The absence of laws of primogeniture and entail, moreover, may have meant that the more "democratic" the distribution of inheritance, the greater the danger to slave families involved in the death of a wealthy owner. Just how such divisions operated after the death of an owner is illustrated in a North Carolina will dated 1833 and cited by Jones:

> With the negroes sent the Executors are constrained to send the suckling infants with their mothers. ... These children are sent as still belonging to the Estate to be disposed of according to the Will. The Executors could do no better than to send them with their mothers or to retain their mothers which they have a right to do for two years, but they prefer to send the Children with their mothers and with the promise and assurance on our part that we will pay those of you who own their mothers for taking care of them until they can be taken away or weaned. ... If you will advert to the will you will see that Burton the Husband is given to D. Hawkins & Siller his wife is given to Mrs. Little. That Sillers Daughter Lucenda who was only 4 years old is given to Mary Jane Hawkins. That Edy the Mother is given to D. Hawkins and Edys small Daughters Martha & Phillis one 6 & the other 7 years old are given to Lucy Coleman & Matilda Hawkins. That Great Ben the only surviving parent is given to Mr. S. Haywood and his youngest child Sarah to Mrs. D. Haywood. That Jesses and Penny are given to me and their small Daughter Penny is given to Celestia Hawkins.

So wrote John Hawkins to William Polk in 1833.[184]

[183] *Ibid.*
[184] Printed in Jones, "A Cultural Middle Passage," pp. 192-193.

None of the slaves mentioned in the letter by John Hawkins would appear in any record of slave sales; neither would slaves given by parents to their children as gifts. Without using plantation records, Stampp and Jones both emphasized the importance of gift transfers on slave family structure and stability. "Affluent parents," said Stampp, "liked to give slaves to their children as presents." He cited a Virginia judge as saying, "With us, nothing is so usual as to advance children by gifts of slaves. They stand with us instead of money."[185] Jones puts it somewhat differently: "Evident among masters and slaves is a curious tendency to differentiate between sale and separation, but the slave family hardly benefited from either interpretation." A master "who would not part with a slave in the market would give one to his children as a wedding or Christmas gift." Jones went on: "Providing a slave [labor] force for a son or daughter who moved into another state to establish a new plantation, for example, divided slave families of several generations in every conceivable manner."[186]

Calderhead's Maryland Study and the So-called Stability of the Slave Family

We return finally to Calderhead's Maryland study to estimate roughly the number of slave sales per slave family. Calderhead examined the importance of Maryland slaveholders to the interstate slave trade and found significantly that all previous estimates — and especially those by Frederic Bancroft —

TABLE 31. SALES OF SLAVES, 1830-1840[187]

Maryland Counties	Number of Slaves	Total Sales	Slaves Sold	Total Sales per 100 Families	Total Slaves Sold per 100 Families
Anne Arundel	10,347	340	1,024	13	40
Prince Georges	11,585	361	1,249	12	43
Kent	3,191	241	480	30	60
Talbot	4,173	225	563	21	50
Harford	2,947	144	268	14	36
Carroll	1,122	135	265	48	95
Baltimore	10,653	390	915	15	34
Howard	2,862	155	273	22	38
Total	46,840	1,991	5,073	17	43

[185] Stampp, *Peculiar Institution*, p. 202.
[186] Jones, "A Cultural Middle Passage," p. 194.
[187] Calderhead, "Border State Slave Trade," pp. 42-55.

were far too high. He makes a good case for the need to revise those estimates, and significantly, too, in a downward direction. He found that of 46,840 slaves, 5,073 (10.8 percent) were sold, but that only 810 (1.7 percent) were sold South. The eight counties studied included two Eastern Shore counties (Kent and Talbot), two tobacco counties (Anne Arundel and Prince Georges), and four central Maryland counties (Baltimore, Carroll, Harford, and Howard). Calderhead failed to examine the effects of such sales on slave families, but they can be estimated crudely by assuming that the "average" slave family had in it four members. Table 31 adjusts the number of slaves to the number of slave families. There was no possible way for Maryland slaves living in families to have escaped from the realities related to the sale of slaves from families other than their own. It happened too frequently in all counties. F + E may respond that most slaves sold were neither husbands nor wives (or mothers or fathers). That was so; most were over fourteen and not yet thirty, the children of slave parents.

The Sale of Older Slave Children from Their Parents as a Neglected Measure of the "Stable" Slave Family

To suggest, as F + E do, that the sale of such persons occurred "at an age when it would have been normal for them to have left the family" not only senselessly cheapens the process by which slave families were involuntarily broken but reveals an ideological bias that has no place in the writing of history, even "cliometric history."[188] F + E's argument here, incidentally, is not original to them. Antebellum pro-slavery ideologues made the same point frequently. Chancellor Harper admitted that the slave was "liable to be separated from wife and child," adding "though not more frequently, that I am aware of, than the exigency of their condition compels the separation of families among the laboring poor elsewhere."[189] Robert Toombs made the same point slightly differently: "The accidents and necessities of life, the desire to better one's condition, produce infinitely a greater amount of separation in families of the white than ever happen to the colored race. This is true, even in the United States, where the general condition of the people is prosperous. The injustice and despotism of England towards Ireland has produced more separation of Irish families, and sundered more domestic ties within the last ten years than African slavery has effected since its introduction into the United States."[190] And the *Southern Literary*

[188] T/C, I, p. 5.
[189] *The Pro-Slavery Argument,* p. 48.
[190] Toombs 1856 speech printed in Alexander H. Stephens, *A Constitutional View of the Late War Between the States,* I (1868), p. 643.

Messenger insisted that "forced removal by sales of the slaves of the South, is nothing more than the application to them by the whites, of the great law of migration, which has governed and controlled the movements which have taken place among the populations of the earth from the beginning of time."[191] The poem "Slave Mother's Reply" responded to such specious arguments:

> Georgia's rice-fields show the care
> Of my boys who labor there;
> Alabama claims the three
> Last who nestled on my knee.[192]

There is no possible way to compare the decision by a white teenage youth to quit his Virginia or Maryland home for Georgia and Alabama to the sale of a black teenage youth from his Virginia or Maryland slave family. No historian has described the difference more precisely than Frederick Douglass:

The people of the North, and free people generally, I think, have less attachment to the places where they are born and brought up than had the slaves. Their freedom to come and go, to be here and there, as they list, prevents any extravagant attachment to any one place. On the other hand, the slave was a fixture, he had no choice, no goal, but was pegged down to one single spot, and must take root there or die. The idea of removal elsewhere came generally in the shape of a threat, and in punishment for crime. It was therefore attended with fear and dread. The enthusiasm which animates young freemen, when they contemplate a life in the far west, or in some distant country, where they expect to rise to wealth and distinction, could have no place in the thought of the slave; nor could those from whom they separated know anything of that cheerfulness with which friends and relations yield each other up, when they feel that it is for the good of the departing one that he is removed from his native place. Then, too, there is correspondence and the hope of reunion, but with the slaves, all these mitigating circumstances were wanting. There was no improvement in condition *probable* — no correspondence *possible* — no reunion attainable. His going out into the world was like a living man going into a tomb, who, with open eyes, sees himself buried out of sight and hearing of wife, children, and friends of kindred tie.[193]

It was as if Douglass was anticipating the nearly unspeakably trivializing proposition more than a century later that most slaves sold away "were at an age when it would have been normal for them to have left the family."

[191] "American Slavery in 1857," *Southern Literary Messenger*, XXV (1857), p. 87.
[192] "Slave Mother's Reply," *Boston Saturday Express*, n.d., reprinted in James Redpath, *The Roving Editor* (1859), pp. 44-45.
[193] Frederick Douglass, *Life and Times of Frederick Douglass* (1962), p. 97.

Douglass gave the reasons then why this kind of pseudo-comparative social history should not be taken seriously.

"Prudish" Slave Sexual Mores

A Confusing Single Measure (the Age of Slave Mothers at the Birth of a First Child or the Birth of a First Surviving Child)

In some cultures, steady and regular labor go along with sexual repression. There is even the suggestion that modernization is the child of a marriage between the Protestant work ethic and the idealization of female chastity. Slaveowners, according to F + E, had unusual success in converting the enslaved to their own standards of sexual and moral behavior. Ordinary slaves lived in stable nuclear families, waited until marriage before having sexual intercourse, and did not marry until they were either "twenty" (women) or "twenty-four" (men) years old. Rational profit maximizers did much more than transform Uncle Tom into Horatio Alger. They also created the conditions — if not the incentives — that made his wife and daughter into prudish women. The absence of any supporting evidence does not deter F + E from describing the owning class as imbued with Victorian beliefs. "Victorian attitudes," the reader learns, "predominated in the planting class. The emphasis on strong, stable [slave] families, and on the limitation of sexual activity to the family [*sic*], followed naturally from such attitudes."[194] Although F + E indicate in volume two that their "analysis of the demographic characteristics of the slave family and of the effects of slavery on family formation is still at a preliminary stage,"[195] they feel sufficiently confident to assert that their *preliminary* demographic findings suggest that the "prevailing sexual mores of slaves were not promiscuous but prudish."[196]

In a paper read just before T/C's publication, Fogel described these "data" in order to tout the utility of "counting": "I want to emphasize the dramatic change in interpretation that may result merely by moving from an impression to an actual count. I want to emphasize that counting is rarely an easy task in historical work. It was, for example, complex, costly, and time-consuming to obtain from archival sources a valid distribution of the ages of slave mothers at the birth of their first child. It required hundreds of man-hours of research and thousands of dollars. Yet this 'mere' act of counting yielded the discovery that half of all slave women were over 21

194 T/C, I, p. 129.
195 T/C, II, 114.
196 T/C, I, p. 138, italics added.

years of age at the birth of their first child — a fact which threw into doubt the entire structure of traditional assumptions about the sexual behavior of slaves."[197] "And the result of all this data," he explained to a Gannett syndicate newspaper reporter, "is an emerging picture of a noncontraceptive society structured around the family, with close knit ties, and Puritanical attitudes about pre-marital sex."[198] "Victorian" and "Puritanical" attitudes among the owners of slaves and the enslaved themselves? If true, these are indeed significant findings.[199]

But the quantitative evidence offered casts no doubt on "the entire structure of traditional assumptions about the sexual behavior of slaves." All of F + E's arguments about "Victorian," "Puritanical," or "prudish" slave sexual behavior rest upon a single set of grossly misunderstood data that have been generalized about in a surprisingly careless fashion. We leave aside their apparent assumption that the sole alternative to "promiscuous" sexual behavior is "prudish" sexual behavior. A whole range of sexual norms and behavior that fall between promiscuity and prudishness have escaped their attention.

We focus instead upon the historical sources used to establish the age at which the typical slave woman gave birth to a first child. Inattentive readers might assume that such information is available in T/C. It is not. Several reviewers have made just this mistake. *Time* readers, for example, learned that T/C revealed "the average age of black mothers at the time of the first-born child."[200] And readers of the Gannett press were told that F + E had "discovered that the average slave mother had her first child at age 22; that the percentage of slave women under age 15 was about the same as it is

---

[197] R. W. Fogel, "The Limits of Quantitative Methods in History," unpublished paper, Conference on Mathematics in the Social Sciences, Southern Illinois University, April 1974, p. 12. In the published version of that paper Fogel reports that probate records indicate only "the ages of slave mothers at the birth of the first surviving child." See R. W. Fogel, "The Limits of Quantitative Methods in History," *American Historical Review*, Vol. 80 (April 1975), p. 337. An improvement, this statement still is incorrect. A probate record gives the age of the oldest surviving child *in the household*. Older surviving children may have left the household. Fogel still insists that such a statistic casts doubt on "the entire structure of traditional assumptions about the sexual behavior of slaves." It does not.

[198] Hansen, "A New Picture of Slavery."

[199] In his interview with Furet and Ladurie, Fogel emphasized these same points (*Le Nouvel Observateur*, 9 September 1974). "[S]lave society," he said, "was rather prudish." A few sentences later, he adds: "So, from many different sources, demographic evidence is accumulating which indicates that there were strong 'Victorian' tendencies among the slaves, as far as sex is concerned. Perhaps the word 'Victorian' isn't all that well chosen, since it implies a lot of other things as well. But in the end, it seems to me to give a fair idea of what we're talking about in this context."

[200] Foote, review of T/C, *Time*, 17 June 1974, pp. 98-100.

in our society."[201] But F + E do not reveal the "average age" at which slave women had their first child. Instead, they report "the distribution of the ages of mothers at the time of the birth of their *first surviving child*."[202] There is a vast difference in the mid-nineteenth century between the age of a woman at the birth of her first child and the age of a woman at the birth of her first surviving child. And especially — as shall be seen — a slave mother. F + E, not their readers or reviewers, are themselves mostly responsible for blurring the difference between the two. In the written text they report "the distribution of the ages of mothers at the time of the birth of the first surviving child." But Figure 37, which illustrates this distribution, is entitled The Distribution of First Births, by the Ages of Slave Mothers.[203] And in the paper cited above, Fogel explained that F + E had obtained at great cost "a valid distribution of the ages of slave mothers at the birth of their first child," insisting that "half of all slave women were over 21 years of age at the birth of their first child." That is not what their data show.

The Essential Argument and the Essential Data in T/C

F + E's full argument is recorded below before the deathly defect in it is discussed. They write:

> An even more telling piece of information is the distribution of the ages of mothers at the time of the birth of their first surviving child. This distribution, which is shown in figure 37, contradicts the charge that black girls were frequently turned into mothers at such tender ages as twelve, thirteen, and fourteen. Not only was motherhood at age twelve virtually unknown, and motherhood in the early teens quite uncommon, but the average age at first birth was 22.5 (the median age was 20.8). Thus the high fertility rate of slave women was not the consequence of the wanton impregnation of very young unmarried women by either white or black men, but of the frequency of conception after the first birth. By far the great majority of slave children were borne by women who were not only quite mature, but who were already married.
>
> The high average age of mothers at first birth also suggests that slave parents closely guarded their daughters from sexual contact with men. For in a well-fed, noncontraceptive population in which women are quite fecund after marriage, only abstinence would explain the relative shortage of births in the late-teen ages. In other words, the demographic evidence suggests that the prevailing sexual mores of slaves were not promiscuous but prudish — the very reverse of the stereotype published by many in both the abolitionist and slave-holding camps and accepted in traditional historiography.[204]

[201] Hansen, "A New Picture of Slavery."
[202] T/C, I, p. 137, italics added.
[203] *Ibid.*, p. 138.
[204] *Ibid.*, pp. 137-138.

Age of Mothers	Distribution of First Births (est.)
Under 15	3%
15–19	37%
20–24	30%
25–29	15%
30–34	8%
35+	7%
N	Not given

The bar chart Figure 37 accompanies these assertions and is summarized in Table 32. F + E's entire argument about slave sexual behavior rests upon the age of slave mothers at the birth of a first surviving child. Surprisingly high average (22.5) and median (20.8) ages convinced them that "the prevailing sexual mores of slaves were. . . . prudish." That only 40 percent of "all first births took place before the mothers were [aged] twenty" further tells "that a significant degree of sexual abstinence among unmarried persons was probably a feature of slave behavior." Although additional data reported briefly in volume two indicate a somewhat younger "average age" for such women, that information does not cause F + E to correct the median and average ages reported so authoritatively in volume one. It merely puzzles them: "Data obtained from the plantation records indicates an average age of mothers at first birth which is approximately one year less than that indicated by the data in the larger sample from the probate records. We have not yet been able to determine whether this difference is due to some statistical artifact or whether it reflects a behavioral difference, such as a lower age at marriage on large plantations."[206] We leave aside F + E's accompanying assertion that "the average age of a [slave] woman at first marriage was 20 and . . . the average age of her groom was 24." Not a shred of evidence in T/C supports these two averages.[207] We consider just the evidence about

205 *Ibid.*, p. 138.

206 T/C, II, pp. 114-115.

207 Plantation records rarely, if ever, indicated the ages of slave husbands and wives at the time of a first marriage. When slaveowners recorded such unions (and that did not happen too frequently), they nearly always listed the names of the couple and the date of their marriage. The only way in which plantation records can be used to learn the age of slaves at marriage is to know the date of their birth. And that requires the study of plantation birth and death records over two or more generations. F + E have examined thirty sets of plantation records in seven states from the period "1800-1865," but there is no indication that these records were used to establish the ages of slaves at marriage. As pointed out earlier, it is not possible to get such data from either probate records or manuscript census schedules.

the "average" age of slave women at the birth of either a first or a "surviving" child. The "averages" — as shall be seen — are based upon a quite erroneous use of probate records and untenable inferences based upon these flawed data. The different "averages" found in the probate records and the plantation records have nothing at all to do with "behavioral difference[s]," and one is not a "statistical artifact." The difference results from a badly used source.

Contrary Literary and Quantitative Antebellum Evidence

Even if F + E used the probate records accurately in arriving at their averages, a vast amount of contemporary evidence — quantitative as well as literary — would nevertheless still contradict their "finding" and the inferences flowing from it. Their misinterpretation of the probate records is examined below, and some of the opposite evidence is reported here. The assertion that "a significant degree of sexual abstinence among unmarried persons was probably a feature of slave behavior" is examined first. F + E seem to argue that only the "racial" beliefs of biased southern and especially northern white contemporaries — beliefs which indeed assumed that promiscuity was rife among subordinate classes, blacks and slaves among these classes — account for the myth of slave "promiscuity." A good deal of evidence, of course, reveals the presence of such racial and class beliefs. But elite northern and southern white observers of slave sexual behavior also generally scorned prenuptial intercourse of all kinds, idealized (in theory if not always in practice) female chastity, and did not distinguish between prenuptial intercourse and promiscuity. Most could not realize that they were describing prenuptial intercourse among the enslaved. The historian of slave sexual behavior should not, however, reject such evidence out of hand. It can be fruitfully used, but only after the class and racial biases built into it have been discounted. F + E dismiss such evidence too easily. The value of such evidence is considered at much greater length in my forthcoming study of the Afro-American family and kinship system during and after enslavement.[208]

Here it is simply worth noting that the prevalence of slave prenuptial intercourse — in itself hardly evidence of promiscuity — among enslaved Afro-Americans was described by contemporaries other than biased southern

---

[208] These matters will be considered in detail in my forthcoming study in chapters two and ten.

and northern white observers.[209] In testimony before the American Freedmen's Inquiry Commission in 1863 and later ignored by the commission in its published reports, black witnesses did not hide such behavior from their Yankee questioners. Then about forty years old, Harry McMillan had been

[209] In his interview with Furet and Ladurie (*Le Nouvel Observateur*, 9 September 1974), Fogel insists that "the fact that, on average, the first baby did not 'arrive' until a woman was past the age of 20 indicates that there was a lot of pre-marital sexual abstinence." He adds: "In the 19th and 20th centuries, twenty-five percent of those white European women living in cities were already pregnant on the day of their marriage. Recently, (after our book had gone to press) a young economic historian calculated the pre-nuptial conception rate for slaves to be about ten percent. This rate is considerably lower than the twenty-five percent that we find in European cities. It's even lower than the prenuptial conception rate found in the Puritan communities of Massachusetts around 1850."

I leave to European social historians the "twenty-five percent" statistic and to specialists in New England social history the "prenuptial conception rate found in the Puritan [*sic*] communities of Massachusetts around 1850." But I have grave doubts concerning the "finding" that "the pre-nuptial conception rate for slaves... [was] about ten percent." Several reasons prompt that doubt. Such information as needed cannot come from manuscript census records or probate records. It can only possibly come from plantation birth registers. But these sources pose unusual difficulties for the student of pre-nuptial conception. Two can be listed here:

(1) *Most* plantation birth registers list *just* the name of the slave mother. How is it possible to determine whether a slave woman was pregnant prior to marriage when the register usually gives no more than the mother's name, the child's name, and the date of birth of the child?

(2) Even where the names of both slave parents are given in scattered plantation birth registers, the same documents do *not* record the date of marriage for these slaves. In my own work, I have studied with some care about a dozen of such registers. Not one tells the date of marriage!

Yet another kind of data greatly invalidates this "finding," and those data come from the *1900 federal manuscript census*. That is the first census in which women were asked to give the years they had been married and is, therefore, the *first census* which allows us to estimate carefully such matters of importance as prenuptial pregnancy and bridal pregnancy.

A small sample drawn from this census allows for a *preliminary* comparison between rural and urban southern blacks, poor rural southern whites, and immigrant Jews and Italians in New York City. The findings for *married women aged 20-29 in 1900* are given in Table 33.

These percentages (and especially in Issaquena County) include a number of stepchildren born in an earlier marriage and therefore must be used with care. I am indebted to Karen Kearns, a City University graduate student, for gathering them for me.

This is not the place to discuss the meaning of these data except as they bear on the unpublished study cited by Fogel. If that study is accurate, are we to believe that the "rate of prenuptial conception" was two to five times greater among the first generation of women born after emancipation than among their slave parents? That staggers the imagination.

TABLE 33. PERCENTAGE OF MARRIED WOMEN TWENTY TO TWENTY-NINE WITH A SURVIVING CHILD OLDER THAN THE MARRIAGE OR BORN THE YEAR OF THE MARRIAGE, 1900

Place	Type of Community and Women	Percentage of Married Women 20–29 with a Surviving Child Older Than the Marriage or Born the Year of the Marriage
New York City	Working Class Jewish Women	5.4%
New York City	Working Class Italian Women	7.5%
Jones County, Mississippi	Rural Poor Southern White Women	9.0%
Issaquena County, Mississippi	Rural Poor Southern Black Women	48.4%
St. Helena's Island, South Carolina	Rural Poor Southern Black Women	29.5%
Jackson Ward, Richmond, Va.	Urban Poor Southern Black Women	21.2%

born in Georgia but had grown up a Beaufort, South Carolina, slave. "Colored women," McMillan was asked, "have a great deal of sexual passion, have they not? They all go with men?" "Yes, sir," responded the slave, "there is a good deal of that. I do not think you will find four out of a hundred that do not; they begin at fifteen or sixteen." The better-known slave Robert Smalls, a black who had escaped dramatically from Charleston with his slave family and some friends by seizing a Confederate boat and who was still in his early twenties, did not differ from McMillan. "Have not colored women a good deal of sexual passion?" a commission member asked Smalls. "Yes, sir," he replied. Asked about "young women," Smalls added, "They are very wild and run around a good deal." "What proportion of the young women have sexual intercourse before marriage?" he was then asked. "The majority do," said Smalls, "but they do not consider this intercourse an evil thing." Smalls and McMillan, incidentally, were the only South Carolina slaves to testify before the commission.[210]

We need not rely solely on the testimony of these two former slaves to learn about prenuptial sexual intercourse among slaves. Plantation records examined by the author indicate that at least one out of five slave mothers had one or more children before settling into a monogamous slave union. Even though most white observers never understood it, most slaves found

[210] Testimony of Harry McMillan and Robert Smalls, American Freedmen's Inquiry Commission, Letters Received, Office of the Adjutant General, Main Series, Reel 200, file 3, National Archives.

prenuptial intercourse and even prenuptial pregnancy and childbirth compatible with subsequent monogamous marriage. F + E appear to believe that prenuptial intercourse followed by a settled union was either uncommon or evidence of moral weakness, and that, perhaps, is the reason they insist "that a significant degree of sexual abstinence among unmarried persons was probably a feature of slave society." Plainly, however, all such inferences rest on the median (20.8) and average (22.5) ages of slave mothers at the time of the birth of their first *surviving* child. But that age is far too old. Plantation records drawn from throughout the entire South and examined over two or more generations make this clear and are reported in Table 34. The age at which sexual intercourse began must have been earlier than 18 or 19 unless one wants to argue that pregnancy and live birth followed immediately after intercourse began at age 17, 18, or 19. More than this, a median masks much about a particular distribution. On the South Carolina Good Hope Plantation, for example, only two women were older than 25 at the birth of a first child. Two others were not yet 15. On the Cameron plantation, one of the twenty-four women was 14 and eleven others were either 16 or 17. Four women were between 24 and 31. The median age at birth of first child among the Cameron slave women was 18.9, but the average age was 17 years. Confirming data exist among other plantation women. A birth register covering the years between 1802 and 1860 of the St. Helena's Island, South Carolina, Fripp plantation, shows that for ten women, five had a child at the age of 19 and two at the age of 20. The other three were aged 15, 16, and 17. The median age for these few women was 18.3, and the average age was about 19, but nearly one-third of them had a first child before their 18th birthday. Records also exist for a dozen slave women on the Virginia Cedar Vale Plantation (1826–1862), and two out of three among them were between 17 and 19 years old at the birth of a first child.[211]

TABLE 34. MEDIAN AGE OF SLAVE WOMEN AT THE BIRTH OF A FIRST CHILD

Name of Plantation	Location	Approximate Years Covered	Number of Women	Median Age
Cameron	North Carolina	1776-1841	24	18.9
Good Hope	South Carolina	1797-1856	31	18–19
Stirling	Louisiana	1828-1865	49	18.7
Watson	Alabama	1843-1865	32	19

[211] Except for the Fripp plantation records, the data summarized in this paragraph are drawn from my forthcoming study, chapters two and three. The Fripp information comes from G. G. Johnson, *Social History of the Sea Islands* (1930), p. 103.

Evidence Indicating the Age of Southern Black Mothers
at the Birth of a First Surviving Child in 1880

What these scattered plantation birth records indicate — and not what F + E report from the probate records — is reinforced by masses of data gathered from the 1880 federal manuscript census for southern rural and urban black women and northern urban predominantly workingclass immigrant and native-born white women. That information, together with the F + E slave data, is printed below, and the differences between the two are vast. (We need, incidentally, to correct the error in how F + E describe their data. Theirs is not a "distribution of the ages of mothers at the time of birth of their first surviving child," but rather a distribution of the ages of mothers at the time of the birth of their first surviving child still living with its mother.) The comparative data are given in Table 35.[212]

TABLE 35. AGE OF BLACK AND WHITE WOMEN UNDER THIRTY AT THE BIRTH OF A FIRST SURVIVING CHILD STILL LIVING IN THE HOUSEHOLD, 1880

Place	Percentage under 15	15–19	20 and Older
St. Helena's Island and Township, S.C.	9%	51%	40%
Lane's Schoolhouse, Miss.	13%	53%	34%
Beaufort, S.C.	11%	50%	39%
Natchez, Miss.	11%	54%	35%
Mobile, Ala., Wards 7 and 8	10%	54%	36%
Richmond, Va., Jackson, Marshall Wards	8%	40%	52%
(F + E Slave Data, undated	3%	37%	60%)

	Mean Age	Median Age
St. Helena's Island and Township	18.6	19.4
Lane's Schoolhouse	18.0	19.3
Beaufort	18.9	19.2
Natchez	18.5	18.9
Mobile, Wards 7 and 8	18.2	18.9
Richmond, Jackson, Marshall Wards	19.7	20.2
(F + E Slave Data, undated	22.5	20.5)
Paterson, New Jersey, Whites		
Irish	21.5	21.9
German	21.4	21.9
British	21.3	21.6
Native White	19.8	20.4

[212] These data are dealt with more fully in my forthcoming study, chapter nine.

There is much to notice in these data. For one thing, and without taking into account probable higher infant mortality rates among southern blacks, the mean age of southern urban and rural black women at the birth of a first surviving child was significantly lower than it was among northern urban workingclass and immigrant women in 1880. (F + E never compare their findings to nonslave women.) Just as significantly, the mean ages of both rural and urban black mothers at the birth of a first surviving child was much lower in all places except the Richmond wards than the age reported by F + E for slave women. Four or so years is not an insignificant difference. Nor is the "fact" trivial that only 40 percent of the slave women F + E studied had a first surviving child by age twenty as compared to the fact that in all places, again excepting the Richmond wards, the percentage ranged from 60 to 64 percent. And, finally, F + E fix the percentage of slave females having a surviving first child when not yet fifteen years old at 3 percent, insisting that "motherhood in the early teens" was "quite uncommon" among slave females. The comparable percentage in the black communities studied in 1880, including the Richmond wards, ranged from 8 to 13 percent. These, too, are not slight differences. And that about one in ten women in 1880 had a first surviving child before her fifteenth birthday is a fact of some social importance, not a "quite uncommon" statistic. Such percentages were far higher in 1880 than among any "comparable" group of northern or southern white women. And that makes them very important.

An Absurd "Explanation" Linking the Data in T/C
with the Data in the 1880 Census

The 1880 data are much more consistent with the ages of mothers at the birth of a first child (recorded in diverse plantation birth registers) than with their age at the birth of a first surviving child (indicated in the probate records examined by F + E). The same data, moreover, are quite consistent with the 1864 observation by Moncure D. Conway (the son of a Virginia slaveholder who became a fierce critic of slavery) that under slavery "the period of maternity is hastened, the average youth of negro mothers being nearly three years earlier than that of any free race."[213] It is possible, of course, to dismiss these plantation birth registers together with Conway's remarks and to reconcile F + E's probate record "findings" with the ages reported by black women in the 1880 federal census. But that involves arguments that F + E surely can not accept and which would run as follows: Before emancipation, very few slave women (about 3 percent) had a first child before their fifteenth birthday. But right after emancipation

[213] Conway, *Testimonies Concerning Slavery*, p. 20.

that percentage increased three or four times. Only two in five slave mothers had a child before their twentieth birthday. That percentage increased after emancipation, too, ranging in most places from three in five to two in three. Quite clearly, the age at which slave females had a first child dropped significantly after 1865, falling rapidly from 22.5 to 18 (or 19). This drop is known by examining the age of the oldest surviving child in southern rural and urban black households where mothers were not yet thirty years old in 1880. The oldest among these women was born in 1850 and was fifteen years old at the time of the general emancipation. Put simply, if the 1880 data and the data drawn from slave probate records are both accurate, one of the great social consequences of emancipation was a significant drop in the age at which black women first had intercourse and then had a first child. For so significant a change in sexual behavior to have occurred in less than a generation is highly improbable unless one is prepared to argue — as F + E surely would not — that emancipation removed the sexual restraints imposed by their owners upon the enslaved. If it happened that way so *quickly*, it would also mean that slaveowners had successfully managed to repress "black" sexual "drives" but had not changed or altered them. Instead, they reemerged quickly upon emancipation.

Such inferences, of course, belong more properly to earlier generations of racially biased historians and social scientists who saw in the behavior of emancipated blacks little more than the unleashing of pent-up Afro-American sexual "drives," "instincts," or what have you. They have no place as explanatory devices in modern historical scholarship. (Such inferences suggest, furthermore, that children born slaves also rejected the sexual practices and beliefs of their slave parents at the first available opportunity: that is, upon their emancipation. That, too, is highly improbable.) A clever historian may yet seize upon such comparative data and write sparkling essays entitled "The Sexual Rebellion of the Children of Enslaved Afro-Americans" or "Emancipation as a Sexual Revolution among Enslaved Afro-Americans." But before these are attempted, it is essential that we have a much more accurate measure of the age of slave mothers at the birth of their first child, not their first surviving child.

The Key Error in T/C, or the Misuse of the Probate Records

No such speculations are really necessary. And the reason is quite simple. F + E have misinterpreted the probate records by failing to correct for the obvious upward bias in a probate record which lists the age of a slave mother and that of the oldest child living with her (*not* surviving) at the time of her owner's death. The magnitude of the error can be illustrated easily, and with that illustration F + E's argument about "prudish" slave sexual mores just collapses. The argument, we recollect, is based primarily on the age slave women had a first child. Put simply, a probate record (like a census enumeration) offers the historian no clue whether the oldest child in a household (or family) was the first-born. Our illustration follows.

A slaveowner named Smith died in 1850. The probate record revealed that he owned three adult female slaves. Mahala, then a forty-year-old slave, had three children. The first was stillborn in 1830. The second — born in 1832 — was sold in 1848. A third child was born in 1835 and still lived with her mother. According to F + E, Mahala was twenty-five when her first surviving child was born. When her first child was born, she was actually twenty years old. The second adult woman, Fanny, was born in 1805. Two children were born to her, the first in 1824 and the second in 1826. By 1850 both had married and lived in households of their own. A probate record would have listed them in separate households. F + E would have counted Fanny as a childless woman. She actually had become a mother at the age of nineteen. The third adult woman, Tenah, was born in 1823. She had children in 1840, 1842, 1846, and 1848. Her first two children died in infancy. The third was given to her owner's daughter as a gift on that young woman's marriage, and the fourth still lived with her mother in 1850. According to F + E, Tenah was twenty-five at the birth of her first surviving child. When her first child was born, Tenah was actually seventeen years old. The probate record revealed a childless woman and two other women each twenty-five years old at the birth of their oldest "surviving" child. Their median and average age, therefore, would be recorded as "twenty-five." In fact, these women had been seventeen, nineteen, and twenty years of age at the time a first child was born to them. F + E take none of these real social facts — a stillborn child, the death of an infant child, the sale or gift of a teenage child, and the grown slave child setting up a separate household — into account in using probate records. The older a child (and especially a slave child, given that most slaves sold were older teenagers and in their twenties), the greater the probable spread between the age of the first-born child and the age of the oldest child living in the household at the time the probate record was filed. That spread would be even greater if the probate sample included a large number of slave mothers aged thirty-five and older.

These illustrations are not far-fetched, and that is seen by examining the behavior of slave women on Lewis Stirling's large West Feliciana, Louisiana, sugar plantation. The median age of mothers who had a first child before 1850 was 18.7 years. The Stirling plantation records listed deaths as well as births. If we take infant deaths into account and assume that the birth of of a child removed its mother from her family of origin, the median age based upon the oldest child in the household rises from 18.7 to 20.6, an increase of just short of two years. The median age 20.6 is a false statistic and tells nothing about slave "sexual mores." So, too, are F + E's "average" and "median" ages of 22.5 and 20.8. Since this evidence serves as the essential data for F + E's inferences concerning "prudish" sexual behavior, that argument needs to be wholly put aside. It is based upon quantitative evidence that has not been used carefully.[214]

[214] Nowhere in T/C do F + E indicate the number of individual probates sampled in their study. In their listing of "Major Bodies of Data Collected by Cliometricians" (T/C, II, pp. 24-25), it is noted that the probate records include observations on "approximately 80,000 slaves from 54 counties in 8 southern states." But the sample size used is never indicated. In examining the occupations of male slaves, those data came from "a sample of 33 estates, ranging in size from 3 to 98 slaves, retrieved from the probate records" (ibid., p. 37). If the same sample was used in figuring the age of women at the birth of the oldest surviving child in the household and the average estate studied had fifty slaves, 25 percent of whom were females aged fifteen and older, about 412 women were studied. But not all of those women lived with their children. Some were single women, others childless older married women, others young married women not yet mothers, and still others older daughters living with one or both parents. When such women are excluded, the sample size shrinks significantly.

Yet another set of "data" dealing with slave sexual behavior needs to be put aside. F + E write: "That marriage altered the sexual behavior of slaves is clearly indicated by the difference between the seasonal pattern of first births and that of second and subsequent births. Data culled from plantation records indicate that for second and subsequent births, roughly equal percentages of infants were born during every quarter of the year. But the seasonal pattern of first births shows a definite peak during the last quarter of the year — precisely the pattern to be expected in an agrarian society in which a large proportion of marriages took place soon after the harvest. Over twice as many first births took place during the last quarter of the year — roughly nine to thirteen months after the end of the harvest, depending on the region and crop — as took place during the first quarter of the year. This pattern cannot be attributed merely to the fact that slaves had more leisure time during the winter interstice, and hence, more opportunity for sexual intercourse. If that was all that had been involved, the peaking of births during the last quarter of the year would have occurred not only for first children but for subsequent children as well" (T/C, I, p. 139). F + E do not report the number of observations on which these inferences are based. Nor do they give the names of the plantations studied. But the pattern they describe did not exist on the two large plantations I examined for this purpose: the North Carolina Cameron plantation (1776-1829) and the South Carolina Good Hope plantation (1790-1857). Nearly 100 first births were recorded on these two plantations: 55 on the Cameron place and 40 on the Good Hope place. "A definite peak" in first births did not occur on either place. About one in four (27 percent) of Cameron first births occurred between October and December and about one in three Good Hope births. More Cameron first children were born between April and June than between October and December. F + E, moreover, present no evidence at all that slave marriages commonly ("a large proportion") "took place soon after the harvest."

F + E's Findings

Even a subject seemingly as unimportant as the age spread between slave husbands and their wives raises serious doubts about the validity of the data used by F + E. Their assertion that a narrow age spread separated slave wives and husbands is wrong. A bar chart (Figure 39) accompanies the following paragraph: "Also fallacious is the contention that slave marriages, since they were arbitrarily dictated by masters, frequently produced odd age combinations — young men married to old women and vice versa. Figure 39 shows that most marriages were contracted among partners quite close in age. The average age difference between husband and wife was just three years. In almost all cases, the man was the same age or older than the woman. Reversals in this pattern were quite uncommon."[215] Figure 39 reads as shown in Table 36.

There is much difficulty with this chart and its percentages. The number of slave marriages examined is not stated. We are not told whether these marriages involved rural or urban slaves, Upper or Lower South slaves, farm or plantation slaves, and so forth. The ages of marital partners are not revealed. Finally, and most importantly, no source is cited for these data. They could not have come from manuscript census schedules, and hardly any plantation owners recorded slave marriages, much less the ages of marital partners, in their business records. The information must come from probate records, and if that is so it is incorrect to report that "Figure 39 shows that most marriages were contracted among partners quite close in age." Probate records tell the age of marital partners at the time of an

TABLE 36. DISTRIBUTION OF AGE DIFFERENCES BETWEEN SLAVE HUSBANDS AND WIVES[216]

Husband's Age Minus Wife's Age	Estimated Percentage
Less than −3	2%
−1 to −3	6%
0	12%
1-3	44%
4-6	19%
Over 6	17%
Total Marriages	Not given

[215] T/C, I, p. 139.
[216] Ibid., p. 140.

owner's death, not when a slave marriage was first consummated. Probate records tell nothing about the length of slave marriages and possible remarriages before an owner's death. Probate records, moreover, are sources which mainly record the ages of older, not younger, slaves and, therefore, are not characteristic of the entire slave population.

Conflicting Evidence

Other data that give the ages of slave husbands and wives soon after their emancipation (1864 to 1866) and in 1880 make it clear that F + E's finding does not describe the typical slave marriage.[217] Slave husbands were often a good many years older than their wives. A summary of those data follows:

(1) The 1864-1865 Mississippi and Louisiana military marriage registers included information elicited from 18,904 slave men and women marrying for the first time or validating with the military clergy a settled slave marriage. All but a handful had been slaves. In the Davis Bend, Natchez, and Vicksburg marriage registers, between 20.5 percent (the husbands of wives at least fifty years old) and 39 percent (the husbands of wives aged 30 to 39) of all men registering marriages were at least ten years older than their wives.

(2) A significant percentage of the husbands listed in the Montgomery County (1866) and York County (1865), Virginia, military population censuses also were much older than their wives. In slightly more than three in ten Montgomery County black marriages, the husband was at least ten years

TABLE 37. DISTRIBUTION OF AGE DIFFERENCES BETWEEN BLACK HUSBANDS AND WIVES, LOUISA COUNTY, VIRGINIA, 1866

| Age of Wife | Years Husband Is Older than Wife | | | |
	Under 5	5 to 9	10 and Over	Number
15–19	29%	45%	26%	58
20–29	44%	23%	33%	427
30–39	38%	23%	39%	346
40–49	42%	25%	33%	198
50–59	52%	16%	32%	114
60+	76%	4%	20%	51
Number	519	273	402	1,194
Percentage	43%	23%	34%	

[217] The 1864-1866 data are drawn from my forthcoming study (chapter eight) and are based upon unpublished Mississippi and Virginia Freedmen's Bureau records, Record Group 5, National Archives.

older than his wife. Black York County couples revealed an even greater percentage of marriages with that large an age spread.

(3) A similar pattern is found in the 1866 Goochland County and Louisa County, Virginia, marriage registers. Depending upon the age of the Goochland County wife, the percentage of husbands at least ten years older than their wives ranged from 30 percent to 42 percent. The pattern did not differ among Louisa County slave couples, as revealed in Table 37.

Why the Age Differences between Slave Spouses Reported in T/C Cannot Be Accurate

These three sets of data — one describing Mississippi and Louisiana blacks and the other two Virginia blacks — raise grave doubts about the value of probate records as a source for demographic data about enslaved Afro-Americans. The ages in these three sets of data were given by the former slaves themselves. The consistency with which Upper and Lower South blacks reported an age difference between a husband and wife indicates that these freshly emancipated slaves had a fairly good idea of their general ages. F + E report that no more than 17 percent of slave husbands were more than six years older than their wives. But Louisa County blacks themselves — as well as blacks in the other places studied — reported that three times as many marriages involved men at least five years older than their wives. What explains this discrepancy? No fewer than 23,000 black husbands and wives gave their ages in these diverse population censuses and marriage registers and reported a consistent pattern. If these blacks reported accurately, it appears that probate records are not an accurate source for gauging the ages of slave men and women. Slaves did not give their ages to those who prepared probate documents. That information was given by owning whites and apparently was not recorded accurately. That is one possible explanation for the discrepancy.

But suppose the age spread reported by F + E is as accurate as the 1864-1866 ages of partners in 11,500 former slave marriages? That would have to mean that large numbers of older male slaves discarded their wives soon after emancipation to marry younger women. It would also mean in these places (except York and Montgomery counties) that these same couples then voluntarily registered their new marriages with military missionaries or Freedmen's Bureau officers. Some men doubtless took new wives — even much younger ones — after emancipation. But that had to happen frequently and in a very short period of time in order to connect the Virginia and Mississippi-Louisiana data with the percentages reported in Figure 39 (Table 36). No evidence of any kind suggests a pattern of massive remarriage among the newly emancipated slaves. And it is unthinkable to suggest that men who dumped slave wives for younger women would then have rushed to celebrate their new marriages before a Yankee missionary or a bureau officer. We need not speculate about these matters. In Rockbridge County, Virginia, for example, 227 men and women at least forty years old registered marriages with the Freedmen's Bureau. That happened in 1866, and only 7 of these persons had been married for less than two years. Two out of three had lived with the same spouse between ten and nineteen years and an additional one in four (23 percent) at least twenty years. F + E's "sample" cannot be correct. Figure 39 needs to be put aside. And we should worry greatly about the value of probate records as accurate sources for describing demographic patterns among enslaved Afro-Americans.

Additional data indicate that F + E have been misled by their data, and they come from the pages of the 1880 federal manuscript census.[218] Six different southern Afro-American communities have been studied, and I record in Table 38 the age difference between black husbands and wives recorded there. The difference is indicated only for marriages in which the wife was at least thirty years old, that is, was born no later than 1850. Most of these 4,446 women had married prior to emancipation, and what they and their spouses reported casts additional doubt on Figure 39 unless we are prepared to argue that emancipation caused a sharp and immediate break with conventional Afro-American slave marital practices. But that would mean that slaveowners had repressed the "natural" (or "social")

TABLE 38. AGE DIFFERENCES BETWEEN HUSBANDS AND WIVES, ALL WIVES AGED THIRTY AND OLDER, 1880

	Women Aged 30 to 49		Women Aged 50 and Older	
Place	Number	Percentage, Husband 5 Years Older Than Wife	Number	Percentage, Husband 5 Years Older Than Wife
St. Helena's Island, S.C.	321	63%	114	58%
Rural Adams Co., Miss.	964	64%	448	50%
Beaufort, S.C.	133	58%	34	53%
Natchez, Miss.	215	48%	112	44%
Richmond, Va. (Jackson and Marshall Wards)	977	57%	256	58%
Mobile, Ala. (Wards 6 and 7)	705	60%	167	44%

[218] These data draw from my forthcoming study, chapter nine.

desire among many black males to marry younger women, a "desire" that fully revealed itself after emancipation in 1864-1866 and became a "pattern" by 1880. That would carry us back again to the kind of fantastical early-twentieth-century Reconstruction "histories" written by biased scholars like Walter Fleming. And, as F + E surely would agree, that is not a route worth traveling. The existence of a significant number of marriages between older men and younger women, incidentally, is not evidence that such marriages had been "arbitrarily dictated by masters." Too little is yet known to explain that difference by this or other reasons. It is clear, however, that a difference existed and carried over into the early decades following emancipation. The relatively high percentage of older men marrying younger women, furthermore, is not found among whites. Questions remain for the student of Afro-American social history. What in their experiences as enslaved Afro-Americans caused so large a number of men to marry younger women? Why did this pattern continue after emancipation? Why did slave and then free black women conform to such a pattern? And how did this pattern affect premarital sexual behavior among slaves and then among emancipated southern blacks?

SLAVE PROSTITUTION

The Conventional View of Southern Prostitution

F + E's idealization of southern white and especially black sexual behavior affects the way in which antebellum southern white and black — as well as slave and free — prostitution is examined. A different error is committed in dealing with this subject: the creation of a non-fact serves as the basis for a totally fanciful discussion of white and black sexual behavior. Not much is known about prostitution in the antebellum South. Nevertheless, it has often been assumed that the relatively easy sexual access to slave women by white men put southern white women on a sort of sexual pedestal. Abolitionist propaganda fed that belief, but it had its roots in the classical pro-slavery argument.[219] Chancellor Harper, for example, denied that free white prostitutes had a place in southern society: "With general truth, it might be said, that there are none. . . . Our brothels, comparatively very few — and these should not be permitted to exist at all — are filled, for the most part, by importations from the cities of our confederate States, where Slavery

[219] See James Redpath, The Roving Editor, p. 263, in which this extreme abolitionist denied that "black prostitution prevents white harlotry." "There are as many, or more, public courtesans of the dominant race in the Southern cities I have visited," said Redpath, "than in Northern towns of similar population. Slavery prevents no old evils, but breeds a host of new ones."

does not exist. . . . Never, but in a single instance, have I heard of an imputation on the general purity of manners, among the free females of the slave-holding States. . . . [C]an it be doubted, that this purity is caused by, and is a compensation for, the evils resulting from the existence of an enslaved class of more relaxed morals?" William Gilmore Simms agreed. "The fact is," said Simms, "that, in the Southern States, the prostitutes of the communities are usually slaves, unless when imported from the free States. The negro and colored woman, in the South, supply the place which, at the North, is usually filled with factory and with serving girls."

Neither Simms nor Harper defended prostitution, but, as the novelist Simms put it, the prevalence of black (or slave) prostitution did not "debase the civilized, as is the case with prostitution at the North."[220] Harper and Simms were not ordinary southern whites. They were unusually intelligent men, and their observations once more reveal how ideology so often blinds men of learning. The antebellum white South had its prostitutes, and from what little is known they were not northern or foreign-born women. That much is learned from a single source — the 1860 federal manuscript census of population for Nashville, Tennessee. It listed the occupations of white and black *free* Nashville women, including prostitutes.

F + E's Study of the Nashville Prostitutes

First examined in a brief descriptive article by David Kaser, inappropriately entitled "Nashville's Women of Pleasure in 1860," the Nashville data are greatly abused by F + E. They write:

> Nor should one underestimate the effect of racism on the demand of white males for black sexual partners. While some white men might have been tempted by the myth of black sexuality, a myth that may be stronger today than it was in the antebellum South, it is likely that far larger numbers were put off by racist aversions. Data on prostitution supports this conjecture. Nashville is the only southern city for which a count of prostitutes is available. The 1860 census showed that just 4.3 percent of the prostitutes in that city were Negroes, although a fifth of the population of Nashville was Negro. Moreover, all of the Negro prostitutes were free and light-skinned. There were no pure blacks who were prostitutes; nor were any slaves prostitutes. The substantial underrepresentation of Negroes, as well as the complete absence of dark-skinned Negroes, indicates that white men who desired illicit sex had a strong preference for white women.
>
> The failure of Nashville's brothels to employ slave women is of special interest. For it indicates that supply as well as demand considerations served to limit the use of slaves as prostitutes. The census revealed that half of

[220] *The Pro-Slavery Argument,* pp. 43-44, 230.

Nashville's prostitutes were illiterate — not functionally illiterate, but completely lacking in either the capacity to read, or to write, or both. In other words, the supply of prostitutes was drawn from poor, uneducated girls who could only command the wages of unskilled labor. Given such a supply, a slaveholder did not have to be imbued with Victorian morals [sic] to demur from sending his chattel into prostitution. He could clearly earn more on his slave women by working them in the fields where they would not be subject to the high morbidity and mortality rates which accompany the "world's oldest profession."[221]

The Nashville data make it clear that Harper and Simms were wrong. The census pages listed 207 Nashville prostitutes, of which nine were free mulattoes and the rest white women. Among the white women, three out of five were born in Tennessee (113), Kentucky, or Alabama. Just 4 were foreign-born. Their mean age was twenty-three. Overall — and this is a startling statistic which does much to demolish the "pedestal" theory as applied to urban white southern women — these 198 self-identified white Nashville prostitutes accounted for about 7 percent of all white Nashville women aged fifteen to thirty-nine in 1860.[222] Such a percentage — one out of fourteen white women — does much more than lay to rest the pedestal theory. It makes it quite clear, as F + E correctly argue, that some white men "who desired illicit sex had a strong preference for white women," strong enough, at least, to explain why so relatively large a percentage of Nashville white women not yet forty years old labored as prostitutes. Nashville, incidentally, was not unusual, and F + E are wrong to write that "Nashville is the only southern city for which a count of prostitutes is available." The Milledgeville, Georgia, 1828 town census used first by U. B. Phillips and reprinted in the 1968 edition of Phillips' essays edited by Eugene D. Genovese listed 346 white females of all ages, 15 among them prostitutes.[223] That means that

[221] T/C, I, pp. 134-135. See also David Kaser, "Nashville's Women of Pleasure in 1860," *Tennessee Historical Quarterly*, XXIII (December 1964), pp. 379-382.

[222] The published 1860 census does not break down the Nashville population by age and sex, so the number of white women fifteen to thirty-nine is estimated from the overall Davidson County age and sex structure. The estimate, therefore, is a crude one. It does not, moreover, take into account the class status of white Nashville women. The percentage of white prostitutes as a percentage of the white lower-class female population must have been greater than 7 percent.

[223] U. B. Phillips, *The Slave Economy of the Old South*, ed. E. D. Genovese (1968), pp. 178-179. Phillips insisted that the town also had "a considerable number of occasional prostitutes among the negroes and mulattoes" but that "police regulations" prevented nonwhites from being "openly professional." If true, that is an unusual way to sanction publicly a sexual racial preference. Phillips offered no evidence. The Milledgeville percentage is a crude one and is derived as follows: it is assumed that the town's 346 females divided by age in the same way as its males, for whom a rough age breakdown was recorded.

between 10 and 14 percent of all Milledgeville white women at least nineteen years old were prostitutes. There is yet much — very much — to learn about antebellum southern white women.

But if F + E are correct in suggesting that the presence of white prostitutes in Nashville (and Milledgeville and surely other southern towns and cities)[224] is evidence that some white males willingly paid a price for white sexual partners, they are quite wrong in all their other conjectures from these data. The fact that the census listed only nine free Negro prostitutes is hardly convincing evidence about the relationship between color preference and sexual behavior. F + E do not tell us the number of free colored women in Nashville in 1860 and the percentage among these women who were "mulattoes" as contrasted to "blacks." Suppose that only fifty free colored women lived in Nashville that year and nine were prostitutes. That is not an insignificant percentage. And suppose, furthermore, that in Nashville as in many other antebellum southern cities most free colored women were mulattoes, not blacks. Then the fact that the census failed to list a single free "pure black . . . prostitute" is meaningless evidence of white male sexual color preference. We first need such data.

The "Absent" Slave Prostitute, or How to Create a Non-Fact

These are mere quibbles. A much more serious error occurs in F + E's use of the Nashville 1860 census data. It is summed up in their phrase "nor were any slaves prostitutes" and in their sentence "the failure of Nashville's brothels to employ slave women is of special interest." It cannot be learned from the 1860 manuscript census whether any slave women labored as prostitutes. The reason is simple: the 1860 census failed to record the occupations of all slave men and women. That is a central weakness in this quantitative source, and it is surprising that F + E failed to take it into account in their speculations. In volume two of T/C, an elegant economic analysis explains why there were no Nashville slave prostitutes.[225] This impressive theoretical display of econometric skills is entirely fanciful because it rests upon a non-fact. F + E seek to explain "the failure of Nashville slaveowners to supply slaves as prostitutes" without supplying evidence that

[224] See, for example, Guion G. Johnson, *Antebellum North Carolina: A Social History* (1937), pp. 215-216, 221. "There is ample evidence to show that all of the largest towns in the State had their 'lewd houses,' and it is reasonable to assume that most of the smaller town did also." "Strolling prostitutes" also were "always present at any large gatherings" such as "public celebrations, the musters, the fairs, and the courts." "It is significant," Johnson added, "that many of these prostitutes were white women." "Race mixing," she said, was not uncommon, but its "extent has often been exaggerated."

[225] T/C, II, pp. 113-114.

Nashville slaveowners failed to supply slaves as prostitutes. The same logic on which this non-fact rests should cause them to write that not a single Nashville slaveholder owned slave washerwomen, domestic servants, carpenters, blacksmiths, and so forth. No one would take seriously the assertion that Nashville slaves did not labor as either house servants or carpenters. And the reason is simple. The failure of the 1860 census to list any slave occupations is not evidence the slaves were without occupations, prostitution among them. It only means that the manuscript census tells nothing about slave occupations. It is, therefore, fanciful to argue that a slaveholder could "clearly earn more on his slave women by working them in the fields" than in "the 'world's oldest profession.'" (Incidentally, the slave women belonging to Nashville whites surely did not labor "in the fields." Most would have worked as domestics and washerwomen.) Slave prostitution and its relationship to white and free colored prostitution are subjects that deserve careful study, but these subjects will not be illuminated by theorizing with non-facts.

Another point about the Nashville census that needs to be made relates to the conjecture that "while some white men might have been tempted by the myth of black sexuality, a myth that may be stronger today than it was in the antebellum South, it is likely that far larger numbers were put off by racist aversions." That conjecture makes far too much of racial beliefs and far too little of social and sexual dominance. Prostitution is just one measure of the sexual contacts between free white men and enslaved black women. F + E pay no attention to the other varieties of "non-pecuniary" sexual ties between such persons, contacts that had much less to do with "racist assumptions" than with the sexual dominance inherent in ownership. We need only to examine the subtle conclusions on this subject by Edward H. Phifer in his study of Burke County, North Carolina, slavery. He examined that county with some care and found much more complex patterns of sexual interracial and interstatus contacts than can be subsumed by mere racial beliefs. Phifer wrote:

> In Burke County a general pattern is discernable. If a bachelor entered into an intimate relationship with a female slave and raised a family by her, but never became promiscuous, the situation did not become a topic of polite conversation it is true, yet there is very little evidence that he was censured for his conduct or that he lost status in the community. Again, if a young boy of a slaveholding family had a child by a female slave, later married and engaged in no further indiscretions, the incident was usually considered lightly and quickly forgotten. But the married slave holder who promiscuously or openly consorted with his slaves became a social outcast, and he was never forgiven nor his actions forgotten so long as his name was remembered.[226]

[226] Phifer, "Slavery in Microcosm," pp. 137-160.

Burke County was not a staple-producing county, and it will be interesting to learn after further study whether the patterns suggested by Phifer applied to staple-producing counties, much less to towns and cities. Phifer himself, of course, examined these patterns from the perspective of the slaveholding and nonslaveholding white communities. He did not — in his otherwise useful study — suggest how the enslaved themselves dealt with and interpreted such diverse sexual ties with white males. That, too, is a subject that badly needs to be studied, but it will not get too far if we start off with such dicta as "it is likely that far larger numbers [of whites] were put off by racist aversions." The three patterns described by Phifer depended for their success first upon the dominance inherent in all master-slave relationships, not upon "the myth of black sexuality." All three were shaped by the relative social powerlessness of enslaved black women, not by one or another racial belief. Beliefs concerning the alleged sexuality of blacks, slave or otherwise, and lower-class whites need to be examined in any study of sexual contacts between dominant and subordinate social classes. But such beliefs exist in a concrete social setting. By emphasizing a "myth," F + E fail to give attention to the real social world in which one or more myths competed and helped shape — but did not determine — sexual behavior by the dominant classes. It remains much easier to measure the changing price of slaves or staple crops than to measure racial, class, and sexual beliefs (or "myths"). Prostitution is a single indicator of real sexual behavior and belief. Examined alone, however, data on prostitution do no more than peel away one of the heavy layers of myth that continue to hide from us the realities of sexual behavior among antebellum southern whites and blacks.

F + E on the "Stable Slave Family": The Absence
of Positive Evidence in T/C

What does T/C, finally, tell us that is new about the "stable slave nuclear family," about slave sexual behavior, and about the relationship among slave socialization, the slave family, and master attitudes and behavior? Not much. The book contains erroneous and misleading data meant to show that the enslaved had internalized sexual values resembling "Puritan," "Victorian," or "prudish" beliefs. T/C furthermore contains no positive evidence showing that "both moral convictions and good business practice generally led planters to encourage stable nuclear families" and that "slave life pivoted around stable nuclear families." The only evidence in T/C suggesting slave family stability is negative evidence: the so-called low incidence of slave marriages broken by sale. This evidence, too, is flawed. A relatively low sale figure might be interpreted as evidence that enslavement had a benign effect on the Afro-American family, but fifty (or even twenty-five) thousand sales a year is hardly a low "estimate." In itself, that simple statistic irreparably damages the proposition that planters "encourage[d] stable nuclear families." A good deal of other evidence considered elsewhere convincingly shows that slave families and slave marriages were precarious and fragile, not stable. We return briefly to the wartime Mississippi and Louisiana slave marriage registers. Fresh from slavery when they renewed old marriages, the registrants were asked by officiating Union Army clergy about earlier slave unions terminated by sale ("force"), death, desertion, and divorce. Among the registrants, 647 men and women at least forty years old reported the breakup of an earlier marriage by sale ("force"). About two-thirds (63 percent) had lived with a spouse at least five years before sale. About one in six or seven told of an earlier marriage that had lasted at least fifteen years before sale. Were these marriages "stable" before their involuntary breakup by owners? The registrants were not asked about the sale of children, but those with terminated marriages told the number of children born of these earlier unions. Their answers strongly indicate that the presence of children had not deterred owners from separating husbands and wives from one another:

(1) 862 males reported the termination of an earlier childless slave marriage; 45 percent said the marriage had been broken by force or sale.

(2) 991 males reported the termination of an earlier child-bearing slave marriage; 48 percent said the marriage had been broken by force or sale.

(3) 879 females reported the termination of an earlier childless slave marriage; 33.7 percent said the marriage had been broken by force or sale.

(4) 1,054 females reported the termination of an earlier child-bearing slave marriage; 33.8 percent said the marriage had been broken by force or sale.

Even if financial reverses, the payment of debts, and the division of estates explained most of these involuntary breakups, the fact that childless and child-bearing adults reported similar rates of marital dissolution by force or sale strongly suggests that the presence of a "completed nuclear family" did not convince hard-pressed owners to let a spouse live with his or her slave mate. Evidence of this kind — and there is much more of it — is further reason to doubt that planters "encourage[d] stable nuclear families."[227]

Percentages are useful but dangerously deceptive measures of the precarious and fragile social character of slave families and of slave marriages. What percentage of slave families (or marriages) had to be disrupted by the sale of a spouse, a parent, or a child to teach the enslaved that such power rested with their owners and could be exercised as a central ordering and disciplining principle in the day-to-day management of the slave social and

[227] The percentages and numbers cited in this paragraph are drawn from my forthcoming study, chapter eight, in which the wartime slave marriage registers for Mississippi and Louisiana are examined in close detail.

economic system? 5 percent? 8.6 percent? 25 percent? 33 percent? 50 percent? 66 percent? If about 10 percent of slave families were disrupted by owner migration, sale, gift transfer, estate division, or hire, that number would have been more than adequate. And for good reason. The breakup of a single slave family (say the sale of a fourteen-year-old son from his parents) or a single slave marriage had a geometric social meaning among slaves at any place or any moment in time. It, of course, affected a particular family and other kin nearby. But it was also known to slave neighbors and to those who came to know the adult or child sold away from his or her family. Following sale, such social awareness spread over space, and when children were involved, it also moved forward in time. From the perspective of the enslaved, the former Virginia slave Cornelius Garner put the problem well: "Boys git to cuttin' up on Sundays an' 'sturbin' Marsa and Missus an' dey com'ny. Finally ole Marsa come clumpin' down to de quarters. Pick out de fam'ly dat got de mos' chillun an' say, 'Fo' God, nigger, I'm goin' to sell all dem chillum o' your'n lessen you keep 'em quiet.' Dat threat was worsen prospects of a lickin'. Ev'body sho' keep quiet arter dat."[228] The threat made by Garner's owner did not require the frequent dissolution of slave families (or the sale of slave children) to make it effective.

No one, of course, seriously interested in the enslaved Afro-American quarrels with the need for careful analysis of planter patterns of behavior that strengthened, weakened, or entirely destroyed slave marriages and slave families. But such a study barely begins to examine seriously the development of an adaptive family and kinship system among enslaved Afro-Americans. The volume of annual slave sales hinted at in T/C (fifty thousand a year) is sufficiently large to pose a series of pertinent questions entirely neglected in T/C. Put simply, how did enslaved Afro-Americans like Cornelius Garner deal with the reality of familial dissolution under slavery? How, for example, did the reality of migration, sale, gift transfer, estate division, and hire affect the ways in which slave parents and other slave adults — not slaveowners — socialized slave children and built kin networks? How did the emerging Afro-American family and kinship system adapt to patterns of planter behavior? These variables find no place in T/C, and that is why it is so inadequate an analysis of "the slave family."

[228] Work Projects Administration, *Negro in Virginia*, p. 74.

An Archaic Historical Model

Black Culture and "Achievement": Sambo and Horatio Alger,
or Stanley Elkins and F + E

"We have attacked the traditional interpretation of the economics of slavery," F + E vigorously assert in their widely quoted conclusion ". . . to strike down the view that black Americans were without [a?] culture, without achievement, and without development for their first two hundred and fifty years on American soil."[229] It is ironic, however, that T/C (perhaps unknown to its authors) reinforces precisely the historical perspective of the Afro-American experience that it professes to criticize so severely. That — not the misused or fragile evidence — is its most serious shortcoming. How that happened is illustrated by examining the model of slave society in Stanley Elkins' influential *Slavery: A Problem in American Institutional and Intellectual Life* and then comparing that model to the one used by F + E. Elkins' conception of American slave society derived from a large assumption about the distinctive social structure and character of premodern American society. "American society, capitalism," said Elkins, "developed unimpeded by prior arrangements and institutions." In its diverse lesser workings, the

[229] T/C, I, pp. 258-259. See the astute comments on F + E's conception of black culture and black achievement in Duberman's review, *Village Voice*, 18 July 1974, p. 32. Duberman writes: "To have been a hard-working, responsible slave is to have been part of the 'positive' development of black culture, to have contributed to the saga of black 'achievement.' F & E berate Stampp and Elkins for having portrayed slaves who lied, stole, feigned illness, acted childishly, shirked their duties — as if these traits *necessarily* reflect badly on black personality and culture. But they do only in the context of a Calvinist work ethic and the Boy Scout pledge to loyalty and cheerfulness. F & E might have profited from a quick course in situational ethics: lying to avoid the lash is not the same as lying to deceive a friend. . . . Themselves equating 'efficiency' with 'achievement' and eager to award blacks their credentials in middle-class white culture, F & E reject any suggestion that a slave's *refusal* to become an effective cog in the plantation machine can itself be seen as an achievement, a testimony to black ingenuity, resistance, pride. Indeed they impugn 'racist' motives to any historian who makes such a suggestion."

society-at-large revealed in many ways "the dynamics of unopposed capitalism." The particular harshness of Anglo-American enslavement, according to Elkins, simply reflected this larger national process: "The presence or absence of other powerful institutions in society made an immense difference in the character of slavery itself." Social arrangements and institutions rooted in earlier cultural formations had no place in American society ("unopposed capitalism"). As a result, enslaved Africans and their descendants became the most "individualized," or socially isolated, of all Americans. The law granted absolute power to the slaveowner, a power unchecked by traditional institutional restraints. Their legal and institutional powerlessness was reinforced by the slaves' own social and cultural rootlessness, which followed from the harshness of initial enslavement. "Much of his past," said Elkins of the first-generation African slave in the British mainland colonies, was "annihilated." The enslaved therefore had a single choice. "Where, then," Elkins asked, "was he to look for new standards, new cues — who would furnish them? He could now look to none but his master, the one man to whom the system had committed his entire being." A dependency relationship set in early, the start of a long and seeming self-fulfilling historical process. So it happened that several generations of slaves underwent socialization in a most oppressive circumstance. The "sanctions of the system" rested only with the owners of the enslaved and "were in themselves sufficient to produce a recognizable personality type."[230] The reality of "Sambo" as "the typical plantation slave" flowed easily from this analytic model of American society and of slave society.

The many Sambos that Elkins created have become the many "diligent workers" in T/C. Sambo and the slave Horatio Alger are very different men. But the model which has created the archetypal enslaved Afro-American remains the same. In both models, the enslaved are "made over" by their owners. The "inputs" and "outputs" differ, but the process does not. The enslaved live in a Skinner Box. The "sanctions of the system" flow in one direction over time. The sanctions differ, but not the direction of the flow. Slave socialization remains oversimplified, and one-dimensional. Sambo and the diligent field hand turn out to be opposite sides of the same coin, both minted in factories, each in a factory with a different manager. But if the plantation was not a "concentration camp," neither was it a mid-nineteenth-century vocational high school. "Unfettered capitalism," note David and Temin, in a neat summary of T/C, "led to a form of slavery which was peculiarly benign insofar as concerns the social and material circumstances of its human chattel."[231] F + E have indeed turned Elkins on his head. But

[230] Stanley M. Elkins, *Slavery: A Problem in American Institutional and Intellectual Life* (1959), *passim*.

[231] David and Temin, "Slavery: The Progressive Institution?"

they have used his flawed model of slave socialization in doing so. And that model is their undoing, too.

T/C as Reductionist History and as Consensus History

This overriding criticism should not be misunderstood. Fogel and Engerman are well-known economic historians. They are not racists and are men of much good will. By reputation, they rank among this country's most talented and prolific economic historians. They have pioneered in developing "cliometric" history. Why, then, should they have written so flawed a work, one that uses new materials ("quantitative") and new methods ("cliometric") but nevertheless ends up as very dated history? It is not primarily that their enthusiasm over the "findings" has caused gross statistics to become easy explanations of slave belief and behavior.

The historians David Fischer and Harold Woodman indicate in different ways the fallacies involved in such explanations. A narrow "economic" analysis often results in what Fischer calls a "reductive fallacy," the "confusion of a causal component without which an effect will not occur, with all other causal components which are all required to make it occur." That often happens, Fischer wisely remarks, "in causal explanations which are constructed like a single chain and stretched taut across a vast chasm of complexity."[232] In T/C, the beliefs and behavior of enslaved Afro-Americans are not bound by the legal realities of ownership but by constricting cliometric chains. Woodman puts it differently, reminding the "econometrician" that "aggregate" data ("averages") tell little about "individual motivation" and splendidly pointing out the methodological flaw that weakens so many narrow "one-factor" quantitative studies: "The assumption ... is that the existence of an economic factor is adequate to explain behavior, or, to put it negatively, other causal connections must be sought out *only* when an economic connection is absent. It is true that if behavior does not correspond to the hypothesis designed to explain that behavior, the hypothesis must be rejected or modified. But it does not follow that the reverse is necessarily true; the hypothesis might not be inconsistent with observed behavior, but it might not explain it either. Behavior might be explained by another, quite different (although not contradictory) hypothesis."[233] Woodman made these comments before the publication of T/C in a superb review-essay of an earlier volume of cliometric work edited by F + E. But in reading T/C, it

[232] Fischer, *Historians' Fallacies*, p. 172.
[233] Harold D. Woodman, "Economic History and Economic Theory: The New Economic History in America," *Journal of Interdisciplinary History*, III (Fall 1972), pp. 324-350 and especially pp. 334-335. This is a brilliant review-essay, and I have learned much from it.

167

is as if these criticisms were never written. We need not even depend upon Woodman and Fischer for such methodological acuteness. In a quite different setting and much earlier in time, Thomas Carlyle pointed out the dangers in reductionist economic analysis: "He who reads the inscrutable book of Nature as if it were a Merchant's Ledger is justly suspected of having never seen that Book, but only some School Synopsis thereof; from which if taken for the real book, more error than insight is to be derived."[234] (It is said in jest of a distinguished contemporary British social historian by an admiring but critical colleague that if asked to study the Crucifixion, he would first count the number of nails in the body of Jesus Christ. But that information is useful only to the student interested in the demand for nails nearly two thousands years ago.)

T/C is dated for yet other reasons than its emphasis on a monocausal explanation (rational, profit-maximizing slaveowners). One could, for example, make the case that T/C should have been published in the 1950s because it is a quintessential example of "consensus history." The consensus historians of the 1950s (Kenneth Stampp was *not* one of them) criticized an earlier generation of historians for exaggerating the theme of conflict in the nation's history and for failing to examine how shared values often bound together political adversaries. Despite its limitations, that school valuably criticized the limitations of earlier and oversimplified conflict models. But the consensus historians had much difficulty fitting the Afro-American — and especially the enslaved Afro-American — into their new synthesis. Except for a tiny minority, blacks never had much of a chance to participate fully in an achievement-oriented society. F + E have succeeded, perhaps inadvertently, in fitting the ordinary enslaved Afro-American into that type of society. They, too, had a chance to rise, and, like their white Yankee and Cavalier brothers, they, too, bit the bait. Some among them even fixed the bait to the hook. None, of course, owned the fishing line. In its own way, then, the American Dream had its slave version. Enslavement had its nightmarish qualities (F + E admit that). Rags-to-riches was not a possibility; but enslaved Afro-Americans could act out a modified version of the American Dream. Field hands could become artisans, drivers, and overseers. Profit-maximizing owners encouraged such aspirations by developing a system of positive labor incentives. Enough slaves made it to the middle or the top of *slave* society to reinforce those incentives. Resistance, or conflict, therefore remained narrow and limited. Fogel [(F + E) — E] made precisely this argument in an interview with a *New York Post* reporter a few months after the publication of T/C: "Those who struggled ["rebelled," "protested," and so forth] should be extolled to the highest. But what about those who just maintained their dignity? Shouldn't they get credit? They were a lot of

[234] Quoted in Fischer, *Historians' Fallacies*, p. 91.

ordinary Joes who didn't *know* they should be revolutionaries, who became skilled craftsmen. They weren't untrue to themselves."[235] We have seen that there is good reason to question how many "ordinary Joes" became skilled slave craftsmen. It needs also to be pointed out that "dignity" for "ordinary Joes" came in many ways other than by conforming to owner expectations.

Old and New "Models" Meant to Explain the Beliefs and Behavior of Enslaved Afro-Americans

T/C is even more dated in its underlying model than this comparison to the 1950s suggests, and that is because in explaining the beliefs and the behavior of the "ordinary Joes," it uses an analytic model as old as the pioneering work of U. B. Phillips and one that had its most sophisticated expression in the writings of Stanley Elkins. Neither Elkins nor F + E, of course, share in any way the mistaken racial assumptions that irreparably damaged all of Phillips' writings. They, nevertheless, share a conceptual model with this founding father. Phillips sought only to answer the question: What did enslavement do to Africans and their Afro-American descendants? That is the same question asked by Elkins and F + E and one that is essential. Without answering it, the history of enslaved Afro-Americans cannot be written. Phillips' answer runs something like this: Nothing much; the planters tried and failed; the African remained an African; racial factors proved insurmountable; the planters tried so hard they went broke doing it; slavery was therefore unprofitable. F + E argue the opposite case: planters labored diligently to transform the slaves and transformed them into diligent laborers; their success helps explain the profitability of slavery and the behavior of the enslaved. It has been known for nearly half a century that slavery was profitable, and F + E deserve credit for reopening that question and focusing on the reasons for its profitability. But neither the profitability of slavery nor the efficiency of the plantation system is a sufficient determinant of slave belief and behavior. Like Elkins and like Phillips before him, F + E have worked with a model which views slave belief and behavior as little more than one or another response to planter-sponsored stimuli. That remains their cardinal error, and that is the reason T/C ends up being so old-fashioned a work. Errors mar F + E's basic findings on slave sales, slave marriage and family ties, slave sexual behavior, slave punishments and rewards, and the urban and rural slave occupational structure. But if the estimates were more accurate and the quantitative data examined more soundly, the model meant to explain slave beliefs and behavior would still be inadequate.

[235] Edward Newton, "Slaves and the South . . . New Input and Feedback," *New York Post Magazine Section,* 27 July 1974, pp. 24-25.

More needs to be asked than the question Phillips posed. Simply changing the factors in the Phillips equation and, of course, rejecting his racial assumptions does not necessarily make for more truthful answers or better social history. We need to know in close detail what enslavement did to Africans and then to their Afro-American descendants. But we shall never comprehend slave belief and behavior by just asking that question. We need also to ask what Africans and their Afro-American descendants did as slaves. That is a very different question, and the answers to it are not the mirror-image of what owners did to slaves. The novelist Ralph Ellison put it well in criticizing the main thrust that has informed the writing of much Afro-American history. His criticisms apply just as well to T/C. "Can a people . . . live and develop over three hundred years by simply reacting?" asked Ellison. "Are American Negroes simply the creation of white men, or have they at least helped create themselves out of what they found around them?"[236] The anthropologist John F. Szwed makes the same point somewhat differently: "[F]rom the beginnings of slavery Afro-Americans exercised the capacity to perpetuate and create means of comprehending and dealing with the natural and social worlds surrounding them — they were culture bearers and creators as well as receivers and learners. In other words, although slavery, poverty, and racism have severely circumscribed the exercise of this capacity, even sometimes driving it underground, these constraints can in no way be seen as the sufficient cause of Afro-American behavior."[237]

Ellison and Szwed pose alternate ways of studying slave beliefs and behavior and reexamining entirely neglected dimensions of the social history lived by enslaved Afro-Americans. Not a hint of this perspective penetrates the pages of T/C. Ellison and Szwed tell historians to put aside the Skinner Box model of Afro-American history. New questions cannot be asked from inside that Box. Sophisticated measuring techniques cannot change the shape of the box.

The best way to begin reexamining changing patterns of slave belief and behavior, of course, is not by putting aside the study of planter belief and behavior. But it does require the examination of the ways the enslaved themselves accumulated historical experiences over time (culture), and the ways in which these accumulated experiences helped shape slave belief and behavior. At every moment in more than two centuries that preceded the general emancipation, planter policies, whatever their content, encountered slave beliefs and practices that were much more than the sum of planter

---

[236] Ralph Ellison, *Shadow and Act* (1964), p. 315.

[237] John F. Szwed, "The Politics of Afro-American Culture," in Dell Hymes, ed., *Reinventing Anthropology* (1972), pp. 166-167.

beliefs and practices. Put differently, slave work habits, the slave family, slave sexual behavior, and slave culture itself require the study of the manner in which Africans and their Afro-American descendants adapted to enslavement and to changing patterns of enslavement. Some slaves, of course, adapted by conforming. Some became Sambos and others Horatio Algers. But even these kinds of adaptive responses to enslavement were much more subtle historical and complex cultural processes than mere imitation. Diffusion of an important kind occurred. But the ease with which F + E transfer the Protestant work ethic from owner to slave rests, I fear, on their implicit and possibly unconscious acceptance of an imitative model for the development of slave culture. It never was that simple. And that is why Eugene Genovese is far too generous in saying that even though T/C "hardly discusses black culture and initiative at all, ... it does make the useful contribution of showing how the living space for such a culture and initiative was created."[238] That "living space" had as much, if not more, to do with the initial adaptive capacities of enslaved Africans and their early Afro-American descendants than with the economic calculations of their "capitalist" or "pre-capitalist" owners.

T/C uses new methods and new data, but neither the data nor the methods answer the questions posed by Ellison. Its assumptions (model) — as contrasted to its methods and some of its data — flow from a tradition of archaic historical scholarship. Old questions are answered in a new way. But if the answers to old questions are new, it does not mean that they are accurate. Ellison poses new questions, and only when they are answered by using appropriate methods, quantitative and otherwise, can we write with some satisfaction about a "new" history, cliometric or otherwise. T/C does not ask and, therefore, cannot answer such questions. That is why it is so disappointing a book. F + E have done a service in calling attention to the need to explain the profitability of slavery. Answers to that question will be forthcoming. We will need then to know how the enslaved dealt with the ways in which their owners organized the factors of production. But those answers will come only after rejecting the lopsided analytic model that continues to dominate the writing of so much Afro-American (and American) history.

Three examples may explain these theoretical points more directly. In the winter and spring of 1862, South Carolina Sea Island slaves ("contrabands"), then supervised in their labor by the Union Army and a few missionaries, refused to grow cotton, wanted to plant corn, broke the cotton gins, hid the iron work, and finally agreed to grow cotton but planted corn between the rows of cotton and then refused to pay the military rent on the

[238] Eugene D. Genovese, Review of T/C, *Washington Post Book World,* 1974.

171

land where the corn grew. A Yankee entrepreneur among them learned that "nothing was more remote from their shallow pates than the idea of planting cotton for 'white-folks' again." One Sea Island black quit a church during a sermon given by a northern white that year and was heard to mutter, "The Yankees preach nothing but cotton, cotton." Four years later, Augusta, Georgia, blacks, nearly all former slaves, greatly amazed the Freedmen's Bureau officer Davis Tillison. Much material suffering had followed emancipation. "I know of colored men who work hard all day and into the night, and who give one third of all they earn to the poor of their own race," said Tillison. "This I learn," he added, "not from their own lips, but from those of their white neighbors." Even before this, Liberty County, Georgia, blacks, their exact number unknown, gathered in a local church and picked five among them to plead before the Freedmen's Bureau concerning their material condition. Their petition follows, and the italicized portions were so underlined in the original document:

> We the People of Liberty County . . . appeal to you asking aid and counsel in this our *distressed condition.* We learned from the Address of *general Howard* that We Were to *Return* to the *Plantations* and *Work for our Former owners* at a *Reasonable contract as Freemen,* and find a *Home* and *Labor, Provided We can agree. But these owners of Plantations . . . Says they only will hire or* ———— the *Prime Hands* and our *old and infirm Mothers and Fathers* and *our Children Will not be Provided for* and this Will See Sir Put us in *confusion . . . We cannot Labor for the Land owners . . .* [while] *our Infirm and children are not provided for, and are not allowed to educate or learn . . . We are Destitute of Religious Worship, having no Home or Place to Live When We Leave the Plantation, Returned to our Former owners; We are a Working Class of People* and We are *Willing* and *Anxious* to worke for a *Fair Compensation;* But to *return to work upon the Terms that are at Present offered to us, Would Be We Think going Backe into the state of slavery that We have just to some extent Been Delivered from.*
> We *Appeal* to *you Sir* and through *you* to the *Rulers* of the *Country* in our *Distressed State* and ———— that *We feel, unsettled as Sheep Without a Shepard, and beg your advice and Assistance,* and *Believe that this is an Earnest Appeal from A Poor But Loyal Earnest People.*[239]

These three illustrations are not cited to either idealize or romanticize enslaved Afro-Americans before or just upon their emancipation. They serve instead as examples of slave beliefs and behavior that cannot be explained by the analytic model that infuses the pages of T/C. These blacks were "ordinary Joes," but they did not live in the world the cliometricians made. They may even have been diligent workers before 1860, and surely they were

[239] I am very much indebted to Edward Magdol for bringing this petition to my attention.

Protestant in their religion. But refusing to grow a commercial crop, breaking cotton gins, giving away income to less fortunate former slaves, and describing themselves as "*a Working Class of People . . . Willing* and *Anxious* to Worke for a *Fair Compensation*" hardly serve as evidence of an internalized " 'Protestant' work ethic" as defined by either Bennet Barrow or F + E.

No one, neither the enslaved nor their owners, lived in the world the cliometricians made. Such a world, even as measured by the flawed evidence that fills the pages of T/C, did not exist. The criticisms that have filled this review-essay, however, should not be misunderstood. They are not a Luddite-like attack on quantitative methods. Quantification, used properly, is very useful to the social historian and especially the social historian concerned with dependent and exploited classes. It helps to establish regularities, and regularities help the social historian to define different aspects of otherwise often obscure social experiences. It is important to know what percentage of slaves were artisans, how frequently slaves were whipped, the typical age of slave women at the birth of a first child, the approximate number of slave families (or marriages) broken by force or sale, and so forth. Such information provides clues to the beliefs and behavior of the enslaved. But that kind of data, like any historical data, must be used with great care. The right questions must be asked of it. The inaccuracies in the data must be accounted for. A sound historical framework must exist within which the data are studied. Assumptions about the real world which such regularities partially describe must be rigorously and critically examined. An adequate theory of human behavior is needed. These are some of the essential preconditions for using quantifiable materials in creative and scientific ways. It has been seen that many of the data and many of the most important generalizations in T/C fail to meet these preconditions.

Just before the book's publication, co-author Fogel explained to the Conference on Mathematics in the Social Sciences at Southern Illinois University that "the 'new' urban history, the 'new' social history, the 'new' demographic history, the 'new' political history" were "all . . . attracting young disciples." He identified T/C with this "new" history, pointing to "the intense prepublication debate that has been touched off by *Time on the Cross.*" He explained:

I regret the immodesty involved in this statement. Yet the fact remains that many historians are now predicting that this book will force the issue of the role of quantitative methods in history. For *Time on the Cross* has assailed a problem which historians agree is at the very center of their discipline, and has reversed, or at least brought into question, virtually every major assumption connected with that problem. Moreover, it is undeniable that this reversal arises directly out of the analytical methods we have employed. Under these circumstances, the methodological challenge cannot be avoided. Those who reject our findings will be forced to fight, to a considerable extent, on the grounds and with the methods set forth in *Time on the Cross*.[240]

T/C is not "new" history. All it does is answer old questions. It has been seen that the answers offered to explain slave beliefs and slave behavior are wrong. Neither the data used nor the analytic methods employed have "reversed, or at least brought into question," a single major assumption about the behavior and beliefs of enslaved Afro-Americans. That has been seen in these pages by a close examination of the quantitative data bearing on slave beliefs and behavior. That is the test ("fight") Fogel set for critics of T/C. T/C fails that test. But this work is not the one to "force the issue of quantitative methods in history." That is an unfair test.

Quantitative methods — that is, the use of numerical data to establish regularities in all sorts of social behavior — have a place in the writing of social history and of Afro-American history, but as just one of many techniques available to the modern historian. T/C might have been a much better book if its authors had read and taken seriously the appendix in Harriet Beecher Stowe's *Key to Uncle Tom's Cabin* (1854). The appendix is a brief essay entitled "Fact v. Figures; or, The Nine Arab Brothers. Being a New Arabian Nights' Entertainment." Its author — perhaps Stowe herself — began by quoting a shopworn commonplace: "It is a favorite maxim that *'figures cannot lie.'* " The author went on:

> There may have been days of pastoral innocence and primitive simplicity, when they did not lie. When Abraham sat contemplatively in his tent-door, with nothing to do, all the day long, but compose psalms and pious meditations, it is likely that he had implicit faith in this maxim, and never thought of questioning the statistical tables of Eliezer of Damascas, with regard to the number of camels, asses, sheep, oxen, and goats, which illustrated the prairie where he was the time being encamped. Alas for those good old days! Figures did not lie then, we freely admit; but we are sadly afraid, from their behavior in recent ages, that this arose from no native innocence of disposition, but simply from want of occasion and opportunity. In those days they were young and green, and had not learned what they could do. The first inventor, who commenced making a numeration table, with the artless primeval machine of his toes and fingers, had, like other great inventors, very little idea of what he was doing, and what would be the mighty uses of these very simple characters, when men got to have republican governments and elections, and discussions of all sorts of unheard-of questions in politics and morals, and to electioneering among these

[240] Fogel, "The Limits of Quantitative Methods in History," unpublished paper, pp. 8-9. These sentences do not appear in the published version of this essay (Fogel, "The Limits of Quantitative Methods in History," *American Historical Review*, pp. 329-50). Since the publication of T/C, it is possible that the "challenge" has been withdrawn.

poor simple Arab herdsmen, the nine digits, for their votes on all these complicated subjects. No wonder that figures have had their heads turned! Such un-
precedented power and popularity is enough to turn any head. We are sorry
to speak ill of them; but really we must say that like many of our political
men, they have been found on all sides of every subject to an extent that is
really very confusing. Of course, there is no doubt of their veracity *somewhere;*
the only problem being, on which side and where. . . .

Political and social adversaries gathered "figures" concerning the great controversy over slavery, firing them "as two opposite cannons." Such combat,
however, had "no particular effect, except the bewilderment of a few old-
fashioned people, who, like Mr. Pickwick at the review, stand on the middle
ground."

There was also the example of "Mrs. Partington, . . . like most unsophisti-
cated old ladies, . . . a most vehement and uncompromising abolitionist." If
only she knew the statistics "in favor of slavery, she would take off her
spectacles and wipe her eyes in pious joy, and think that the Millennium,
and nothing else, had come upon earth." Mrs. Partington felt the middle
passage "horrid," but figures fairly presented would have convinced her
otherwise:

> "By no means, my dear madam," says the illustrator, whisking over his papers,
> "I have that all in figures — averages of deaths in the first cargoes, 25 per
> cent. — large average, certainly; they didn't manage the business exactly right;
> but then the rate of increase in a Christian country averages 25 per cent. over
> what it would have been in Africa. Now, Mrs. Partington, if these had been left
> in Africa, they would have been all heathen; by getting them over here, you
> have just as many, and all Christians to boot. Because, you see, the excess of
> increase balances the percentage of loss, and we make no deduction for in-
> terest in those cases."
>
> Now, as Mrs. Partington does not know with very great clearness what "per-
> centage" and "average" mean, and as mental philosophers have demonstrated
> that we are always powerfully affected by the unknown, she is all the more
> impressed with this reasoning, on that account; being one of the simple old-
> fashioned people, who have not yet gotten over the impression that "figures
> cannot lie."
>
> "Well, now, really," says she, "strange what these figures will do! I always
> thought the slave trade was monstrous wicked. But it really seems to be quite a
> missionary work."

The author worried about the many contemporary Mr. Pickwicks and Mrs.
Partingtons.[241]

To judge from the early reactions to T/C, Mr. Pickwick and Mrs. Partington are still very much alive. Why has a book filled with such glaring errors

[241] "Fact v. Figures; or, The Nine Arab Brothers. Being a New Arabian Nights'
Entertainment," appendix in Stowe, *Key to Uncle Tom's Cabin,* pp. 505-508.

attracted such favorable notice? A Columbia University economist explained to readers of the *New York Times Book Review* that "if a more important book about American history has been published in the last decade, I don't know about it." He is convinced that F + E have "with one stroke turned around a whole field of interpretation and exposed the frailty of history without science."[242] *Time* readers learned that T/C "more or less proved that traditional 'impressionistic' historians persistently wrote about American slavery in delusive and polemical stereotypes" and that "the moonlight and molasses nostalgia of a Stephen Foster may somewhat more accurately describe the average relationship between slave and master than any serious historian has been willing to admit for years."[243] (The very next sentence tells that F + E "blend statistics on everything from the percentage of blacks in skilled plantation trades to the average age of black mothers at the time of the first-born child." It has been seen that each of these numbers is wrong.)

What explains such uncritical enthusiasm? Is it simply evidence that contemporaries of the computer stand in even greater awe of the power of "numbers" than did those of our forbears who lived in the time of Liza, Simon Legree, and Uncle Tom? Or is it evidence of a deep flaw in the national culture that finds comfort in learning the "fact" that the great-grandfather of a ghetto Afro-American was neither an Uncle Tom nor a Nat Turner but a black Horatio Alger? We need no longer use the successful immigrant as the counterimage to the late-twentieth-century ghetto Afro-American. Now it can be argued, "Look, brother, your great-grandfather made it 'under adversity.' You can too. Just straighten out your sexual mores, live in a stable nuclear family, and work hard. Remember that it paid off for your great-grandfather. He started out as a field hand and became an overseer. Now, just straighten up, man. . . ." Whatever their intentions, it may yet turn out that the authors of T/C have written a book that will serve once again to "blame the victim." It is important, therefore, for readers of *Time on the Cross* to realize that it is a book filled with egregious errors meant to measure "black achievement under adversity." It really tells us nothing of importance about the beliefs and behavior of enslaved Afro-Americans.

[242] Passell, review of T/C, *New York Times Book Review*, 28 April 1974, p. 4.
[243] Foote, review of T/C, *Time*, 17 June 1974, pp. 98-100.

Index